D# 198480

check Bib

SURVIVING
The Best Game on Earth

SURVIVING
The Best Game on Earth

Norie Huddle

Foreword Based on an Interview with
Studs Terkel

Schocken Books • New York

First published by Schocken Books 1984
10 9 8 7 6 5 4 3 2 1   84 85 86 87
Copyright © 1984 by Eleanor Huddle

Library of Congress Cataloging in Publication Data
Huddle, Norie, 1944–
   Surviving: the best game on earth.
   1. United States—National security—Public opinion.
2. Public opinion—United States.   I. Title.
UA23.H73   1983   355'.033073   83–42722

Designed by Edward Smith
Manufactured in the United States of America
ISBN 0–8052–3871–9

To my parents, Frank and Clare Huddle,
    who encouraged me to keep asking the
    "impertinent" questions,
    and
To all of the children who are counting on you and me
    to do our parts now.

Until one is committed, there is hesitancy, the chance to draw back, always ineffectiveness. Concerning all acts of initiative and creation, there is one elementary truth, the ignorance of which kills countless ideas and splendid plans. At the moment one definitely commits oneself, then Providence moves, too. All sorts of things occur to help one that would never otherwise have occurred. A whole stream of events issues from the decision, raising in one's favor all manner of unforeseen incidents and meetings and material assistance which no man could have dreamed would come his way.

I have learned a deep respect for one of Goethe's couplets:

Whatever you can do or dream you can, begin it:
Boldness has genius, power and magic in it.

—William Murray
(Member of Scottish expedition to Mount Everest)

Contents

**Foreword Based on an Interview
with Studs Terkel**   xiii

Acknowledgments   xix

Introduction   xxi

The Interviews

Paul Green   3

  Director of Public Relations, Committee on the
  Present Danger

Sue Shetrom   11

  Schoolteacher near Three Mile Island;
  "conservative housewife turned activist"

Greg Akili   22

  Union Organizer

Ed Johnson   32

  Truck Driver

Elmo Zumwalt   38

  Retired Admiral; former member, Joint Chiefs of
  Staff

Pat Mische   46

  Co-Founder, Global Education Associates

Melor Sturua   59

  Washington Bureau Chief, *Izvestia*

Gene La Rocque   72

Retired Admiral; Director, Center for Defense
Information

Lester Brown   79

Director, Worldwatch Institute

Rob Caughlan   86

Co-Founder, the Roanoke Company (an
environmental PR firm)

Russell Means   96

Leader in the American Indian Movement

Richard Falk   102

Professor of International Law, Princeton
University

Hazel Henderson   110

Author and Lecturer

Edgar Mitchell   120

Former Astronaut; Business Consultant

Edward Teller   128

Scientist; Inventor of the Hydrogen Bomb

Shigetoshi Iwamatsu   134

Professor of Sociology, Nagasaki University;
Survivor of the Atomic Bombing of Nagasaki

Joanna Macy   145

Social Change Activist; Creator of the "Despair
and Empowerment" Workshops

Harvey Cox   151

Theologian, Harvard University; Antinuclear
Activist

B. F. Skinner   159

Behavioral Psychologist and Researcher, Harvard
University

Howard Kurtz   165

Director, War Control Planners, Inc.

Buckminster Fuller   176

Inventor, Author, Lecturer, Philosopher

Eldon Byrd   181

Scientific Researcher, Naval Surface Weapons
Research Center

Yuri Antipov   192

Former Member, Soviet Delegation to the United
Nations

Bob Aldridge   204

Former Developer, Ballistic Missile Systems,
Lockheed; Author, Lecturer, and Critic of Current
Defense Policies

Seymour Melman   219

Professor of Industrial Engineering, Columbia
University

Dick Gregory   227

Comedian; Peace Movement Activist

Ina May Gaskin   232

Midwife and Member, The Farm Community

James W. Prescott   239

Neurophysiologist

Robert Muller   251

Secretary, Economic and Social Council, United
Nations

Tony Buzan   256

Educator and Lecturer; Founder, The Learning
Methods Group

Conclusion   267

Questionnaire   275

Foreword
Based on an Interview with Studs Terkel

People have a lot to say. They deserve far more credit for understanding what is happening than is shown by the media. As Ed Sadlowski, a young steelworker, says, "There's more to these working men than a guy with a flag on his hardhat." Many of these guys are worried about their homes, their families, and their jobs. They're tired all the time and they worry about what has happened to their energy. They look for beauty if they have a chance to; if a guy had a chance to read a book, he'd read it. There's more to these people than is offered by the Hollywood image or the Six O'clock News. As this book tells us, we can find the truth and regain our energy by starting to listen to each other. Today we hear all sorts of talk about "national security." What does it really mean? Every construction worker on the air says "We've got to build bigger bombs than the Russians have." That's all we hear on the media—nothing about their lives and what they really want in order to be secure.

If you go to the streets and talk with the people you find they all want food, clothing, shelter, and a better life for themselves and their kids. They want good schools, the mortgage lifted on the house, and a sane world. Everybody wants that. There are fears, of course, offered each day. Some fears are real. It's all connected. How come the streets have crime? Well, if there's unemployment, there's crime. If you have young kids hanging out on the corner, not working, the energy has to go somewhere. If it can't work toward something social, then it goes toward something antisocial. There's no mystery about this.

Author, actor, critic, folklorist, lecturer, and broadcaster, Studs Terkel is perhaps most well known for his best-selling book, Working, *and for his daily radio program on station WFMT (Chicago). He has received numerous awards and is active in community affairs. We conducted the interview on which this foreword is based in his Chicago office during the fall of 1980.*

Who's running our country? The guy in the White House? The multinationals? Agribusiness? It's a combination of them. The people on top are few in number but powerful; they determine what we see on the networks and drum into us the "Russian menace." No doubt the Russians *are* building up. So are *we*. If we can knock *them* off fifty times over and they can knock *us* off fifty times over, what is the fifty-first time for? Our government assumes that we have white hats and they have black hats, but I don't believe that. Both our hats are white and black; we both must fear one another. In a big sense they are the metaphor for our daily lives, because we fear the stranger, don't we? We shut the doors. In the old days during elections you'd knock on doors and give them your talk. Now they shut the door in your face. We are taught to fear—the different-colored face, the different idea. As a result Russian-American tensions are building up more and more. If it continues like this, finally there'll be a blowup that no one really wants.

Why are we so attuned toward death rather than life? People know that for the same amount of dough more people can get work building a mass-transit system than a missile. We already know that more jobs mean less crime, right? The mass-transit system would also reduce the clogging of the highways and cut pollution. It would save energy—and isn't *energy* one of the main things we're thinking about going to war for? If you put it *this* way to someone, he says, "Well, of *course* I'd rather have a mass-transit system than a missile." If people were offered this explanation and these choices as often as they're offered the fears, they'd make a more humane decision. So when you hear the guy with the hardhat saying that we should "nuke the Russians," it's as though he were preconditioned to say it. A great many don't feel that, you see. They're the ones we don't usually hear about. We can hear more from these people by putting them on the air. By having Mary Lou Wolf say her piece—a mother of nine kids in Chicago who suddenly found a voice in stopping an expressway that everybody said couldn't be stopped. By letting Joe Begley, general storekeeper in a ghost town in eastern Kentucky, speak his mind about those who make war and about those who strip-mine his land. These are the ones we need to hear from.

Where does the news come from? Think of the Vietnam War. For so long we heard "Now I don't know if the war's wrong or not, because the guys up there know more than we do, don't they?" How often were you told that? Well, now we know: they *didn't* know more than we did. Indeed they were deceiving us. Consider Iran. Of course holding hostages is a terrible and stupid thing, but unless we understand Iranian grief, unless we learn the lesson in what we did in overthrowing a legally elected government, we won't understand Iranian rage. What did we see on TV during all those days the hostages were held? We saw fists shaken in Teheran; we heard Khomeini's incredible comments and chants of "Down with Carter!" But we've got to understand the Iranian mothers who cried for thousands who were killed. I'll read you something from the *New York Times* of November 29, 1979, from a town called Shah Abdul Azim:

> A cold rain drives through the cemetery. In the failing after-noon light, hundreds of men and women and children, some with umbrellas, most with jackets or robes thrown over their heads, walk silently toward a large meadow. . . . We see young faces, faces of the dead. Their photographs framed in glass and mounted over the simple stone slabs for burial. . . . Azizah Aman Zade, her traditional black robe wrapped loosely around her frail body, rivets her eyes on the picture of her son, Goam Rezah. He was 23 years old when he died at the hands of the Shah's secret police last January. "Come back, my loved one," she says in soft Persian. "My loved one, you are down there where it is too dark. You are alone there, aren't you? And we are alone. Come back to us, my beloved son."
>   . . . The graves are in neat rows, thousands of them, all who died at the hands of the Shah's secret police. . . .

Imagine, then, American mothers watching an Iranian mother weep for her lost son. Did we see this on ABC, CBS, or NBC during these hundreds of days? Why not? Why just the clenched fists? This article appeared way back on page 17 of the newspaper. You never saw it, did you? But you sure as hell knew about those raised fists: "Down with Carter! Death to Carter!" We know nothing about the Iranians or the Russians as people. That makes it easy for people to say "Let's go in there and bomb 'em."

The news, as it is offered, is deceitful and venal. We've got to grow up. Our people have a great capacity for catching onto events and growing up. But it seems as though "they" won't let them grow up. As a nation we need to learn to say "*We were wrong!*" If we could admit our mistakes we would win the affection and admiration of the world. Strong power says, "Yes, we were wrong; we're human, and it was a mistake." What is wrong with apologizing for errors? *That* is what would help this nation's security, *not* the loony MX missile project and all the rest.

It's as though we're erasing history. When former President Ford was asked about Vietnam, he said, "Let's put Vietnam behind us." Santayana said, "He who does not study history is condemned to repeat it." During an early session with the press regarding Iran, Carter was asked, "Do you have any second thoughts or apologies?" He said, "None." "1953?" asked the journalist, meaning when we overthrew Mossadegh. Carter's response was "That is ancient history." If *that* is ancient history, how will our kids know of *any* past? The new kids who come up might not even know of Vietnam, and so they might say, "Yeah, let's bomb 'em." A sense of history is important; it gives people a great capacity to learn and grow.

I imagine the Russians are as scared of us as we are of them. Brezhnev said, "Nobody can win a nuclear war." He was right. But eventually irrationality takes over in one of these buildups. In this country we're ignoring all the stuff *we've* been doing and refusing to change. In a way we are saying, "We never did wrong." And that's a lie.

I think that deep, deep down inside all of us there's a sense that we did wrong in Vietnam. How do we admit that? We simply *admit* it! The fact is that if a powerful country says "We were wrong," the rest of the world will look at it and say "You're a country of highly civilized human beings, not a country of robots and machines and technicians who move along as though nothing happened." We would not be groveling or losing face by apologizing; if anything, our faces would be glowing and beaming out into the rest of the world. And that in itself would affect the Russians.

You always hear that "power corrupts, and absolute power corrupts absolutely." That's only one side of it. The other side is that powerlessness corrupts, and utter powerlessness corrupts absolutely. The kids on the street corners feel they are nothing, so they slug each other. In my newest book, for example, Vernon Jarrett, a black columnist for the *Chicago Tribune,* speaks of a corner. The black kids hanging out there say "What's another dead nigger? It's nothing." They hate and kill each other, and others too, because they're powerless. Power over yourself builds real strength. If you have a job and bring home some money, you have a sense of dignity plus the actual energy of working. This is all related to national security. Something good happens to a person who's working at a satisfying job. When people are unemployed they're lost; they feel rotten. And sometimes, if you're young and full of energy and you feel rotten and no good, you're going to let that energy out by hitting or shooting or mugging. If there's the Russians to hate, it can end up getting expressed in a war.

There's not just crime on the streets that makes this country insecure. It's an old phrase, but we should emphasize a little more "crime in the suites." What greater crime is there than polluting the air we breathe? It's a crime against millions. Or the chemical and nuclear leakages that occur? God knows how many people have been affected in Arkansas, at Three Mile Island, at Love Canal. We have been lucky so far.

How do you value human life? You watch a newsreel and a woman carries her baby out of a fire—dead. Then cut to a sweet matronly woman telling how good this detergent is. Life is as valueless as the detergent. *That's* the message. All this is related.

What's going to kill us may not be the bomb. It may not be chemical leakage or strangulation of people by pollution. What may kill us is *banality*. Hannah Arendt spoke of the "banality of evil" in her book about Eichmann and Jerusalem. The Germans were not beastly; they were just ordinary people. Even those in the SS were ordinary people, capable of extraordinary brutality. They were banal people, without imagination. What we get on TV is a steady diet of banality. It stunts the imaginations and possibilities of people that I meet. Banality is a shroud. Day after day after day on radio and TV we get these ten-second or thirty-second spots, again and again. This is banal stuff, and now they're using little children as peddlers and hawkers and pimps and whores and liars. This is what banality does to us. The very language we use becomes the language of TV. At the time of the

Christmas bombings of North Vietnam I asked a cabdriver what he thought about it. He said, "We can't be a pitiful, helpless giant." He picked that up from Nixon on TV! He said, "We got to be Number One." I said, "Are *you* Number One?" And he paused; no one had ever asked him that question before. He said, "I'm Number *Nothin'*." Then he told about his wife leaving him; his daughter is round-heeled, his boy's on drugs, he hates himself. But if you are Number Nothing, you've got to be part of something else, no matter how brutal it is.

Why does a poor white guy join the Ku Klux Klan? Because his life is rotten he wants someone even lower—the "nigger."

Being patriotic is more than waving the Stars and Stripes. It's understanding the nature of America and how it came to be, understanding the idea of freedom of expression and every man being a king. Everybody must be free to express his real thoughts without being called a traitor just because he disagrees with the official position.

There are impertinent questions not being asked. The "impertinent question" is a phrase used by J. Bronowski who did the Public Television program "Ascent of Man." In one of his lectures he said, "The great scientists and poets always ask the impertinent question." Einstein asked it and Newton asked it. The technicians, who are banal men, never ask; they just go along. Right now we are in the hands of the technicians. It's time for the scientists, poets, and all the so-called ordinary people who have poetry in them to have their say. *We have to get equal time,* in all the media, on behalf of sanity and survival. And that's what this book is all about.

Acknowledgments

I deeply appreciate the many people who have made this book possible, particularly the nearly 400 people I interviewed who so generously shared their insights and concerns—and often their homes as well. I only wish I could include all of their excellent ideas in these pages.

In addition to the interviewees, numerous people in a variety of capacities have given me support. I owe a particularly deep debt of gratitude to three of them. My mother, Clare Scott Huddle, has given me invaluable support and editorial suggestions—as well as working with me to prove there need be no generation gap. Dr. Mel Gurtov of the University of California (Riverside) worked closely with me on an earlier version of this manuscript and gave me a remarkable experience of what true collaboration can be. Finally, Dr. Edgar Robinson, Professor Emeritus of The American University (Washington, D.C.) has given me constant encouragement and support in this project.

Unfortunately the limits of space prohibit my giving full credit to all of the other friends and colleagues who have supported my work over the past five years. A few individuals to whom I give special thanks are: Alison Allan, Frank von Hippel, Randy Mack, Leigh Ann Ffansler, Marilyn Asbell, Chris Kirtz, Pat and Louise Patteson, Richard Perl, Vince Darago, Linda and Chucky Blitz, Joshua Mailman, Bob and Magda Mazer, Lianne Sorkin, Fleeda Darby, Marty Edelston, Rob and Diana Coughlan, Phil Nelson, Peter Russell, John Cox, and Carl Fismer. In addition, I am grateful to Milton Taubman and the Peace Development Fund for timely financial assistance which enabled me to complete this manuscript.

I also deeply appreciate the people at Schocken Books for their faith in me and in this book, in particular, Peter Bedrick, Betty Gold, Irene Williams, and Julius Glaser.

And last, but not least, I thank God for the privilege of having been given such an inspiring "assignment"—and for living in a country where carrying out such work is possible.

Norie Huddle

Introduction

When I first got the idea for this book I thought it would be easy to write. After all, for my first book, on Japanese pollution, I had to learn Japanese, and for the second I had to bicycle for nine months across the United States. This new book would be interviews done in English, on the very question of how to survive. Publishers would love it, talk-show hosts would crawl over each other to get to me first. . . . It'd be like falling off a log, and I couldn't wait to get started.

Boy, was I wrong! One early interviewee, excited by my approach, urged me to go to her literary agent. "B.R. will *love* the idea." I went to New York City, was kept waiting for ages, and when I was finally ushered into his spacious office, he cut me off as soon as I said ". . . book of interviews on national and global security . . ." and ran a ten-minute monologue of which I remember most vividly the line "If it's not about sex and not about money, it'll never sell."

"What if it's about survival?" I asked innocently.

"Nope, sex and money. That's all people are interested in. And the publishing world is getting very tight these days."

"But . . . *survival?*" Maybe he didn't get it: if we didn't survive, there wouldn't be any sex or money.

"Yeah, yeah, I know. It's an important issue, but people don't read books anymore. They watch TV."

I walked out of there, stunned both at his utterly discouraging remarks and at the obviously low image he had of the American public's reading habits. Before long, however, I bounced back, joking to my friends, "I'll change the title to *Sex, Money, Violence, and National Security*—on the cover, Brooke Shields or Dolly Parton, naked from the waist up, a bandolier of bullets slung between her breasts, one hand with long red fingernails grips a machine gun, and the other a hand grenade. *That* ought to make it sell!" But I was secretly discouraged. Was it true? Did people really only want to read about money and sex? Didn't we care about our own survival?★

★ As it turned out, several interviewees made fascinating arguments that survival and security were very directly linked to issues of sex and money.

My project had been born during a ten-day period of fasting and meditation over the Christmas holiday of 1979. Frustrated from a year's intense work of large-scale organizing in the antinuclear movement, I had reached the conclusion that although mass demonstrations and direct confrontations possibly had an important role to play in changing society, surely there must be a better way. Although I felt deeply moved by the obvious commitment and concern, I had also become burnt out on what one friend called the "hostile pacifism" of a few members of the peace activists' movement: A. J. Muste's quote "There is no way to peace, peace *is* the way," made a lot of sense, and I couldn't find any projects which inspired me to become involved. I was offered an attractive job to lobby against nuclear power in the Congress and felt compelled to turn it down; I was tired of arguing in favor of a certain position and felt I needed to understand better why it was that certain people were so adamantly in favor of building nuclear weapons, even though it seemed clear that was such a dead-end street. Within me there grew a gnawing conviction that I had a particular "assignment" to carry out, yet I had no idea what it was. In late December, right near the end of my retreat, I had the clear impression of a voice in my head which said, "Go interview all sorts of people on their ideas for what will make America and the world more secure." I was ecstatic; it felt like the right assignment: a "Studs Terkel approach" to national security.

I wrote up a prospectus to raise money so I wouldn't have to live on a frayed shoestring. Nobody liked my concept. "It's too broad," they said. "Why don't you just write about nuclear war?"

"I see the issue as much broader than that," I said, "and I don't just want to write about how awful things are. I want to show that by actively listening to people we can all improve our understanding, and at the very least, improve the quality of the debate on national security." By this time I was beginning to wonder if I was overestimating my interviewing skills and if I myself really could make a difference. In frustration I asked Hal Feiveson, a Princeton professor and friend, if I could demonstrate my approach by interviewing him. At the end of an hour he had come around 180 degrees, saying the words I'd been praying for: "*Now* I understand what you're trying to do. This is very important; this could really make a difference."

Over the months that followed I developed a basic set of questions:

1. Tell me about yourself and your work, particularly as it relates to creating greater national and global security.
2. How can we make America and the world more secure?
3. What is your positive vision of the future? How, specifically, can we create that vision?
4. How can we stop and reverse the arms race? How can we improve relations with the Soviet Union?
5. How can we improve relations with the Third World?

I also developed a loosely styled interview technique which brought results that sometimes astonished me. Basically I would remind myself before each interview that I was not there to convert but to understand. After all, it seemed reasonable to assume that each person had developed his or her worldview based on personal life experiences. Instead of debating points of view and thereby focusing attention on how our ideas were different, I simply asked them to explain their ideas in a way that I could understand them. In communicating successfully to me they had to hear themselves, including any inconsistencies in their logic, and the debate could take place where it was most appropriate: in each of our own heads. At times interviewees became angry or defensive. Initially I took this personally, feeling that I had failed in my aim of creating a really safe environment for them to share the truth of their experience; later I realized that their anger came from fear—after all, the threat of nuclear war hangs like a sword of Damocles over the heads of all of us, and we instinctively realize this. Perhaps it also came from a sense of despair, a lack of conviction of personally being able to make a difference in preventing a holocaust. At times, to my amazement, when I was able to give people the opportunity to express themselves fully, including some rather unpleasant opinions, remarkable shifts would occur. Several people told me after the interviews, "I didn't plan to tell you the truth, but I couldn't help myself." Others, complaisant in the beginning, by the end were practically begging me to tell them how they could become more involved. Some even wept, and I found myself at times moved to tears as well. I was deeply moved to discover how hungry people everywhere are for engaging in effective action.

During the first year I interviewed people primarily in the Washington, D.C., area who had been in or were currently serving in the government or military, or people in conservative political organizations and the peace movement. I selected interviewees largely by word of mouth: "You should interview so-and-so." As I became more experienced and self-confident I broke through an initial shyness and hesitation to "bother" important people and grew bolder in my approach. One day, while hunting for a number in the District of Columbia telephone directory, the name of a very high-level former government official leaped off the page at me. I gathered up my courage and picked up the telephone. To my astonishment, five minutes later I had an appointment to interview him. The interview, several days later, was somewhat of a disappointment. Indeed at the end of it I turned off the tape recorder and said to him, "Mr. C., I really don't want to be rude, but I feel as if I've been fed a bunch of canned pabulum."

"I've been trying to give you accurate information," he said.

"I'm not questioning that. But you're basically giving me the same sort of stuff I can read in the newspaper daily. What I'm asking you is how we can make this country and the world more secure. From where you have been in government, sir, you must have some *wonderful* insights into this. Why won't you share the benefits of your experience and explore this question creatively?"

"Well," he said, carefully, "one doesn't want to appear foolish by indulging in speculation on anything."

"Excuse me," I said, getting somewhat exasperated. "We're talking about possibly destroying civilization as we know it. You're sitting on information and experience that could possibly make *the* critical difference in whether we make it or not, and you're talking about *looking foolish*?! What good is it to have freedom of speech if we don't exercise it because we're afraid to share the truth of our personal experience and the insights gained from that?"

We smoothed it over, had a fairly diplomatic departure, and I caught the bus home. Once safely in the house I burst into tears, feeling more desperate than before. If *this* was the attitude of the people in power or formerly in power, why, *we were in deep trouble.* I also felt very moved by Mr. C., who seemed intelligent and well meaning but nervous about telling me what he really thought. A friend pointed out that maybe at some time he had been burned by a reporter. I thought, *"If we all drag around so much of the past with us, how can we ever be free in the present to create a decent future?"* Our minds will be too cluttered with fearful images based on crummy past experiences for us to maximize present opportunities. I also became deeply concerned about the exclusive use of "worst-case scenarios" in developing strategies: if we constantly assume the worst and react on the basis of negative assumptions about what the Soviets are going to do, and if they do the same, then there is little reason to expect that we will find a way of resolving difficulties peacefully. Why couldn't there also be "best-case scenarios" in which everybody wins? The phrase "Seek and ye shall find" came to me with new meaning.

It became increasingly clear to me that the world seen from Washington allowed only a fairly narrow range of thinking to be considered "realistic," so I decided to take my questions on the road. Surely, I thought, *in the collective wisdom of all of us there must be the answers we need.* A few days before I left, a Canadian friend, Alison Allan, came down to join me.

On our 12,000-mile odyssey in my ancient Volkswagen bus we found people everywhere deeply appreciative of the chance to talk about the issues I was raising. Even outside the formal interviews, no sooner would I tell people my questions than they would pour out their ideas, many of which were excellent. Indeed I became convinced that schools, churches, businesses, and communities could do much to contribute to our national and global security by exploring these same questions within their organizations and with their elected officials at all levels of government. I found a great hunger for accurate information and clearer thinking, as well as a deep sense of concern for the future course of our society. This matched well with one recent nationwide poll which found that 76 percent of Americans surveyed believe that war is probable in the next few years; another 1982 poll found that fully 80 percent of college students interviewed believed they would die in a nuclear war.

Discussing these issues and their deeper roots wasn't always easy, however. I found a number of people terrified to talk: "You can't fight City Hall," or "What's the use? We're doomed," or "You have to watch what you say or 'they' will get you." One bus driver told me candidly that he thought powerful vested interests had sold America's national security down the river: "Before long there'll be a revolution and the gutters will flow with blood." He added a word of kindly advice, "Lady, if you continue to ask the kinds of questions you're asking, I'll bet that within ten years the little men in white coats will come to get you." Other people pointed to the assassinations of the Kennedy brothers and Martin Luther King to justify their fear of talking. Briefly, I found their warnings disconcerting and disempowering until I remembered that fundamentally we all want the same things in our lives and that in our essence we are truly all born of one life spirit. Whenever considerations of my own safety would begin to plague my mind, I found myself recalling the words of Christ: "And ye shall know the truth, and the truth shall make you free." How else, except by committing ourselves to the pursuit of truth and asking questions that lead us forward, will we come to know what will make the world work better for all of us and discover our freedom? And so I continued to ask my questions.

The results of these interviews—nearly 400 during four and a half years—have given me a renewed sense of hope that America can, and indeed *is,* changing—because we are awakening to the realization that we *must* change in order to survive. Despite their great diversity, all the people with whom I spoke—male and fe-male, young and old, conservatives and liberals and radicals, intel-lectuals, blue- and pink-collar workers, bureaucrats, national secu-rity professionals—recognize that we are in a state of great crisis. Today as I continue to ask my "impertinent questions" every-where I go—the post office, the grocery store, friends' houses, the bank—I find that people are increasingly talking about the danger, the horror, and at times the "inevitability" of nuclear war. Such talk is disquieting, for, as I remind them and myself, if we focus exclusively on the negative and believe it to be inevit-able, that might well be precisely the trigger for nuclear war: the proverbial "self-fulfilling prophecy."

Nuclear war does *not* have to happen. You, just like me, can and do make a critical difference in choosing and helping to create the sort of future we want. The first step in this process is to ask ourselves and those around us the right questions. We must begin to see how the problems are interconnected, rising from a deeper rupture in the fabric of our lives and thinking. We must commit ourselves constantly to saying what is really true for us about our current situation, personal and societal, for although this may seem dangerous or overwhelming in the short run, *it is only a collective sense of integrity which will give us the vision and the strength to transform ourselves, our nation, and our world.*

As we start to pool our information and insights we can build a collective set of visions and revise our institutions in a manner appropriate for this day and age, for as Thomas Jefferson wrote,

> I am not an advocate for frequent changes in laws and constitutions, but laws and institutions must go hand in hand with the progress of the human mind. As that becomes more developed, more enlightened, as new discoveries are made, new truths discovered and manners and opinions change, with the change of circumstances, institutions must advance also to keep pace with the times. We might as well require a man to wear still the coat which fitted him when a boy as civilized society to remain ever under the regimen of their barbarous ancestors.

Our effectiveness in carrying out this task will depend on the level of integrity and commitment we each bring to the "new American revolution." In examining the strength of our commitment, we can learn much from the example of our Founding Fathers, a handful of diverse individuals of varying fortunes and talents whose concern blossomed into a commitment so strong that they could write ". . . we pledge our lives, our fortunes and our sacred honor . . ." to the task of carrying out the first American Revolution.

Looking back at our history, it is easy for us to imagine how much simpler were the tasks our Founding Fathers faced. Today the complexity of industrial society, the proliferation of knowledge and technologies, the explosion of our national and global population and pollution problems, the large numbers of weapons of massive destruction all converge to make it sometimes appear as if we face an impossible task. Yet the same process that worked for our Founding Fathers still functions today—and functions well. The new American revolution begins in the hearts and minds of each one of us. It starts with telling the truth about what we experience, and then with creating opportunities for others to share *their* experiences. As we really listen to each other, remembering that all of us have changed some of our own deeply held convictions in the past as we have found them to be counterproductive to our safety and happiness, we begin to move beyond our "prerecorded tapes" to discover our shared concerns and visions. This was brought home to me in a stunning fashion in late December 1980 as the long interviewing trip around the United States drew near the end. Over eggs and toast in a Mississippi truckstop, I got into a brief conversation with Kevin O'Brian, a Sacramento-based trucker in his early fifties. When I asked him what he thought would make America and the world more secure, he slugged down some coffee and grinned: "Easy. Kill all the Russians." He watched for me to react; I took a deep breath and smiled sweetly.

"Really? Kill all the Russians? You think that'll do it?"

He shrugged. "Why not? We've got two different and incompatible thought systems and don't seem to be able to work through the differences, so I guess we should kill them. What do *you* think?" He turned the question back on me.

"Well," I said, "I guess I'm a softie because I don't like the idea of killing people and the Russians are people too. At one time they were even our political allies. So how can we resolve our differences in a peaceful fashion?"

He shrugged again. "Beats the hell out'a me. I'm just a trucker. Why don't you ask the folks in Washington? That's *their* job. That's what we're payin' them fancy salaries to do."

"I've talked with a number of them," I said, "but I think we need more folks *outside* of D.C. involved in thinking through this whole national security thing. In Washington you can get stuck in a mental rut that's pretty narrow."

He studied me for a moment and his voice tone changed. Then, "Excuse my French, lady, but what I said about killing the Russians was bullshit. *Of course* you're right: the people over there are just people too, partly good and partly bad. It's government and big business that get us in trouble. People in power get greedy. What we need are people-to-people cultural and educational exchanges of all sorts, so's we can see their art and culture and they can see ours. If more ordinary folks were going over there and coming over here, I think we'd find we have less to fight about and more to cooperate on. We have wars because that feeds certain businesses and keeps the economy going. We got our fingers in pies all over the world, so we sell weapons to all sorts of totalitarian governments and send down our agents to help them repress the poor people and maintain power. And then our government bitches at the Russians for doing the same kind of thing. Vietnam should've taught us that this was a losing game, but somebody in D.C. ain't catchin' on." He shook his head in frustration. "The funny thing is that those politicians in Washington think us folks out here are dumb because we don't have college degrees and don't wear fancy suits to work. But there are some damned smart truckers out here on the road and we're getting pretty pissed."

This experience and similar ones made me wonder how many people are putting forth ideas they don't really believe deep inside—in order to create an effect on their listeners, or to protect themselves from "them," or simply to avoid thinking about painful subjects they think they have no power to change. Whatever the reasons, *can it be that right under the surface of the quick responses we might find a wholly new reality?*

There is an American Indian saying, "Do not judge a man until you have walked a mile in his moccasins." As you read the interviews in the pages that follow, imagine that you are joining me on my journey through the minds and values of a broad spectrum of thoughtful individuals whose diverse life patterns have trained them to experience the world and themselves in quite different ways. Although some of the ideas presented may seem farfetched or ridiculous, the people holding those ideas probably believe them as much as you and I believe ours; and most of them would probably be willing to embrace new ideas if they were convinced they would work better. When you have finished, I would really like to hear personally from you, your response to the questions asked and, particularly, what you personally are doing to make things work better. It's an honor and a privilege to be working together on such an important task.

THE INTERVIEWS

Paul Green

Because the Committee on the Present Danger was receiving a good deal of unfavorable commentary from antinuclear activists I interviewed, I very much wanted to understand its view of the world and of Soviet policies. In late 1979 I met with Paul Green in his office in Washington, D.C., part of a large suite rented out by the Committee.

Since college I've been very interested in foreign affairs and national security. My parents were immigrants from Poland, which also influenced me a lot. When he was growing up my father was considered a young radical and was always interested in Russia. He was part of an organization called the Bund, a group of Jewish socialists. They were for the socialism of Eastern Europe and were concerned about anti-Semitism. He came to America when he was about seventeen and worked as an embroiderer, which was a very skilled trade in those days and quite well paid. He was a hard worker all his life and got little in return. I am very proud of him. I grew up during the depression and it was a difficult time economically; we lived from hand to mouth. I'm still tainted by it; I hate to see food wasted. My kids grew up thinking everything is plentiful and their wastefulness drives me batty.

Since we were Jewish, when World War II came along I was particularly interested in seeing Hitler defeated. I joined the air force, and with my degree in journalism fairly soon got an assignment with the *Stars and Stripes*. With that I went to North Africa with General Patton. We went into Tunisia, Sicily, southern France, and finally into Germany. I distinctly remember meeting the Russian troops, and a real sense of camaraderie between them and the American GIs. I hoped this might help alleviate what I knew was going on in Russia. You see, with my parents being Polish I was particularly aware of the disillusionment of radicals under Stalin, his shooting of the Bolsheviks, and the liquidating of his top military leadership. Stalin's trials of dissidents created a furor in New York City and in Europe; we followed them very carefully. I was among those who were against the trials. When the Nazi–Soviet Pact was signed, our group became anti-Soviet. As a result of the war I hoped there might be an alleviation of the brutal Soviet dictatorship.

After I left the *Stars and Stripes,* I came back to Washington and returned to my job with CBS. I was a reporter from the newsroom; Eric Sevareid was there. I was here a year and then the lure of being overseas kept pulling me, so I left CBS and signed up with a little news agency and went over to London. I covered Western Europe for them.

Eventually I came to work at the Committee on the Present Danger. We're not a mass organization, only about twelve thousand, but we manage to get our people in the news pretty well. We have a pretty mixed membership and stick to dealing with national security in terms of the military balance between the United States and the Soviet Union. Our people go along with the theory of MAD [mutually assured destruction] that says you can prevent war by being strong enough to deter the Russians from attacking. We believe in that, and we think that the Soviet Union does too.

I don't think things have changed much in Russia since Stalin's time. It's unfortunate, because I like the Russian people very much. I think the Communists have rigid control over the government apparatus and that it's worse than ever. Although I haven't been to Russia myself, I'm in touch with people who have. One young couple, my close friends, are scientists and go over every year. They know Russian scientists intimately, and their view of Russian leaders is pretty critical. I think the Russian people are generally hardworking and would like to get along with the rest of the world. They do have a certain degree of paranoia because of the conflicts Russia has been involved with over the years, but often Russia has been the aggressor as well as the aggressed-on.

The Russians see us Americans as being very lucky. I've been interviewed by a number of Russians. They always bring up the fact that "You were one of the ones who attacked us, trying to destroy the Russion Revolution," and "You don't know what it means to be living under the gun." Which is true. In America it's been a long time since we fought a major war on our soil. In every country in Europe the people have a much different perspective from us. But, anyway, I think there is essentially no difference in character and personality between the dictatorship today and the one before the Bolshevik Revolution. The same types of people gravitate to the top. As for the revolutionary fervor and reform that the Marxists advocated, those ideas lasted a very short time and then, with the realities of the postrevolutionary era, they went completely by the board. I don't think there's anything left of the original fervor and reform, and there hasn't been for decades. The ideals were good ones, as Lenin translated them, and it became Marxist-Leninism. But more and more of the idealism went out of it. The Russian people were perfectly justified in having a revolution because of the stupidity and tyranny of the Russian tsars and the people around them. There was terrible brutality, more horrible even than it was under Stalin. What was the original slogan? "Bread and Land for the People." Originally I suppose they had land for the people for a very short time, but they soon collectivized the entire country. Stalin murdered all the *kulaks* [wealthy and middle-class peasant farmers and landowners]. Now you have collectivization of the country and nobody owns anything. They are all working for the state, which is a monster. Maybe they have more equitable distribution of food than they did under the tsars or under Stalin, but their economic system is terrible.

Lenin capitalized on the fact that the peasants wanted to own a piece of land. The original way he got them out of World War I was by promising to give land to the people. Today they have a bit of those privately owned plots of land, but there is very little, and they circumscribe it by all sorts of conditions. It helps a little bit, but just about all the cultivated land is collectivized year after year after year. Meanwhile the Soviet Union cannot grow enough wheat to feed itself. They have some of the finest wheatlands in the world, millions and millions of acres, yet they have to buy wheat from the capitalist nations. How do you explain that? I say it's because the peasants aren't interested in working for the state. They'd get a heck of a lot more if they worked for themselves.

The economic system as structured by the Soviet Union doesn't work and it wouldn't exist without tyranny. That's the only thing that holds it together. Now they do spread some of the benefits over the managerial and technical class who do have a stake in the system and who live quite well, but they're living off the backs of the peasants. The peasantry is absolutely aware of this but there's nothing they can do about it. They had a revolution under the tsars, but they can't have a revolution under the Soviets because the grip of the military is too strong. The Soviet people have lived under the Soviet regime for . . . let me see, 1917, that's sixty-two years. Every organ of communication, from the radio to the press, is in the hands of the dictatorship. They tell people only what they want them to know. People who are sixty-two years old have been born under this kind of regime, and this is all they know. They don't know what is going on in the rest of the world.

They have the traditional Marxist view—that the United States is imperialist, that we're in the last stage of capitalism, and that eventually this will lead to the great dawning of the proletarian revolution. They are intent on world domination because they see that as the way to carry out the principles of Marxism. The only way they think they can do it is through military force because, although they have tried, they cannot persuade other countries to go Marxist. I don't think the people in Russia know what's going on in the rest of the world. If the Soviet people found out what kind of a democracy we have here I think they'd be a little envious. But they're never going to find out. Some of the Russians who come over here see it, but the Russians who come over here have a stake in the government.

You have to make a distinction between the Soviet Union and Eastern Europe. Even though the countries in Eastern Europe are technically Marxist, there is no love lost toward the Russians among the people who are relatively free, who realize what is going on with the Soviet Union, and who want to be different. Even though they are tied to the Soviet Union in economic, political, and military ways and have to make the best of it, that doesn't say that they love the Russians or admire the Russian type of government. In Eastern Europe they do have a press that is controlled, but not rigidly so. Our material does get in there. They have a much better idea of what's going on in the rest of the world, so if we continue what we are doing, and continue to set an example of democracy—like, not get into any more Vietnams—we'll get along with them. But we can't do that in the Soviet Union because of the rigid control there.

With that much rigid control, the Russians are not going to negotiate their power. They want SALT II because it will give them an advantage over us. But they'd never agree to proper monitoring and verification. They did under the Helsinki agreement and have been violating it ever since. I don't think there is anything that we can do to make them yield their own power. I think you'll find me on the pessimistic side. In the transfer of leadership, perhaps when Brezhnev dies, if there is a struggle for power. . . . But I don't think there is very much we can do to have an effect on that either.

Huddle: If the leadership is feeling threatened militarily by the United States, is there a chance that we could help push a hawk into a position of leadership?

Green: I don't see how they can be more hawkish than they are.

Huddle: Well, if they actually *used* their weapons, that would be more hawkish.

Green: They're realistic. They have nothing to gain by launching a war; they would lose just as much as the other side—although the Soviet military *do* conceive of the possibility of a nuclear war. That is different here in the United States. I won't say that there aren't individuals here who talk about nuclear war. But our basic national strategy is predicated on avoiding nuclear war. And theirs is not.

Huddle: I sense there is a lot of confusion about this at this time in America.

Green: That's because of our democratic form of government. A lot of different voices speak in various ways. Anyway, our feeling at the Committee is that we'll only make progress in arms reduction if the Soviets perceive that we are strong. We intend to remain strong and won't let them get the jump on us. The Soviets are realists; they always have been.

Huddle: Since the Soviets perceive that we are intent on world domination through capitalism and imperialism in its final phase, is there a danger that they might also perceive our weapons buildup as being something threatening to them, that *we* might seek to destroy *them*?

Green: They have military people and political people who understand military strategy and military weapons. They know by looking at their weapons and what they're building that this is not for self-defense; it's simply far beyond what they need for self-defense. So in the Committee our feeling is that they are thinking far beyond self-defense, that it can only be a threatening stance to the rest of the world. In other words, we believe they are trying to gain superiority over the United States—just as we had superiority over them twenty years ago in the nuclear field.

Huddle: How do you think they view our plans to develop the MX and the cruise missiles? Would they see that as some kind of buildup or threatening stance on our part?

Green: They see that as a sign that we will not permit them to become superior.

Huddle: It sounds to me as if what we have are two big kids on a block that are facing off with some pretty big slingshots. . . .

Green: I don't like these analogies. I don't think you can compare two sovereign nations to kids with slingshots. . . .

Huddle: Only nowadays, it's nuclear weapons, not slingshots. You know, Paul, maybe you can explain something I just can't understand in your position and really want to understand. It seems that what you're saying boils down to this: we're afraid of the Russians and their ambitions to dominate the world, so we need a Big One. Then they're afraid of us and our economic system and our Big One, so *they* need a Big One. Then we need *two* Big Ones. Then *they* need two Big Ones. Then we need four and they need four; then eight and eight. . . . When do we have enough? Where do we stop?

Green [in a loud, angry voice]: Well? What is *your* solution? WELL, WHAT IS *YOUR* SOLUTION?

Huddle [startled]: I don't *have* a solution. That's why I'm writing this book, interviewing all sorts of people. I'm really hoping that somewhere in the collective wisdom of all of us we will find the answers we need. I mean, it seems as if we have created a *terrible* situation that is becoming increasingly dangerous, a situation that no one wants. If there is a nuclear war, most likely we'll all die. You have children, right? And I hope to have children someday. We're all in this together.

Green: You're very clever, very clever.

Huddle: No, really, Paul, I'm not particularly clever. I really am trying to understand your position. I think it is terribly important that we in the United States really understand these issues and try to find some answers that will work. [*At this point another visitor arrived and the interview was terminated.*]

Although my initial reaction to Paul Green's outburst was that I had somehow failed, several days after the interview I wrote him to say how much I had enjoyed meeting him and to express my hope that we could keep channels of communication open between us. In my letter I told him how difficult it had been for my father and me to communicate with each other during the early days of the Vietnam War, but that our efforts to bridge the gap had been extremely important in helping each of us to modify our positions. "We can," I stressed, "learn a lot from each other, precisely because we have different backgrounds and perspectives." Then a week or so after I mailed the letter I telephoned him. He had received the letter and appreciated my effort to communicate; he put me on the Committee's mailing list.

Two years passed and I gave him a second telephone call. To my surprise he remembered me immediately, and actually seemed very pleased to hear from me. We arranged to have lunch together a couple of weeks hence. When we finally met, it felt like "old friends." He was very interested in what I had been learning in my research; had I gotten any important insights? Indeed, he interviewed me this time! He also expressed understandable pride in the fact that about forty of the Committee's members (including President Reagan) were now in high positions in the new administration.

Toward the end of our lunch I leaned forward and said, "Do you know, Paul, I think that in some way you hope that I'm right in terms of my vision."

"What do you mean?" He looked somewhat startled.

"As far as I can understand the position your organization and other conservative groups are taking—and correct me if I'm mistaken— you don't offer any hope. Just more and more weapons, probably leading to a nuclear war at some point. The most positive outcome I've generally heard expressed is that it will 'only be a small nuclear war.' Now we've never taken on a challenge this big before, but at least my way offers hope and a new vision for America."

He looked at me thoughtfully for a moment and then said, "You may have a point there." Then he invited me to stop by his office. There he gave me a stack of literature and, opening the brochure which listed the forty Committee members appointed to high positions, he said, "Now, I think you should try to interview this one . . . and this one would be really interested in your questions . . ." and listed seven or eight people for me.

I practically floated home: surely, with caring and mutual respect, we really could begin to break down the walls that separate groups within our own country . . . and wasn't this a beginning?

Sue Shetrom

Sue Shetrom lives with her husband and daughter in a once-again quiet suburban area not far from the defective Three Mile Island nuclear reactor. Under the veneer of the fairly conventional suburban lifestyle, however, little remains unchanged. The interview was conducted in the fall of 1980.

I grew up in central Pennsylvania, in a rural community similar to where I live now. My family was small and conservative. After graduating from Lewisburg State College I moved to the Harrisburg area and began teaching mathematics in a high school. I taught there about six years before my daughter was born, then quit teaching and stayed home for two years. After a divorce I needed a job, so I went back to work for a couple of years. It was really a very conservative, quiet life. I was not involved politically. About a year ago a reporter interviewed me one night in the rain and freezing cold outside the governor's mansion. I had a cold at the time. He asked me, "Why are you doing this? Have you always protested things?" I said, "No." Despite the fact that I was in college in the sixties, I never protested anything; I never sat in, I never did anything of that sort. I was very content with my life the way it was, and it took the accident of Three Mile Island happening practically in my backyard to wake me up to the fact that things weren't being done the way they should be, and that my trust in my government was a little off. I lived here thirteen years before the nuclear plant was built, and I just assumed that if the industry and the government were permitting something like this to happen, that they obviously knew what they were doing and that my safety would be *the* priority. So it came as rather a rude awakening to me to realize that the so-called experts *didn't* know what they were doing and that an accident that they said would never happen had actually happened and was jeopardizing my family.

The accident actually happened at four A.M. on a Wednesday morning, but we didn't learn what really happened until Friday. We were told at that time that nothing much had happened: they had a little problem, there were a few little releases. But things like this had happened before. We were told they would shut it down and it would be back on line within a week. On Friday I was teaching over in York when I found out how serious it was. News reports started coming over the radio, telling us that pregnant women and children to the age of five should leave the area. People were coming in, knowing that I live near TMI, saying, "Oh, I hear that they're going to evacuate; you probably won't be able to get home, the roads are blocked." All sorts of rumors were circulating. My husband was only a few minutes away and our daughter Jenny was in a private school a few minutes away, so I wasn't terribly worried about them. We were all close enough together. Being a responsible teacher I had to stay in my classroom, close the windows, and keep the kids calm. We dismissed school a few minutes early and I came home not knowing what I was going to find. Bill was here and we turned on the television.

Before that day I never really thought about how close we were to the TMI nuclear plant. If you stand out here on a clear day you can look over and see a little bit of the towers. When we discovered on the news reports that we were only three to four miles away, I said, "Okay, Jenny is six, not under five, but I'm not really sure why this cutoff point exists, and I don't want to take any chances." So we packed up and took her to my parents' for a couple of days. We came back Sunday night thinking, "Well, they're saying everything is much better so we'll go home." It was really horrible because there are no streetlights here and it was pitch black. Nobody else came home. There was one other family way up the end of the street, but you couldn't see any lights. You looked out every window of our house and it was totally black. It had been raining those two days and was really foggy. It was just like the end of the world coming. We were sitting here totally alone. I thought that if we were home we'd be able to get more news about what was going on, but it wasn't any more accurate than what we were getting eighty miles away.

On Monday morning Bill went to work. School had been cancelled because so many families were gone. A neighbor came home and said that they were going to evacuate and that we'd be allowed to take pillows and that was it, and get on the bus. I said, "No, that's not going to happen." So I went around the house and got together all our clothes, photographs that I wanted, and valuable papers. I put those in the car and got ready to leave and go be with my husband.

When I left, the most frustrating thing to me was pulling out of this driveway, because as I pulled out, an employee of Metropolitan Edison Company, which owns the TMI plant, was pulling up to read our meter. You kind of stop dead in your tracks and go, *"Wait a minute, I'm leaving my home thinking I may never be able to return, looking back at my house and kind of mentally taking a picture of it and thinking this is the end of all of this, and you're going to read my meter to send me a bill for my electricity!"* I have never been so angry! I am not a violent person but I think I would have shot him if I'd had a gun.

Anyway, we stayed down in York that next day. I had work to do and kept busy, and the radio was playing in the hall so you could hear what was going on. We came back home again at the end of the day. By then they did seem to have things under control a little bit.

That was the end of March and beginning of April. April and May I went on with my teaching. I still wasn't committed to being an antinuclear activist or anything like that by any means. There was just something wrong somewhere that I wanted to take a better look at. There were still people saying to me, "Well, you know we need nuclear power," and I was still thinking, "Well, maybe we *do* need nuclear power." But I was starting to read things and ask a lot more questions. In May we went to our first rally. That was an eye-opener for me. It took place in a little grove in Reading, Pennsylvania, where Metropolitan Edison has their offices. The first thing that struck me was the diversity of people—from senior citizens to little babies. It wasn't the hippy-type rallies that you had in the sixties. We were a lot of mothers and fathers with our kids, all very well mannered. When we left the place, you never would know anything had occurred there. It was incredibly nice.

But surrounding this whole, peaceful, lovely gathering and spring sunshine were these policemen in their cars and helicopters over us, watching us. When we walked down a road, out to the offices of the plant, they were there in riot gear with the helmets and guns. I thought, "*Wait a minute, I'm just a housewife with a little kid. What are you going to do with that stuff?*" You know, the barricades were set up, and it was really frightening, and it was like suddenly *I was the enemy.* I am going, "*No,* wait a minute! *You* people are the enemy, *you* are the ones that have put my life in jeopardy and my child's life in jeopardy, and *you* are standing there with guns looking at me as if I had done something wrong!" It was so twisted!

By the time school let out in June I was committed: we didn't need that nuclear plant and I didn't want it. I had to do something. My feeling was that I would not be able to live with myself if, say, thirty years from now my daughter had a child that was deformed or if she developed cancer or leukemia. If that happened I would just be so wiped out. If she were to turn to me and say, "Mother, why didn't you try to do anything?" That is what motivated me to begin with. It was totally selfish. Now I have changed to the point where I see it's a bigger issue. It is no longer just my responsibility to myself as a person. I can't sit back anymore and leave it up to somebody else. The problem is worldwide, people all over the country and world are suffering and being used as guinea pigs, and I feel a commitment to do something to help them. At the same time each of us has only so much energy, and sometimes we have to focus on work in our backyard.

At first it was just "I'll offer to type, staple, and stuff envelopes; I'm sure I can do that." Before you knew it it was "Sue, would you pick up the radio and do an interview with so-and-so," or "Write this press release," or "We need somebody to go down and make a statement at the courthouse." It just kind of grew and grew. "Would you help organize the teach-in?" "Will you be on the TMI Legal Fund?"

In April I was asked to go down to Washington to speak at the Citizens Hearings for Radiation Victims. That weekend was an eye-opener for me. It was really intense. Bill, Jenny, and I went with a friend of mine, Pat Smith from Newberry Town. When we walked in people were just socializing, having drinks, standing around talking. A couple of fellows walked up to us and started talking. One of them showed us a picture of himself, standing watching an atomic bomb test. You could see spots on his clothing from fallout. And then he pulled up his shirt and showed us the tumors, and then pictures of his deformed children. I realized it wasn't just nuclear power plants. I met widows of people who had worked in enrichment plants or uranium mines. One man had been given excessive radiation exposure to cure a rash and the whole lower half of his face is all plastic surgery and just grotesque. Spending the weekend with those people was *such* a moving experience. Just hearing them tell what had been done to them and how badly they had been treated, with no compensation at all, how the government just denies any responsibility for this at all . . . you were either hugging people or you were just sitting, sobbing. That experience changed me. After that I no longer thought of the problem as just Three Mile Island; it is *so* much bigger.

The word "acceptable" comes up all the time—"acceptable risk." It is as if they are saying, "Well, what are a few people? We can give them up, and our *country* is what's most important." I agree that our country is important, but I can't believe that you can just wipe people off as being unimportant or insignificant. Aren't *we* the country too? We're just sacrificing human beings, and I don't like it that a few people somewhere have the right to decide who they will be.

During the course of all this I have also become aware of the toxic chemicals, the waste–dump situation in our country. Again, I think it's a matter of companies' denying their responsibility for what was happening to the people. Lois Gibbs, from the area where the Love Canal scandal developed, showed me pictures of the school built right on the chemical dumpsite. You see chemicals oozing out of the ground and children coming home with the stuff all over them, unable to get it out of their clothes or off their skin. They had to go through enormous difficulties to make the government recognize the situation. She and another woman had to go door to door and collect all sorts of statistics before any government agency would finally listen and then verify their findings. People actually had to *die*! Although the city government has finally moved families out and given people money for their homes, the city now plans to sell those houses to low-income families! Even though it has been proved conclusively that people died from the chemicals and that it is still a very dangerous place to live, they are going to give low-income people all sorts of inducements to buy those homes, like great mortgages and low interest rates. According to Lois there are families who have said, "I will buy one and move in there, because I am now living in such a desperate situation—in a ghetto where my son will be on drugs, my daughter will be raped, and my child may be murdered in the streets. I would rather take my chances with chemicals than stay where I am."

It is so infuriating that some government official is going to allow this to happen. These people are criminals if they do something like that, and they should be tried and prosecuted. It's like they are destroying our security from *inside* the country.

When I think about national security, I do believe that we need to look strong to the world. No so much just to give the *appearance,* but we need to *be* strong. But now, what is *strong*? I can't agree that it's having all these nuclear weapons. That to me is total insanity. When I read that the government feels we need more missiles and more nuclear weapons, I know this will increase the uranium mining, enrichment programs and so forth. It is *incredible* to me. This is causing people to die, so what they are really saying is that *we can sacrifice our people for these weapons which will then make us strong.* Yet we already have enough weapons to destroy the whole world time and time again.

Our real strength and security are going to come out of the people working together. I have read articles recently that there are small groups, such as the ones I'm part of, that are growing up all over the country, people who are saying, "I can no longer sit back and let somebody else do the job, because they are not doing it. They are not being responsible." A terrible thing has happened to the American people. We have been lulled into believing that, being a democracy, all we had to do was show up at the polls and vote for somebody, and then they would go ahead and just take care of us, and we could sit back and enjoy our tennis and our swimming pools and whatever, and life would be fine. But this isn't the case. We're not informed voters. We're not sending to Washington people who can do an adequate job; and then, once they get there, we're letting them on their own. *Now* we are changing, but it took a really horrible accident to wake us up to the fact that we had to do this. I think it is a good sign that these groups are springing up all over the country. What really frightens me is that the government and the powers that be see *us* as a threat. *We* are not the threat; *they* are. I've heard stories of people sitting at the governor's office and having meetings on how they can hush up political radicals such as myself. It is obvious the governor won't meet us. He won't talk to me for five minutes on the telephone. He doesn't want anything to do with us.

We are going to support each other and we're going to keep growing and building to the point where someone is going to have to deal with us. They are already finding that they have to deal with us on some level. We just have to keep working at it and working at it until we really have a voice, until other people see that we are making progress. A lot of people say, "It's all in God's hands, there is nothing we can do. God will take care of it." Well, I believe God has a lot to do with it, but at the same time I believe He gave me a brain for a reason, and He expects me to do something. I just get so furious with people who say, "Well, there is nothing I can do" or "God will do it" and just sit around and do nothing. I have a lot of resentment at times for these people who are doing nothing. But maybe as they see that we are making progress, they will join too.

What has happened to me in a year and a half is a whole turnaround from somebody who was so trusting, who never would have done anything. I mean, I *never* would have thought of going to a rally, of marching into John Aherne's [head of the federal Nuclear Regulatory Commission] office and telling him what I thought. I *never* would have thought of becoming involved in civil disobedience. Nothing like this had ever occurred to me. But in a year and a half this is where I am. If this can happen to *me,* what kind of changes can happen to people who are *already* disenchanted with their government? It won't take much to turn them around or even to bring them further, where they might be the ones to use bombs and to undermine our democracy. I really don't want to see it come to that, where there is an uprising against the government. I still think our country is great and that democracy is the way to go, but I think it must be strengthened. It has to be strengthened by people being actively involved, by being able to make input into government decisions, and by having our leaders really listen to us.

Children are being very much affected by what is happening. Although I feel it's very important not to bring these issues into my classroom, that my responsibility there is to teach mathematics, between classes and whenever the children asked me about it, I certainly have felt free to tell them how I feel. I find them to be very open in their thinking, more so than adults. I point out that it is their future. The other morning I spoke to a school assembly in New Hampshire and said, "You have a *right* to be angry about what is being done to your country." Somebody said to me later, "That's probably the first time they have ever been told to get angry." I think that may be true, because we are forever telling them to "be nice little children, be quiet, we'll take care of everything," and I am saying to them, "No! That's *not* happening, and *you're* the ones who are going to have children who are affected by radiation and chemicals. We adults have simply not done what we should have done, and I feel very guilty to some extent about that, and now I'm trying to make up for it. But you're still young and you have a lot to learn. *Please* go out and ask questions, get angry, and try to straighten this all out."

With adults I often talk about rate withholding. I tell them, "They're in this business for money. Our lives aren't important; it's money. And so we've got to make them understand that we are going to put them out of business the only way that we can." A very large number of people come up to me afterward and want to know "How do I do this?" I tell them how I've been doing it. When it first started, I found out what percent of the rate base has to do with the amount of power generated from nuclear plants. So I used all these wonderful little formulas to figure out a fair amount to withhold, Now, though, I just see it as a whole system that I am opposed to. Depending on how mad I am at the time I write out the bill, that is how much I deduct now. I send them little notes and address my bills to "Murder, Inc.," and tear off the little numbers to make it harder for them and write notes all over the envelope. It's a good way to vent anger.

You know, it's very hard for the people here to be living on top of a plant that is so badly damaged, knowing that the cleanup is going to go on for maybe another five or ten years, knowing that they are constantly venting krypton, and that it is very dangerous, and knowing that they are constantly playing little games. I'll never let John Aherne forget the story he told me about how the cleanup of Three Mile Island is "like a game of pick-up-sticks." That's the way he described it. I sat in his office and he said to me, "It's like a game of pick-up-sticks, we've never done anything like this before, and so what we have to do is go down there, do one little procedure, remove one little stick, so to speak, and then we take a look at the situation and see what it looks like and, well, let's try this now." And I said, "*Pick-up-sticks?* You just bump one little stick the wrong way and the whole thing is destroyed." He kind of smiled at me, like, "Yeah, well, that's true." And I thought, "Yeah, and *I'm* the one sitting right on top of that thing that could be destroyed by that one little wrong move. And I know that the people in charge down there don't know what they are doing, and you are saying to me, 'Now be calm and rational about the whole thing.' " It's very hard to be calm and rational.

All this tension. . . . It's not like having a fire or flood in my house and coming home and cleaning it up. In those cases at least there is something I can do. With Three Mile Island I am being shoved out of the process as much as possible, and at the same time I am being told to just sit here and be calm and rational. That's hard to do. The more involved you get, the bigger the issue becomes and the more upset you get about things. The tension at times is really very difficult to deal with.

Some of us have had some help. We met here with two psychologists and just talked about what we were going through, sharing with each other how we've learned to handle our anger. I've learned to justify a lot of things that ordinarily I would have thought were just totally crazy. I find the tension builds during the day, so you come home and you try to get dinner, and you are just very upset and the news is on, and you are hearing things that upset you. Anytime that I have veal or round steak or something that needs to be pounded, I give it names. "Okay, John Aherne, this is you, and I am going to beat the hell out of you," and I swear at him and beat it, and you get some really terrific food that way because you really put everything into it! But at the same times it releases your anger in an acceptable way. My family may look at me like I'm a little strange, but I haven't hurt anybody and I have gotten something out of my system.

The main thing I tell people is that before this accident at Three Mile Island, accidents were always something that happened to somebody else, never to me. Okay, but now it has happened to me and to a group of very conservative people; and it happened here for a reason. That plant wasn't put here without somebody doing a lot of studies. They knew that we were people who would accept the plant being put here, and that after an accident like this there would still be a lot of people who would remain conservative and trusting and leave it up to somebody else. And so I tell people, "Look, it happened in my community, but it could just as easily have happened in yours. And why wait until that happens? Why wait until you have to evacuate your home? Why wait until you are put up against a government that doesn't want to do any studies, even though you can see what's happened? I think it was deliberate that TMI was put here and that throughout our country nuclear plants are being put in rural areas. They are saying to us that the people in rural communities are not as important, because nowhere does the nuclear industry say "safe"; they always say "acceptable risk." My life is an acceptable risk. They will accept my dying. Well, I don't accept that. I *can't* accept that. But that's what they're telling us.

There is no security for the American people at this point. People ask me, "Why don't you move?" I say, "Where should I go? Not very far from me is a nuclear power plant. Not very far from these people you have a waste dump. Over there is a uranium mine where radioactive tailings are piled up. To me, there isn't any safe place in our country to live at this point." I also tell people that I can't fight for them. I can come and talk to them, and I can tell them what's happened to me and to my neighbors, that my home isn't worth anything anymore. I can tell them about the "For Sale" signs up and down the streets. I can tell them what they are not hearing in the news and what they're not being told from studies. I live there and I know. And I can say, "Okay, now before this happens to you, *at least ask questions.* Find out what's going on and get involved."

One positive thing that has come out of all this is that I now find myself able to say that I love people in a totally different sense than I had ever used the word before. Before, I had love for my husband or my child or my parents. This is a totally different love, and I found that I have it for many people. I have learned to know them, to see how much good there is in them, and what they are working for. I have a great deal of admiration and respect for them. I see them as our country's real patriots.

Recently I've been looking more closely at my lifestyle. I have started to do some reading, thinking that perhaps a vegetarian diet would be better for my family. We eat all this junk food that is not good for us, and what can we do about it? We can look at how to make our homes more energy efficient, because I don't believe anymore that we need so much electricity. Our whole country has become so accustomed to having plastics and chemicals and electricity, and we don't need those things. We are so spoiled. The accident, if nothing else, brought me to the point where I can say, "All this stuff isn't important."

Greg Akili

Greg Akili is secretary-treasurer of the United Domestic Workers of America. He does union organizing throughout California. Akili also serves on the national executive committee of the Democratic Socialist Organizing Committee and the executive committee of the Campaign for Economic Democracy in California. When not on the road, he lives in San Diego. We did this interview in the summer of 1981.

I grew up in the segregated South, in Florida. I was a petty hoodlum and had no formal education; I attended school, the buildings, but got no real education. My mother died when I was fourteen. After her death I spent another year in Florida and then came out to California to live with my father. I was fifteen then. I'm thirty-three now. I have two daughters who think I walk on water; that's because they don't live with me all the time.

Early on in my life I saw the contradictions—between white and black, rich and poor. There were black people who couldn't go to certain places or do certain things. Once you live in a segregated society you can be invaded at any given time; that lays the basis for insecurity. As a result of thinking about those contradictions I am a social activist now. I saw them back then but I didn't understand them. I got involved in the civil rights movement without really knowing why; it seemed like the hip thing to do. So I would always be around activism—except when the work went down, and then I'd be gone.

Insecurity has been with me since I was a kid. For instance, the white police could ride in on us and take us anytime they wanted to. Agents of the police, or at least people with the quasi-sanction of the police, or organized groups like the KKK, could do the same thing. That makes you feel really vulnerable.

Another insecurity came out of the fact that I was a light-skinned, curly-haired black in the South. I had two choices: I could try and pass as white, if there was a social-economic basis there for it; or I could become a gut-bucket nigger. Since my family was poor I became a gut-bucket nigger, which is one step away from being a petty hoodlum. The other thing about being light-skinned and curly-haired is that it created an unnecessary pressure on me because I was supposed to "live up to my potential." Teachers and relatives would say, "You're a bright boy. Why don't you do more, apply yourself?" There was a basic insecurity; so I recoiled, and instead of applying myself I just rebelled against all that.

I used to hang around with older guys, hanging on their every word. They could get me to walk through hell with gasoline drawers on. They were older; I was looking for a father image. When it was time to do something it was "send the go-fer to do it; he'll do it," and I'd do it—and get in trouble. That came from another insecurity—the desire, like most Americans, to belong. This society breeds that fear of being ostracized more than any other society I know because it's so consumer-oriented. If I'm made to believe that if I use the right kind of deodorant, for example, something good's going to happen—like a woman's gonna pop up—then I'm going to go out and consume. Or that buying this car is going to put me in a class that I ain't in economically, then I buy the car. I'll buy whatever is needed to make me belong. So I did the go-fer thing that allowed me to belong until I got locked up in federal prison in 1969. For smuggling.

I went through a series of changes after I got locked up. I said to myself, "Hey, you gotta do better than this, brother." I decided I would let my work speak for me. Like a lot of young blacks in the black power movement, I knew all the rhetoric but didn't really do anything; I could quote Malcolm X just as good as anybody else, but I didn't really apply anything or give up anything. We started a group in prison called the Afro-American Cultural Workshop to bring a sense of Afro-American culture to blacks. It worked. For a little while the brothers were saying, "Hey, man, I ain't gettin' involved in that 'cause it'll mess up my parole." But we got some books in and put together a play, and they thought, "Hey, that ain't so bad," and then they got involved. At that point I decided to let my work speak for me, instead of spouting off a lot of rhetoric and bullshit.

At age twenty-two I came out of prison and started working in a group I'd been involved with for a long time. I kept my mouth shut and worked. That group evolved from a black cultural nationalist organization to a multicultural and multi-issue organization, to a labor union. You see, in 1972 we thought the revolution would soon be over and we'd have seized state power. We were mistaken. So we looked around and saw that half the stuff we had talked about wasn't there, that much of our failure was due to internal, not external reasons. The biggest failure was that we didn't organize people; we mobilized them, we used a lot of rhetoric, but we never organized them. We never got people to take a first step in their own behalf, and we never left a structure behind so they could do things for themselves. We could get two thousand people in the streets to march, but after the march was over, what happened to the people?

Second, although we did a lot of consciousness-raising which broke the mold and allowed us to think of ourselves differently, we didn't popularize black power as something people could grasp. "Black power" was stated over and over again, but what was it? *Self-defense, self-respect,* and *self-determination.* But then you have to break down those three, and we never could do that. We got involved in trying to get black faces in high places. We did a lot of changing of the scenery, but we never left the land.

There were also external reasons for our failures—the fact that we were marked by the FBI, the national police. They did a very good job of taking advantage of our internal contradictions and effectively destroyed the black power movement. So one lesson I learned is that it requires internal and external situations to destroy anything. I cannot collapse solely from the outside; there must be something inside that first weakens the structure.

That relates to national security: There's a saying that it's people who win the wars, not weapons. We should have learned that from the Vietnam fiasco, but we didn't. Now we're going after more sophisticated weapons to do more damage; but if people ain't got nothing to die for, what's to say they're going to use those weapons? What's even more important to national security, we need to have something to *live* for, and a lot of people don't. You don't have security when you have disgruntled people. If we were attacked, there'd have to be a lot of whipping of the patriotic drum to get people up. You know what I'm talkin' about? I know a lot of brothers in New York who'd say, "Shit, the Russians might treat us better. They might have somethin' I can use. Let 'em in. I know what the *Americans* are all about; let's check these others out." You draft them and you're liable to put guns in the wrong hands. These days I'm more concerned about an *American* attacking me than I am about a Russian. But you've got to have somebody—a foreign power or a foreign threat. If there was no Soviet Union we'd have to go find one or make one up. Otherwise we couldn't mobilize. You can't cut billions of dollars in social programs, ask for fifty-four billion more in military spending two weeks later, and then talk about reducing the federal budget. Someone, somewhere along the line is going to be stuck with the bill. Johnson stuck me and my daughters with a bill for the Vietnam War. Consequently we got stuck with inflation and a very weak economic infrastructure. He was not prepared both to fight this war and also to pay for it. That's why it was stopped: Congress stopped appropriations. I see Reagan doing the same thing. They can't carry this *macho* shit too far. That may have worked for my father, who fought in World War II and showed the world how great we really were after that, but I don't think it's going to work for people my age.

We live in a finite world, with finite resources. I can close my eyes to things and live my life to get all I can for myself, or I can recognize the contradictions and work with other people to correct them. Everything in nature is balanced; it is only things in man that become unbalanced. We have the capacity to reason, but sometimes we use that capacity to rationalize and cover things up. Man is the only creature I know that tries to alter his own environment. Most animals live within their environment, taking what they need and giving back to it. We alter ours—and we pay for it. It's conceivable that there will be a generation of children who don't know what clean air is, who have to play with gas masks on or live in an enclosed city. They may not know what clean water is or what *plants* are. We're out of balance, and the question is if we can restore it. I have to think we can; if I didn't, I'd give it up and stick my head in a hole.

The first kind of balance is economic. There are over four

billion people in the world and about half of them live below acceptable standards. Someone once said, "We are going to wind up on an island of affluence in a sea of starving people." Hunger is the strongest urge to insecurity that I've ever seen, because it causes you to do things that under normal circumstances your values and your culture say you don't do. We have to learn that in order for America or Europe to be rich, somebody somewhere had to give up something. My ancestors provided the wealth for this country and Western Europe; Africa was pillaged and raped.

The greatest resource of any country is its people. If you destroy them, you don't have nothing. You can have all the gold, all the diamonds, all the minerals; but it is people that put all those things to use. To my mind the greatest threat to security in the world today is our taking people for granted and disregarding their value. Every major change in this world has been due to people. They've come together and decided, "Oh, wow, let's change this shit." It took time but they did it. And it's going to be people that either decide to balance things out or to tip over the balance till there ain't nothin' left. I'm on the side that wants to balance out the world.

We can learn a lot from China. A quarter of the world's people live there, and they've done an effective job of making sure that people get fed. India, their neighbor to the south, also has a huge population but many of them are starving. So what's happening? I don't care what people say about China's form of government; the fact is, *they're feeding their people.* Before 1949 that didn't happen. So why is it that in China they're feeding people while in India people are starving while they're building a nuclear reactor? Those choices say something about the people. It is a sad commentary that I live in the richest country in the world, and that millions and millions of people go to bed hungry every night. It really hurts me that we have the machinery to destroy the world in thirty minutes but don't distribute our wheat surplus to help feed the world's hungry.

I realize that I'm simply a link. What I'm doing, somebody's been doing before me and somebody will be doing after me. I am part of a larger process. If I can move this country and this world a half inch, then I'd be satisfied. I have long since accepted the fact that what I want won't be realized in my lifetime. I'm hoping that my daughters pick it up; and they, or somebody, will. I think that people are going to work to balance out this society and their lives, to try to live a more harmonious life. So how do you live in harmony? There has to be tolerance, communication, understanding, and openness. Since you *are* different from me, it's easy for me to say, "That person is different." And the next step I could take is to say, "You're not only *different,* you're *stupid.* And not only are you *stupid,* you're *slow.*" And then I can do a whole series of other things that reduce you; once I reduce you, I can move on you. I can say, "Since she's different, stupid, and slow, maybe she should work for me, 'cause I'm tired."

Racism develops like that. Generally racism is expressed in three ways: an ideology, imposition, and institutional arrangement. That is, I've got to be able to impose an ideology that says you're inferior or stupid. Then I set up institutions that reinforce that and carry it on. How can we eliminate that? This brings back the question of harmony. If you talk about security—world, national, and personal—then you have to deal with each level. If I'm not secure within myself, then no matter what happens outside me I'm going to perceive an outward insecurity. That's why I say that *if a thing is strong within, it will match the pressure from without.* If something is weak and decaying, it won't take much from the outside to make it collapse. That is how most great societies declined—from within. I think that both this society and the Soviet society could be headed for that kind of collapse.

We have to organize people here to prevent that collapse and build something new. If you believe you're powerless or vulnerable, then you think, "Why do anything—I'll only get hurt?" But if you see that there are other people out there who want the same kinds of things, you think that maybe something can be done. Then you may take a first step. Right now most people believe there's nothing we can do; we've abdicated most of our responsibility to professionals, experts, politicians, teachers. First, we don't take personal responsibility, then we don't take community or national responsibility. We want other people to do things for us; and usually there are those who *will* do things for us. In organizing, on the other hand, we say, "Take a step; your taking a step is going to double my efforts and build a structure so that no matter what happens to me, you can carry on. But," I tell people, "you've got to take that first step; you've got to go outside your house, go to a meeting, or do something that *inconve-*

niences you. If it only inconveniences me, then I'm the only one who benefits. You have to break your normal pattern; *then* we can talk. If you're not willing to do anything, then I don't care how good my intentions are or how sincere I am, I can't move you."

People have to feel that they can win. One of the most rewarding things about my work—which is why I can do it for thirty-five dollars a week plus room, board, and transportation— is that there is a *psychic* income. I see people transform their lives. Meeting a woman who doesn't have much confidence in herself, and telling her she can get better pay or be treated decently; and she says, "Yeah, sounds good, but . . ." You work with her to take that first step and she agrees to come to the meeting. Five other people are there and we each talk about what's bothering us and how we can change it. We get each one of those persons to have a house meeting in rotation; and we watch a person go from not believing in themselves or even wanting to get involved, to saying, "Hey, not only can it be done, it's *got* to be done, and I can do it." They start to challenge the assumptions of this society. I have worked with much older women and watched them grow; I feel like a parent—and I'll be gone when the time is right, because they can stand on their own. *That's* a kind of reward that money can't buy. And if tomorrow I found out that we weren't goin' to get nothin', no pay, I'd *still* do this work.

Society's experts say, "We know better than you what's good for you." When people organize, however, they take back that responsibility and say, "You may *know,* but I've got to *do.* There are decisions, especially economic decisions, being made by people I don't know, I can't elect, and I have no influence over. These corporate heads who sit in some interlocking directorate don't ask *me* nothing, don't consult *me.* . . ." I mean, there's this bullshit that people can *choose* whether or not to buy a particular product; but that line confuses mobility with freedom of choice. It's like, if I lock you in this room, you can walk around inside but you can't go out the door; you're mobile but you don't have freedom. There are some decisions I think I ought to be part of; but we don't have equal access to information, for one thing. So we've got to struggle. What I do is organize people so they can sit across the table from somebody else as equals and say, "Listen, you are buying my time. You are giving me some money and I am giving you a service. Since that's the case, here are some things I think I ought to have. Can I get this? All right, how about this? *What* can I get? The first thing I want is some dignity, some respect, and to be treated seriously. Can I get that? If not, I can leave and *you* get somebody else." So that's the whole idea for organizing these women.

Applied to the arms race, I ask this question: Who benefits from the annihilation of the world? Of course, you say, nobody. Then who benefits from getting *just this close* and then backing off. Now, *somebody* benefits. We need to really look close at that one. Historically, man created weapons presumably to defend himself; but inherent in everything is its opposite, for the same weapons created to defend can be used to attack. So in these two super-powers, who's benefiting? In the Soviet Union, which is pretty much totalitarian, people don't have a lot of say. It's a different scenery here. I can talk about Reagan being *bad,* about his momma being *bad,* and nothin' happens, nobody arrests me. And people say, "Wow, one of the benefits of America is that you can talk bad about the president or the mayor." So what? Where it counts is if I start talking bad and find somebody else who talks bad, and then we find somebody else. And then we start organiz-ing and becoming a movement. That's what I can do. Now I want that same political process to apply to *economic* decisions because we have political mobility but we don't have economic mobility. Corporate decisions are made without consulting any-body. People create systems, like governments or corporations, and then use or misuse them. I've never seen a system hurt any-body: people hurt other people, using the system to do it. In America we have one called "capitalism" that has been around for a couple hundred years. Capitalism served a purpose: it organized the collection of wealth for some people and made them wealth-ier. We hear how capitalism is what made this country strong and great, but that's bullshit! Capitalism made a few people *rich,* I'll grant you that; but it's only the working people who made Amer-ica great, and they did it by organizing themselves and saying, "I deserve more of this because I'm producing it." It was you and I, and our parents; it was black slaves that made the South great; it was the coolies out West here, laying the railroad.

We've allowed the acquisition and investment of capital to become more important than the people that do something with it. The system has gotten completely out of balance. You hear about that "trickle-down" stuff—you know, "one tide comes in and all the boats rise," that kind of shit? The kind of mentality that says, "The rich are good-hearted and so of course they'll give you something." Which I think is absurd, since they didn't get rich by doing that. They got rich by conniving, generally, by beating somebody else out of something. In this society you cannot be rich without taking from somebody. Otherwise we'd have a more egalitarian society.

Now in the Soviet Union you have another form of control, based on the state. The corporate bureaucracy here and the state bureaucracy in the Soviet Union are just about the same. That's not to say that I'm against socialism. Socialism, in my estimation, is an infant in world history. What are we talkin'? Sixty, seventy years in practical experience? So give it some time. To hold the Soviet Union up as some expression of communism, of socialism, is absurd nowadays. But I think there are other people, in the Third World and in Europe, who are trying to apply socialist concepts in the context of their own societies and cultures. But the practical expression of socialism is still in an embryonic stage.

Ultimately you cannot hand people their freedom; they've got to take it. The same with privileges and rights. That's why I keep stressing getting organized: it's the best way groups can make an impact. Sooner or later that's what will happen with the Soviet people. It won't be easy. The Soviet people are walking with a weight on them, that is, a repressive government. But you hear about dissident movements—writers, scientists, people being sent into exile. And if that kind of thing is going on, you can believe there's a whole underground thing happening over there. The same thing is going on, differently, here in America. There's a weight oppressing people here too, and it doesn't make any difference if it's a hundred pounds of steel or a hundred pounds of aluminum—it's still a hundred pounds. It's just a question of time for their people and for ours.

There are some good things in the Soviet system, just as there are in ours. For example, the plurality that we promote is good, although plurality without tolerance and understanding is bullshit. Also, our problem-solving approach is often good here, in that people can get together on a small level and work things out, as long as structures don't intervene. In the Soviet Union I think the emphasis on working people is good. There's a question about how *real* that emphasis is, but at least there's an ideology about working people playing an essential role in society. So we have to learn the best that each of our societies has to offer. And we both can learn from other societies: for example, from how the Chinese are feeding their people. One important step would be to set up some kinds of exchanges.

One thing I learned from growing up in a segregated society is that I could at least *live* near white people—"Whoa, look-a here, touch 'em" and stuff. And white people could learn "Hey, this nigger's all right." That comes from *communication*. If you feel like I'm a nonthreatening entity, then we can deal. Black, white, green, short, tall—we can deal. But if you're intimidated by me, then you've got a problem with me no matter *what* I am. That certainly relates to U.S.–Soviet relations: we're equally imposing on each other. It's very interesting, all this saber rattling, drawing the lines in the dirt. It's like two kids—you dig it?—going to the store and buying these plastic soldiers. Except we ain't talkin' about plastic soldiers; we're talking about the existence of the world as we know it. Any morning could be our last.

I'll bet you that if the American *people* and the Soviet *people* were allowed to communicate directly, they'd find they have a lot in common. That could be the catalyst for change in *both* our societies.

I've learned about a certain theory of trust which is based on the idea that I shouldn't look to you for trust; I should trust you first and build on that. That's hard in this society. People are putting bars on their windows, locking themselves up. Well, I've *been* locked up; I damn sure am not going to lock *myself* up. To me, national security means not having to live locked up like that; it's not having to buy thirty-five dogs and a gun. National security is walking across the street without having the adrenaline run fast. National security is sending your kids out to play without having to be with them every minute. National security is people having a sense of security about themselves and their families. Bombs don't give us that kind of security. The military talks about "peace through strength." To me, that *should* mean having inner peace and strength in every person on every block. We need to start there—secure people and families make a secure neighborhood, and with enough of those we'll get a strong, secure nation.

Ed Johnson

Ed Johnson is an independent trucker whose homebase is near Philadelphia. We conducted the interview at a truckstop near Detroit, Michigan, in the fall of 1980.

I grew up in Yeadon, near Philadelphia, in a big family of five brothers and sisters. It was a poor family; I only went to seventh grade. Guess I've done okay for a boy with a seventh-grade education, but if I had to go back all through my life, I'd have got an education. But at the time, somebody offered me a job driving a truck, so I've been doing that now for twenty-seven years. I just continued and changed jobs wherever I thought things were better. Finally, I found where it was better: I have my own truck now, and I lease it back to a company.

The way I look at national security, getting out of debt is the main solution to our problem. Our money isn't worth nothing nowhere in the world. The country is nearly a trillion dollars in debt. You can't continuously do deficit spending because it devalues the dollar even more. But most people just can't visualize a billion dollars. Look at it this way: if your father went into business the day that Christ was born, lost a thousand dollars a day ever since then, he'd still have enough money to last him for another four hundred years.

I really feel the inflation. When I started with my own truck eighteen months ago, diesel fuel was fifty-two cents a gallon. Now it's a dollar and eighteen cents. I used to buy a tire for a hundred and twenty dollars; now it's two hundred and sixty-five dollars. That's only eighteen months ago. In fact we are one of the *lucky* countries with the inflation rate we have; these other countries have a *fantastic* rate of inflation. The only thing I can think that causes it is deficit spending. Government has got to pay the bills or cut the services. So if they don't have the money, they borrow it and push up interest rates. Then they raise our taxes. We need to have a balanced budget every year for as many years as it takes. To do this, we have to cut back some on defense spending and on social services. We have to cut out some of the windfall profits.

The government actually wastes money. For example, they pay farmers not to grow wheat. Famine is going to be one of the biggest things in this world in ten years, yet here we are today paying farmers not to grow grain. Why do we have that policy? Most of the people getting this big money are senators and congressmen that have fantastic farms, and they've passed a law that favors *them*. The same way with the oil interests. There isn't a senator that ever voted against an oil concern yet. When you get out West, you'll see one of the biggest retailers and refiners of oil in the West is Kerr–McGee. They were the two senators that supported the oil industry for years. They have retired from the Senate and now they just run their oil company.

This goes on throughout the government now. You get an allotment for the year. If you don't have your money spent by the end of the fiscal year, you've got to get rid of it or they're going to cut your budget that much next year. This is wrong. There's *millions* being thrown away this way. The GSA [General Services Administration] caught one outfit in D.C. that had several hundreds of thousands of dollars left over from their budget, so they went out and they bought office desks. Then the GSA found a whole warehouse full of them down the street that they bought two years earlier, too.

People make the problem worse with their own variety of deficit spending. That's why it's becoming a plastic world with credit cards. If people don't have the money, they just go out and buy it on a credit card, and they build up a false economy. They're stealing from one place to pay another.

You know, I don't think we have to be so afraid of the Russians. They're looking out for their self-interest, like we are. They can't be frozen out of the Persian Gulf either. That's the most strategic place in the world today. That's all the Russians are doing: looking out for *their* Number One. That's all they've ever done. They've created a buffer state of Communist countries between East and West. To get to Russia you have to go through them satellite countries first. It's protection for them. The big problem, of course, is that our interests conflict with theirs. This could cause World War III. But I doubt it will be fought with nuclear weapons; the first man that trips the trigger knows that *he's* going too. Also, as far as I know, once we send off nuclear missiles, there's no self-destruct in them. Once they're gone, they're gone. That's why they have such an intricate system for firing even one.

I don't know what we as individuals can do about national security things. You're talking about fighting City Hall, and that's tough. What can we do? I have no idea. Protesting? That doesn't work. All you get is a confrontation with the police and it doesn't seem to accomplish nothing. Look how long those demonstrators have been up at the nuclear power plant they're building in Seabrook, New Hampshire. They're tearing down the fences and everything else, but they're still building the plant. That's what I mean by fighting City Hall. If you do something they don't like, they'll tell you to stop. If you don't stop, they get the state police to stop you. If you go against policy, they have the power to stop you. It would take building new policy, but you're talking about a long process. Our basic attitude needs to change.

Part of our attitude now is that since our standard of living is higher, we think we're higher than them other people. But this doesn't rightly make us any better than they are. Also, we are the most wasteful nation on the face of the earth. We have either wasted or destroyed almost everything we've ever put our hands to. I'm not exaggerating. It's greed, like those big, monstrous tankers like the *Torrey Canyon*. Oil is money, and so the more oil you move at one time, the more money you're going to make. It's the human element. I find it in myself too. Like, I work Saturdays when I know I shouldn't. I work Sundays if I have to, you know, if there's a dollar involved in it. You accumulate more than you had two days before that. That extra buck makes me feel like I got more than I had the week before—until the government takes the rest of it off me in taxes.

I do the work for the money. Living on the road is like living like a bum, if you want to know. You're away from your home for five or six days at a time. You're stopping in old, decrepit truckstops like this. You eat what anybody throws at you. It's not really my idea of living. I do it strictly for the income, that's all. I don't know how to do anything else, to be truthful with you. So far this week I've worked two days and I've made twenty-three hundred dollars. And I'm going to work maybe three more days this week. And there's no limit to how much I can make. This is what I'm telling you—it's greed, just plain human greed. It's a basic element.

I'll tell you one thing I have thoughts about. America moved too far too fast, and we left a lot of important things undone. Like our mass transportation system. We have none. Every country in Europe has one. Another thing, in Muslim countries, if you get caught stealing they'll cut off the hand you stole with. That's Muslim law. Under *our* system of justice some judge will probably let you go with a stern lecture. People don't have much respect for the law. I'm for stricter laws and punishment governing crime. In England, if you commit a crime it has a penalty, but if you're carrying a gun it has a death penalty. They've made it so hard to carry a gun in England that nobody wants to get caught with one. In turn, the police don't need guns. The result is that they don't have all the shootings and all the deaths that we have in this country.

A safe nation is part of national security. I'd really like to see it be a little safer for people. You can't be in the cities at night because you're not safe in there. More severe penalties for crime would help. I would also like to see them close down this twenty-four-hours-a-day, seven-days-a-week shopping. There's no reason for it. So it'd just mean getting used to doing it different. They do this all over Europe: if you don't buy it by noon Saturday, you don't buy it until Monday morning. And nobody seems to suffer. If we did this, it would give people more time to spend with their family and friends. It would make homelife more important to them. If you can sit down on Sunday at dinner and talk over your troubles and whatnot, it makes for a closer knit family. It goes back to the same basic principle of human greed. If Gimbels is open on Sunday, Wanamakers has to be too. A person only spends so many dollars a week no matter how many days you're open.

Going back to the national and world level, I think we could improve relations with the Russians through cultural programs. Bring enough of their people over here and let them see how we live, and take enough of our people over there and let them see how they live. We don't understand the Chinese or the Russians because we've been isolated from them for so long. Travel has been banned and it has been just threats and cold war. We're just coming down to the point now that the common, ordinary man can now go to China. Before that, it was only cultural groups approved by the State Department.

Another big problem in our national security is that we don't trust people. In the American way of life, when somebody's doing you a favor you figure they're up to something. Well, maybe there are a few good ones, but generally speaking people do not trust each other. I'll give you an example. Two weeks ago I read in the paper where some guy fell off the subway elevated platform in Chicago. He had one arm in a sling and was trying to crawl up on the platform. A train was coming but nobody offered him a hand. Sixty people stood and laughed and jeered while the train squashed him up against the end of the platform. Yet everybody could see he had one arm in a sling. How are we going to change people like that?

That's the whole thing—to change people. That's the answer to the whole thing. We have to go back to our basic principles of justice and what determines justice, we've got to tighten our justice system.

Fear is one way to change people and eventually to bring respect for the law. I'll give you a good example. Three years ago, down in Wilmington, Delaware, a man that was used to having money got in a bind and needed some money real fast. So he invited his mother- and father-in-law to spend Christmas. Two days before Christmas, while they were sleeping, he "got sloppy" with twenty gallons of gas and the house burned down and killed them. The only mistake he made is that his sixteen-year-old daughter burned to death too. Well, the cops figured out what happened and eventually he was tried and convicted on three counts of premeditated murder. They gave him three life sentences. About two weeks before he was convicted a federal judge said the prison was overpopulated by two hundred and sixty people. They said to him, "Who do we turn loose?" and he said,

"I don't care who you turn loose; just turn loose two hundred and sixty people." And they turned that man loose!

Next he decided to sue State Farm Insurance for a quarter of a million dollars for his house. State Farm said, "Oh, no, you burned the place down." He said, "Well, *I'm* not suing you; my wife is; I didn't have her permission." Do you know, State Farm had to pay him a quarter of a million dollars? He murdered three people, had three life sentences over his head, was walking just as free as a bird up and down the street, and had a quarter of a million dollars in his pocket. Now is *that* justice? There's *no way* you could consider that justice. Nowhere *near* justice.

It's not only here. There's a case in yesterday's paper. A U.S. sailor was over in Kenya. He was on liberty. It seemed like he got tied up with a prostitute, him and her didn't agree, so he beat her over the head with a beer bottle. When the beer bottle broke, he cut her throat. What do you think he got fined? Yes, fined! He admits he murdered the girl! Seventy dollars! Because the United States won't let Kenya have custody of him. Now is that right? Is that justice?

You must have laws and they must be upheld. If they're not upheld it breaks down the whole system. That's the secret to the security thing. It goes right back to the politicians. When they get caught stealing they just get a slap on the wrist. How many of them go to jail? None of them. But like I say, everybody's got a Maker and we've all got Somebody we've gotta answer to in the end.

One thing I'd do different if I was starting over is that I'd have a little bit more religion. But the way I look at it, you don't have to go to church to be religious. You have to watch out for your fellowman, take care of the poor people, and do what you can. When you're feeding somebody that's hungry, or giving clothing or shelter to the poor, you don't have to fight City Hall to do it. If you're going to try and change the whole country's views of national security, you're going to have to fight the system.

Elmo Zumwalt

Admiral Zumwalt was formerly chief of naval operations (1970–1974), and is currently president of Admiral Zumwalt and Associates, Inc., in Arlington, Virginia, where he resides with his wife of thirty-eight years. He serves on the boards of seven corporations. This interview was conducted in the spring of 1982.

I grew up in Tulare, California, the son of two doctors practicing in that town. I attended the U.S. Naval Academy and graduated in the wartime class of 1942. I saw action during World War II in the Pacific on board destroyers. During the Korean War I was navigator aboard the battleship *Wisconsin* and commanded the destroyer escort U.S.S. *Tills*. From 1968 to 1970 I commanded our naval forces in Vietnam and completed my career as chief of naval operations and a member of the Joint Chiefs of Staff from July 1, 1970, until June 30, 1974. Prior to obtaining flag rank I attended the National War College and served a two-year tour as the director of arms control for the secretary of defense during negotiation of the Nuclear Test Ban Treaty and during the Cuban missile crisis. In these experiences, and also while serving as executive assistant to the secretary of the navy, I had the opportunity to participate in the formulation of policy at the national level.

I have lived long enough to see that democracies traditionally have a problem of maintaining adequate strength in peacetime to deter aggressive dictatorships, while dictatorships have no problem maintaining military power. Democracies are run to meet the will of the people, and leaders, in order to be elected, promise what they think people want to hear. This means that those calling for the kinds of sacrifices really required to have adequate deterrence tend to get defeated. We saw this happen before World War I, between World War I and World War II, and between World War II and the Korean War. In all these cases we found ourselves, because we were democracies, forced by circumstances into wars with losses of hundreds of thousands of men. If we had been strong enough to *deter* war we would not have gotten into war and lost those men.

The struggle continues to the present, with the Soviet Union being quite clear in their messages to their own *apparatchik* [bureaucratic machinery] and to the world, that they intend to have political, military, and economic hegemony over the globe. They have been permitted in recent years by the failure of democracies to hang tough, to obtain overwhelming nuclear superiority and significant conventional superiority. Today they are proceeding to use that superiority as a shield to screen themselves from any counteraction by the United States while they proceed to conquer other countries, either directly as in Afghanistan or indirectly as in the Libyan seizure of Chad or the Cuban- and Soviet-supported conquest of Nicaragua. So they are gaining foothold after foothold in other countries in pursuance of their objective of world domination.

The basic weakness the Soviets can exploit in Third World countries is military inferiority. Libya could seize Chad because they were militarily superior, having been armed and equipped by the Soviet Union. The Sandinistas were able to destroy their despotic dictator, but more important, they came to power by virtue of the fact that they had superior military power in Nicaragua with what they were supplied from Russia. Obviously it is easier for the Soviet Union to do their mischief when a combination of factors exist, such as economic chaos and political instability.

Huddle: Some of the people I've interviewed believe we would do more for American security by assisting Third World nations in building up their internal political and economic systems so that they would have more resilience on their own. These people feel that the reason the Soviets make inroads into these countries is that they have a message that appeals to people who are deprived, illiterate, and suffering under the sorts of despotic dictatorships you mentioned earlier.

Zumwalt: I think you have to lay out the whole argument. I advocate that we ought to do more to help Third World countries build themselves up economically and in terms of education and so on. But people who say we should do those things frequently say we should do *less* in the way of defense. And it is *that* kind of thinking that has led to the tragic decline of democracy and the historical descent into war. If one goes back and reviews what the elites were saying prior to World War I, World War II, and Korea, and if one believes what the media wrote, you would see that the elite were saying the same kinds of things that are being said by that school of thought today: that we don't need a strong military capability. People back then were criticizing the military in the same way, saying that the military never felt it had enough, that it was bloated, and so on. In each case we got into a war because we were tragically short of what we needed, and the enemy knew it. I am in favor of a broad-scale approach to dealing with the corrupt and venal dictatorship in the Soviet Union, for containing them until their dismal system gradually changes from within, for sufficient defense and adequate foreign aid, and for a good psychological-warfare approach which emphasizes the benefits of our system compared to the Soviet system.

Huddle: At the same time, we're cutting off a lot of our foreign aid right now, which isn't helping the Third World countries make the needed changes.

Zumwalt: The tragedy is that for a decade and a half we have allowed ourselves to be badly outspent in the military field. A nation that has only sixty percent of our gross national product has been outspending us by threefold in the strategic nuclear field and by sixty percent in the conventional military field. As a result we are in the gravest danger of my lifetime. How does our nation, which has so badly let its defenses down that it is heading for war, get out of that predicament at a time when it is also facing economic hardship and an inflationary spiral from years of excessive and deficit spending? Compromises have to be made. Given the great danger this country faces because of its military inferiority, I believe the Reagan administration is dead right in increasing the defense budget while cutting back on all the other things. We face a national emergency.

Huddle: Some people I've interviewed say that our defense has been based on the premise that the more insecure we can make the Soviet Union, the more secure we will be in the United States. Do you agree?

Zumwalt: Tragically, in the absence of a world rule of law, where you have over one hundred fifty sovereign nations, deci- sions tend to be made based on the power that one has. The Soviet Union has clearly abused its power in order to expand. How is it possible for a peace-loving, democratic nation to deal with that? In the absence of a world rule of law it takes coun- tervailing power. We are only going to have such countervail- ing power by achieving the capability of frightening the Rus- sians so much that they are deterred from expanding.

Huddle: Within that maneuvering, is there the danger that we might, through no one's will and through that kind of "action– reaction, action–reaction" pattern, stumble into a war?

Zumwalt: Let's reformulate that question. There isn't action and reaction. Former Secretary of Defense Harold Brown was quite accurate in reporting that history shows that when we increase our military capability, the Russians increase; when we *de*crease, they still *in*crease. Every year, regardless of our ac- tions, they have added five percent in real dollars to the amount of money they spend on defense. The Russians say that they intend to have military superiority and they have achieved it. And, yes, there *is* danger of war.

Huddle: Do the Russians perceive it as superiority or as parity?

Zumwalt: From the reports I see, they believe they are superior to us. Brezhnev is talking differently in Europe because his objective is to woo the Western European nations away from a close alliance with the United States, and to make them more frightened of the United States, while he deploys an additional SS-20 missile every week. From all the intelligence, the Rus- sians recognize their superiority. Our president has told us that we are inferior; our secretary of defense has told us the same thing. Those of us who have served on the Joint Chiefs of Staff have been reporting that to the Congress for a decade. The fact of that imbalance is that the Russians have become very aggres- sive now. It's always dangerous when an inferior power tries to catch up; but it's even more dangerous to let the Russians con- tinue to exercise their superiority to seize one objective after another as they have been doing. If we think we can avoid any real risk of war by just permitting the Soviets to continue what they are doing, we will at some point reach a line beyond which free men cannot retreat.

Huddle: Looking at the lessons of history, do you think we will have demonstrations in response to the military buildup, as we did during Vietnam?

Zumwalt: No, I think the demonstrations were the result of the fact that we were fighting a long, drawn-out war in which there was no intention of winning a military victory. After only four years of the Korean War the public was similarly beginning to get fed up with war. In a democracy it's more difficult than in a dictatorship to hold onto the same kind of firmness of purpose in war. There are always politicians who try to capitalize on the public mood to the disadvantage of the country. Indeed Mr. Nixon was elected because he created the perception that he had a solution to the Vietnam War. I don't think the people in this country have ever objected to having military parity or superiority; as a matter of fact the polls show that during a presidential election between Mr. Carter and Mr. Reagan, people were deeply concerned because they perceived that the Soviet Union *had* achieved superiority. Even on the campuses at the height of the Vietnam War . . . the first question I would ask was "How many of you believe we should cut our defense budgets?" Everybody always voted for that. And the second question was "How many believe we should be militarily inferior to the Soviet Union?" Only the five or ten campus socialists would put their hands up.

Huddle: Many of the people I've interviewed are concerned about cutting back on social spending. They feel we are destroying our society from within by pulling resources out of modernizing our productive capabilities and out of research and development, weakening our society's long-term viability. They feel we need a whole new way of looking at the whole security question which would involve a more global approach.

Zumwalt: My thought is that that is just a new form of Chamberlainism. That is, inventing reasons not to do the necessary and putting a mantle of idealism over it. The same arguments were put forward by those wanting to see the defense budgets cut back in each of the periods between wars which I talked about. The facts are so stark and so clear that it's difficult nowadays to believe that anyone could fail to perceive that our military inferiority has led to the most serious kinds of consequences. Unless we realize that the first basic requirement of any sovereign nation is to be able to survive, many of the other problems are going to be inconsequential. The Finns survived and have sovereignty today, even though it's quite heavily deferential to the Soviet Union. What limited sovereignty they enjoy is due to the fact that they spent far more than average for defense and were able to win on the battlefield the right to survive and negotiate an outcome, rather than the outright conquests of Latvia, Estonia, Lithuania, Poland, and all the rest, where adequate armaments were not maintained.

Huddle: So you aren't particularly worried about the cutbacks' in social spending leading to major demonstrations?

Zumwalt: There will always be demonstrations in a democracy. The only time we won't have demonstrations is if the Russians move in. There will always be discontent in a democracy: we all dream for better things. What I'm saying is that in this imperfect world, where you have a society like the USSR which has been ruthlessly constituted on a theory of achieving global hegemony, if America wants to survive as a society that has meaning, we've got first to look to our defenses. That means we can't do as much as we would like to do in the domestic field. We can't help foreign nations in other ways, as we would like to do. We must have a balance. But my perception of a balance differs wildly from, say, Paul Warnke's [chief U.S. SALT II negotiator] perception of a balance.

Huddle: Some of my interviews make me wonder if we are not causing some kind of major split in our country which maybe wouldn't be necessary if we thought through the whole issue in greater depth and had more people participating in the debate. Could you comment?

Zumwalt: So far, the things you have identified are part of the "better Red than dead" school. And there are people who freely admit that they'd rather see this nation occupied by the Soviet Union.

Huddle: I think their point is that they see great disparity of wealth between the rich and poor in the U.S., and their analysis would be that the U.S. in many ways is not much better than the Soviet Union—that we're pushing our own form of global hegemony via the corporations.

Zumwalt: That's the Communist line. There are many who adhere to it who are not Communists. The ones who admit they prefer that course to continuing on the course I advocate are, in my opinion, nobler citizens than those who believe but won't admit it. There are many who argue for lower defense budgets who really are of the "better Red than dead" school but won't admit it. I think it's very difficult to argue with that point of view because those who could claim that the differences in wealth encompassed in the United States are a worse problem than the total lack of freedom in the Soviet Union leave you with no basis for discussion. Anyone who says that simply doesn't understand what a democracy is all about.

Huddle: Could you express what democracy means to you and what totalitarianism of the Soviet variety means to you?

Zumwalt: Soviet totalitarianism means the exercise of near total power by a band of ruthless men who have struggled to the top through a tyrannical system. It is the enslavement of millions of people, by a combination of terror and brainwashing and scrubbed news, into sullen support of that power system. It is the creation of much greater discrepancies of wealth than we had in this country when the so-called robber barons were first establishing their fortunes. Mr. Brezhnev has a private lane of highway on which no one else can drive, a fleet of cars, and dachas in many locations in the USSR. He is a man of far greater de facto wealth than the first Rockefeller ever purported to be. Our system is one in which free men have the ability to elect leaders who lead them until they are dismissed from office. With all the imperfections that it carries with it, our system has the ultimate strength that free men continue to control their own destiny by being able to turn these leaders out.

Huddle: What do you see are some of the differences between what it means to be a Soviet citizen and American citizen in terms of day-to-day affairs?

Zumwalt: The average Soviet family which thinks in terms of going overseas immediately has to be frightened about whether or not one of the family members will have to remain behind as a hostage. In a very large percentage of the cases that happens. "Will our dossier begin to show that we have talked to foreigners?" "Will this affect opportunity for promotion?" "If I go to a cocktail party and am indiscreet in criticizing my government, what will that impact be?" "Dare I say to this good friend what I really think about Brezhnev?" It's a life of constant fear. The nature of the fear has changed somewhat. In the days of Stalin they used to take people out of their bedrooms and slaughter them by the millions or send them off to slave labor camps. Today it's psychiatric wards or job loss. But it is still a system that operates basically on fear.

Huddle: What is the response of the people to fear?

Zumwalt: The overwhelming majority shut down and become less courageous, but there are always the Solzhenitsyns and Sakharovs. In Poland there turned out to be enough of them to begin to turn the system around. Whether or not that movement will survive being smashed by the Soviet Union still remains to be seen. But the multitude will cooperate with the government.

Huddle: If we were creating greater fear by building up our military might to contain and deter the Soviet government from aggressive acts, are we contributing to the internal totalitarianism that exists there?

Zumwalt: The Soviet leaders have always created in the Soviet populace fear of the Americans: "The Americans are coming!" That was true when we were superior and it remains true today when we are inferior. "If the Americans are coming," their leaders say, "then you must sacrifice more and we must build more weapons." We must instill fear in the Soviet leaders. It *did* deter them for a long time, but no longer deters them because they are no longer militarily inferior. The only way you regain that fear or respect is to regain strategic nuclear parity. I'm prepared to settle for equality; that's good enough to make the Soviet government take fewer risks.

Huddle: You say that we don't know their system and they don't know ours. Do you advocate more exposure of American people and Soviet people to each other?

Zumwalt: Yes, I strongly advocate all possible communication back and forth. When I talk about a balanced program, I could go on for an hour about all the things we ought to be doing. For example, first, we must regain a sufficient military capability to deter them. Without that, in my judgment nothing else will do it. Number two, our Central Intelligence Agency must regain a capability behind the Iron Curtain. Number three, there must be the coordination of a vast psychological campaign which would allow as much travel as possible to Russia: cultural exchanges, trade in all but the kinds of things that help them perfect their war machine, assistance to Soviet clients such as Poland which are trying to break away from the total clutch of the Soviet Union—every possible way of weakening their system, short of going to war with them, must be utilized, as well as every possible means of eroding it from within by communicating to their people.

Pat Mische

Pat Mische is co-founder, with her husband Gerald, of Global Education Associates. Together they wrote Toward a Human World Order. *They both travel and lecture widely. When this interview was done in the spring of 1982 the Misches lived with their three children in East Orange, New Jersey, where they were actively involved in global education activities. Pat is currently working on a book on women, peace, and alternative futures.*

I grew up in a very ordinary labor-class family. My father worked in factories all his life in foundries and on an automobile assembly line. He felt very strongly about the importance of labor unions. When he was about fifteen his father died, and being the eldest of twelve children, he left school and got a job. It was at the beginning of the depression, so he worked with the Civilian Conservation Corps. My grandfather died because of the bad working conditions in the foundry where he worked. The autopsy revealed that his lungs were like concrete from the dust and pollutants he had breathed in. Consequently my father felt very stongly about justice for workers, which had a big effect on me.

My mother was from a farm family and left home after finishing eighth grade. She was the second oldest of twelve children. Since only the boys were needed on the farm, the girls were shipped off to earn an income as soon as they got through the eighth grade. She worked as a maid in a wealthy home in St. Paul, until she met my father.

Both families are very strong church people, but my mother is a Lutheran and my father is a Catholic. When my mother married my father, her side of the family practically disowned her for marrying a Catholic; my father's side of the family was a bit more tolerant: they only feared my mother would go to hell if she didn't convert before she died. I grew up with the strong fear that my mother indeed might not convert before she died; later, when I was older, I was very grateful she had maintained her own beliefs and integrity. Those early tensions later made me very interested in the ecumenical movement and religious tolerance.

The other big influence on me was that my father was gone most of my early years. I was born at the beginning of World War II, and my father just disappeared from my life when I wasn't yet two. We rarely saw him. He was in the navy. He returned at the end of the war, but I always had this tremendous sense that war was "something that took your father away." I envisioned war as a place. We lived next to a cornfield on the edge of a very small town in Minnesota; the train passed near our house. I used to imagine my father going off on the train, which is what he had done, to some place called "World War II," and I always felt this fear that he might not come back.

A more developed perception about war came when I was about twelve. Some years after World War II ended with the atomic bombings of Hiroshima and Nagasaki, the nuclear arms race started between the Soviet Union and the United States. In the early fifties, during the McCarthy era, fear began to grow that the Soviets might use such a bomb against the U.S. At that time the American Legion sponsored an essay contest on "What should you do when the atomic bomb falls?" I won first prize—five or ten dollars and cookies—and I got to read my essay before these women in uniform. While I knew all the "right" answers to their question, I was terrified. The answers made no sense. What I really wanted to know from these women was not what to do when the bomb falls as if it were preordained, but "*Why* does it have to fall?" and "Why aren't all those people in uniform, our national leaders, and our town leaders finding a way to keep it from falling?"

That was the departure point for me—a very conscious departure point. I no longer trusted that America was really secure. All those things our leaders had done from the time I was very young to make us a secure nation obviously no longer worked. Even the people I trusted to protect me in my town could no longer provide real, believable security options against this kind of weapon—*because they weren't asking the right questions.* They *assumed* that the bomb would fall and that the only defense was really no defense: you just accepted that you would die. Or that maybe you'd be poisoned by radiation, or your children would be mutated. So there was no *real* defense.

When I was very young I had always felt that our town was secure. We had an annual Memorial Day parade in which we marched to the river to throw in flowers and boom a thirty-gun salute in memory of the war dead. I had believed that if enough young men were brave enough to go off to war our town and America would always be a very secure place to live. But in writing the essay I lost my faith that weapons would provide any kind of security.

At that age I didn't really do a whole lot with my new worldview, but it stayed with me right through the McCarthy era. I went through high school, was a normal high school kid, went to all the dances, tried to be as popular as I could, tried to be Homecoming Queen, and was all of those things. And still there was this thing always nagging at me. I went through college, where books were being destroyed because of McCarthyism. The college chaplain pulled off the shelves such books as H. G. Wells's *The Outline of History* because he thought it was communistic; Salinger's *Catcher in the Rye* was yanked from student shelves and teachers using Salinger in their classes were fired. For me, that was an incredible experience. I wondered, "How secure is our country if our freedoms can be so violated?"

After graduating I went to Africa for several years in a program called Teachers for East Africa. It was the early sixties when Kenya, Uganda, and Tanzania were preparing for independence from Britain. That experience had a tremendous influence on my thinking for several reasons. First, it was very exciting to see firsthand three countries come into independence out of colonial rule. Second, living and teaching in Africa brought me to see my own value system against that of the Africans among whom I lived and worked. For a period of time I dropped almost everything I believed in and then slowly began to take back into my life those values that I really wanted to hold. But this time I *chose* my values consciously rather than just accepting them blindly, as happens when we are conditioned as children.

Relating this to your question of security, I was struck by the tremendous sense of security among the African tribal peoples. Although technologically they were coming out of the Iron Age to make a leap of four thousand or more years of technological development, they were highly advanced in terms of human development and cooperation skills; probably that's the only way they survived. I was very struck by how simply one could live and still be very happy, and decided to get rid of a lot of the clutter in my life. I found I was happier when I didn't have a lot of things. I didn't feel I was sacrificing anything. I was gaining something. I could focus on things that were becoming more important to me.

Another thing that happened to me in Africa was that my whole notion of history exploded. Coming from the American Midwest, where most towns were young, my sense of history only went back about a hundred years, the length of time Minnesota had been a state. When I studied on the East Coast, prior to going to Africa, I learned to read back two hundred years, to the American Revolution. But suddenly, not far from where I was teaching in Africa, the Leakeys were discovering the oldest human fossil forms. They dated back *two million years*. Now other human fossils have been found dating back *three and four million years*! And I was living with people who spanned four to ten thousand years of human evolution. I was teaching the history of ancient civilizations and I realized that these people were living the hunting, gathering, and pastoral lives that were typical in the Old Testament. I began to feel myself a living part of that old history; I was not teaching something that was remote from me.

At the same time I was also having a tremendous new sense of the *future,* because while the Leakeys were discovering the oldest human fossil forms, John Glenn was orbiting the earth overhead, and satellite monitoring systems were being put up. I began to see the full sweep of human history from origins in the far past to the far reaches of the future. I realized that the history of the United States was just a tiny parenthesis in the full sweep of human history. The big question for me now became not "What does it mean to be an American?" but *"What does it mean to be human? Where are we going as a species?"* It seemed clear to me that while all of the past histories of the separate tribes I taught were now converging in nationhood, at the same time the separate histories of the world's nations were now converging in a new global age. We really had one shared future history. So issues like security had to be looked at not just within an American context, but from within a global context. Where do we want to go as a species, not just in terms of technology but in our values and how we live? What do we want to be as a planetary people?

When I returned I married Gerry, who was very much involved in international development. We dedicated our marriage to building world unity. We made a shared commitment to somehow use the energy of our union with each other to build world unity. Gerry had been training people in self-help projects in developing countries. In the first development decade he had seen the gap between rich and poor grow bigger, not smaller. One reason was that development programs were undertaken only in a local or national context. This was insufficient because part of the problem was international: inequitable distribution of resources between nations, inequitable world trade patterns, and so on. We both began to look at current world systems and at the way in which these affect human development. We concluded that they are inadequate to solve either economic development problems or many other global problems we face, including security. Our present world systems cannot deal with the problem of the arms race or provide real security to nations and peoples. The more we arm, the more we fear these weapons will be used and the more insecure we become. Things are getting increasingly out of control. By the year 2000 we will have thirty-five to forty nations with nuclear weapons and the possibility of their being used by a madman head-of-state or terrorist group, or as a result of computer failure or error, will become greater and greater.

It seemed to us that no nation could be expected to disarm unilaterally; they would not do so in a security vacuum. We also noted that the nation-states system that was developed after the collapse of feudalism over the last four to five hundred years was developed for the purpose of assuring people a greater measure of economic and military security. While it had been the best that could be done for a while, the nation-state system is now no longer adequate. Today's nations have become increasingly *interdependent* and modern weapons can penetrate national boundaries from thousands of miles away. What we really need now is a world security system that can assure nations sufficient security to disarm and get on with their domestic needs. If we are really to have security within our nations, we will have to give priority to meeting people's *real* security needs: employment, sufficient food, education, health care, and safe neighborhoods. Yet in nation after nation the priorities are not being placed on real human security needs. Governments are participating in an arms race under the illusion that weapons will provide security, while in fact the weapons no longer provide security because they are too dangerous to use. Meanwhile we're putting so much money into military expenditures that our *real* security needs are being ignored and put on the back burner. So in the name of national security we have a double erosion of security.

We founded Global Education Associates to explore alternative world systems that could enable nations to safely disarm and attend to employing, educating, and caring for their people. We have associates in about forty countries, who participate in research, writing, and educational programs. Our organizational program has three phases: first, a research and educational stage to analyze the linkages between local and global concerns and to explore alternatives; next, a political stage; and finally, a transformational stage. Right now we feel the main emphasis should be on education because so many people still believe security can be ensured within the national context primarily by relying on weapons rather than looking to such alternatives as negotiation and international law. Recently, however, some of our associates have begun to feel, particularly because of the way things are going in the United States and Europe, that it is time to put more emphasis on political strategies. One group in Oregon has begun what they call the Oregon People's Congress for Peace Through Law, supporting candidates for office who will work for alternative security systems. They launched themselves in February 1981, and we are hoping that will take off. I suppose it will be a kind of alternative to the Moral Majority. Initially we are calling it the "Creative Minority," and we hope it will become the Creative *Majority*.

In looking at the relationship between First and Third World countries, two questions come to mind. One is that of justice: Is it morally acceptable to deny autonomy to a people for the sake of supplying the *American* people with the world's highest standard of living? Should we back totalitarian governments in order to support our own comfort while other people are left to live in poverty and their rights are being violated? That is the fundamental moral question we need to ask ourselves. The second question relates to our national self-interest: Does the support of totalitarian regimes really enhance our national security? Certainly resources are important to any nation's security. Like many of the northern industrial nations our country has become very dependent on other nations for over fifty percent of most of its resources. That dependency is growing. By the year 2000 the U.S. will be dependent on other nations for eighty to ninety percent of most of its resources. At the same time more and more Third World nations no longer accept domination from either the United States or the Soviet Union. They really do want their political autonomy and more equitable trade patterns.

As a nation we have two options with regard to Third World resources. We could seize and try to hold them by force, through the threatened or actual use of our armies, our missiles, and through economic support of dictatorships. That would be extremely costly to the U.S. taxpayer. Our resources come not from just one foreign nation but literally from all around the world. It would require enormous financial resources to support an American military presence around the world and to support the many totalitarian governments involved to prevent popular revolutions. Aside from the moral question, that option would destroy the U.S. economically. Our military budgets would escalate beyond what they are even now. Essentially we would become the policeman of the world for our own profit and gain, arousing hostilities against us all of the time. More and more force would have to be used to keep these hostilities from erupting in open rebellion. If one follows this "need to protect national self-interest" argument to its natural conclusion, it doesn't make any real sense. In the long run resources would not really be more secure.

The only way we will have access to resources is to come to understand better the will of the majority of the people within a country. We must be sympathetic to their concerns for autonomy and self-rule and for participation in their own political processes. After all, that's how the U.S. got its start. And we must understand their concern for their own security. Food, education, and shoes for the children: these are the security issues that the people of El Salvador and Guatemala face. *So why should we by default*

make the Communists appear to be the saviors to so many of the world's
people because they seem the most sympathetic to their cause?

I have lived in and been in many Third World countries and
talked to many people. I have only met a handful of Communists.
But I have met thousands of people who want political participation in their country's governing processes. They don't want foreign rule, whether from the USSR, the U.S., or from Europe.
They want autonomy. And if some are driven to embrace communism as a solution, it is usually only as a last resort. Many start
out simply wanting more political and economic equality. They
want access to land, employment, health care, education, and so
on. Castro didn't start out as a Communist: he started out as a
reformer, and when access to the political process was denied, he
became a guerrilla. Eventually, because the Communists were the
ones sympathetic to their cause, he became a Communist. Even so,
in many Latin American countries many of the guerrillas advocating changes are not really Communists. Many of them are very
committed Christians, and one reason they're in the hills is that
they are on the "kill lists" of their governments. They know their
government wants them dead, and many of their friends are already dead. Some were journalists who wrote critical articles about
the government which got them on the kill list; they have seen
other journalists killed. They have three choices: they can find
some way to get out of the country (which may be impossible
because to get a visa means going through government channels),
they can allow themselves to be killed, or they can flee into the
hills. Therefore many of them join the guerrillas *because they see no
other choice.* Not all of the guerrillas are committed to communism,
but they *are* committed to political and economic reform.

I feel the Communist thing is exaggerated. Although some
guerrillas are certainly committed to a Communist solution, I
really think most are not. Many began by simply wanting social
reforms. Some came from Christian concern. They started out
with the social gospels, the Scriptures, and the corporeal works of
mercy. I interviewed one Philippine priest who was in prison
because he had been helping the poor to organize for land reform.
He had started out preaching the gospel and then got very interested in the situation of his people. Most were very poor and no
longer had any land. They had not wanted to sell their land; it was
forcibly taken from them and those who refused to sell were

killed. He became interested in their grievances and they became interested in the messages of the Scriptures, which told them they had dignity and basic human rights. As their sense of dignity and awareness of their rights increased they wanted to take the next step, which was to ask the government for changes. They told the priest, "If you really believe in this, you should be with us." And he came along. The government then accused him of teaching "subversive activity" in organizing these people to seek reforms, so he was imprisoned. I think that is a common story. Both he and the people were accused of being Communists when actually none of them was; they were coming out of the Christian gospel context.

The world faces a very dangerous situation with regard to resources. As the U.S. and other industrialized nations become more dependent on resources and as Third World countries industrialize, these resources will become an increasing source of tension and competition. This can lead to war—this time, to a global war. We don't have an adequate security system to prevent this from happening. An alternative security system would establish equitable access to the world's resources so that nations with guns and missiles don't control the flow of resources. Also, it would establish resource conservation measures to ensure that future generations will have what they need to sustain them. Finally, we need some way of curbing and finally ending the arms race. All three of those have to be worked on simultaneously.

First of all, we need to educate people and develop the political will to find alternatives. Since the beginning of this century several attempts have been made to develop a world security system based on law and arbitration. The first of such attempts were the International Peace Conferences held in 1899 and 1906 at the Hague. Participating governments at these two meetings were ultimately unwilling to surrender sovereignty to a world body in order to enforce their goals of disarmament. A third meeting was planned for 1916, but before it could convene, World War I broke out. After World War I the League of Nations was launched. Its purpose was to prevent another world war. But once more the participating nations were reluctant to give up some sovereignty to make the League effective. Consequently the League was too weak to prevent Hitler's aggression. Even before the end of World War II people began to realize we needed a stronger world body and began working to draft a United Nations charter. But once again nations were reluctant to give a world body enough authority to manage conflict, arbitrate and settle disputes and prevent aggression. And now once again we are seeing the result of this weakness. We do not have an international body that's empowered sufficiently to deal with terrorism, the seizing of hostages, to prevent aggression, or to proceed toward disarmament. We don't have a strong enough International Court. But the infrastructure for a world security system is potentially there—*if we have the political will to develop and implement it.*

Some of the elements needed in an alternative world security system would include the following: a strengthened International Court with compulsory jurisdiction to rule on questions of international law; a strengthened arbitration and mediation service to manage conflicts before they erupt in armed revolt; and an adequate international verification system for compliance with disarmament agreements. Now with satellite monitoring for the first time we have the technology to verify arms-control agreements. On-site inspection by an international team would also be important because, quite understandably, nations will not reduce their arms until they're absolutely sure other nations are not secretly rearming. We also need to reassess the veto power in the Security Council whereby one nation can veto agreements made on behalf of security for the whole world.

Once these elements are in place we could begin a phased arms reduction. We can't expect nations to suddenly dismantle all weapons systems. The intent for the Strategic Arms Limitation Talks (SALT) was to conduct an ongoing series of negotiations between the two superpowers. The first talks would lead to real disarmament. If SALT II had been ratified in the U.S., the Soviet Union would actually have been obligated to dismantle some of its missiles.

The Soviets really wanted SALT II ratified because without it the lid was off in the arms race. The U.S. could build new weapons systems and outspend the Soviets because we are wealthier and have a stronger economy. The Soviet economy is in much worse shape, and if they continue to try to match U.S. weapons development, they will have tremendous internal problems. They want to get on with SALT III, but they don't trust the U.S. very much. We can better understand the Soviet position by remem-

bering U.S. fears during the Cuban missile crisis. There was tremendous fear of Soviet missiles' being based so closely. America
felt tremendously insecure at that time. The Soviets share thousands of miles of border with China, a country hostile toward
them. What if Canadian missiles were aimed at us? We would be
very insecure. To the west, the Soviet Union has NATO, French
and U.S. missiles aimed at them. To their south nuclear submarines roam the Indian Ocean. U.S. nuclear submarines also dock
in the Philippines. So the Soviet Union is ringed by missiles.

The resulting insecurity within the Soviet Union has to be
tremendous. If you add the fact that the U.S., by dropping atomic
bombs on Japan, has proved its willingness to use nuclear weapons, Soviet paranoia is understandable. Dropping the A-bombs on
Hiroshima and Nagasaki was an act aimed against the Soviet
Union as much as Japan. It was a way to give advance warning
about U.S. intent to use weapons of mass destruction if it is
deemed necessary.

When I talked with Soviet women at a conference on
women and disarmament, some of them said, "We lost twenty
million people in World War II. People starved; our cities were
destroyed. We never want to be vulnerable again." But they are
feeling very vulnerable right now, despite all their recent weapons
gains, and I think we could effectively argue with them that real
security for them as well as us could come through a plan for
phased disarmament and verification. The superpowers also must
realize that the nuclear weapons race involves more than the superpowers; by the year 2000 we may have thirty-five or forty
nations with nuclear weapons. In the Nuclear Age the problem of
security has got to be dealt with in a global way.

For me, it is not a question of whether or not we're going to
have a new world order: we are heading for *some* kind of new
world order. The question is, what kind will it be, on what values
will it be based, and who will be the guiding force behind it? We
could have a new world order coming out of catastrophe, such as
a nuclear war. Following the holocaust there would be tremendous chaos, economic collapse, and devastation of social services.
Out of that, some kind of world order would be imposed to
restore order, but it would not be a very democratic one. A
second path to world order is by drift, which is what we are

doing now with transnationals' assuming more and more economic power. Of the world's hundred largest economic entities,
measured by gross product, forty-nine are transnational corporations; only fifty-one are nation-states. Increasing power is going
into the hands of fewer and fewer economic elites—and that in
itself is the beginning of a new kind of world order. These corporations make their own rules and decisions; they are not subject to
international laws. *They are outside the realm of an effective system of
accountability to the world's people.*

A third approach to world order and security is to move
consciously toward a *preferred* world order based on democratic
participation and on preferred values of peace, economic well-
being, social justice, ecological balance, and democratic participation. Unfortunately most people are not educated enough to
know that we can and need to move in this direction. They do not
know the dangers we currently face, and maybe suffer under the
illusion that we still have national sovereignty. Within our nation
we don't have a general awareness that we have entered an era of
increasing global interdependence where our security and well-
being depend not just on decisions we make here but on decisions
made abroad. It's a very different world and we need new structures and worldviews to deal with the new problems and opportunities we face.

In the United States global awareness is so low. UNESCO
did a study of one hundred nations to measure the global awareness level of the media, and *the United States came in last*! Americans are just unaware of world realities. Only five percent of our
teachers come out of teacher-training programs with any kind of
global awareness courses, so they aren't prepared to educate
young people about the world in which they are going to live. We
are being educated for a world that no longer exists. One out of
every six jobs in America is directly related to foreign trade, yet
we talk about "keeping jobs for Americans." If you work for a
multinational corporation, your job is related to the security and
stability of events in the world; if your corporation is kicked out
of a country tomorrow, it will affect your job.

Although some corporations profit from the arms race, most
do not. So I don't think that U.S. ignorance about world affairs
or our government's commitment to the arms race is a capitalist

conspiracy. We have built our country on the value of self-reliance and tend to think of ourselves as independent, so it's hard for us to think of ourselves as also being dependent.

We have also imaged ourselves as "God's gift to the world," making a religion out of America. So when we talk about living in a new world, in a way we are asking people to have a new religion. Christians in the U.S. have identified their Christianity with America and it's hard now to expand that belief system to embrace all the world's people. If people take their religious convictions to the deepest core, however, the essence of the religious vision is oneness. The word religion—from "religiare"—means to bind together, to make one. This is true whether the vision is Hindu, Buddhist, Christian, or Islamic. Almost every great religious visionary of the major world religions has had a vision of world unity. But so often we've confused our nationalism with our religion and have not gone to the essence.

For centuries Americans have seen themselves as almost immune from outside attack and it's hard now to see ourselves as penetrable. That is the *real* Soviet scare: it's not just the Soviets as Soviets or the Communist system; underneath there's the knowledge that we are now vulnerable. Weapons won't make us more secure because each new weapon system we develop is eventually matched by comparable weapons aimed against us from another part of the world. We need to define national security as we define it in our states: New Jersey doesn't have missiles aimed at New York and vice versa. We've developed interstate law to handle conflicts within our nation. The time has come to do that internationally. We will be far more secure with a strong international legal system to manage our disputes and manage gradual, phased disarmament than we ever could be by continuing the arms race and destroying our economy.

Melor Sturua

Melor Sturua was serving as the Washington bureau chief of Izvestia *(the main newspaper of the Communist party) at the time we conducted this interview in the spring of 1982. He was sent back to Moscow by the U.S. government several months later as a quid pro quo exchange for an American correspondent who was charged with espionage activities and deported from the USSR. He is currently living with his wife in Moscow.*

I am both a Georgian and a Soviet citizen. I was born in 1928 in Tbilisi, the capital of Georgia. I left my hometown when I was fourteen years old and went to Moscow to study at the Institute of International Relations, graduating in 1949. Since then I have worked as a journalist or editor with *Izvestia* for almost thirty-two years now. I also have a doctorate in international law. I spent several years outside of the Soviet Union as a correspondent in London and New York, but in June 1977 I came to Washington, D.C., to serve as the bureau chief of my newspaper. I have published thirteen books, eleven of which are about the United States. I have the honor of receiving the Borowski prize, which is like your Pulitzer prize. I am married, and my wife and I have two sons and two granddaughters. I am also a screenplay writer. I wrote screenplays for several fiction movies and documentaries.

Many of my books and screenplays deal with the most important questions of contemporary civilization: how to survive. I never try to give a "recipe" for how to survive because I don't think there is any one particular person who can prescribe it, but I try to contribute to the solution of this question, showing how

dangerous it is when enmity becomes an obsession among nations—especially between the Soviet Union and the United
States. After all, we can eliminate not only each other but also the
whole earth and all of humanity. I try to educate my readers or
viewers because despite technological development, in the end it is
humankind which has the decisive say. And if we are educated
enough and have the will to defend ourselves, we will survive. So
in the final analysis I am still an optimist. It isn't a rosy optimism—I don't think we can have a lasting peace overnight. We
have to fight for it every day because nothing is given to us just
for the asking. When I say "fight," some Americans may think I
just mean with guns and planes and bombs, but the other definition of this word "fight" is that you try to create peace and
articulate your desire for peace and try to enforce your will on
your government and on the military-industrial complex. This is
a very noble and positive kind of "fighting" and it can be hoped
that sooner or later—perhaps later than sooner—the forces of
peace will prevail.

There are many ways to reach people in governments who
view the other country as the enemy. The simplest way is to meet
them and talk with them personally. This is very important—not
only to ask questions but also to tell them your views. In my role
as a journalist I have had this opportunity both in the United
States and in the Soviet Union. I met President Nixon several
times, Mr. Kissinger, and other leading political figures. The
same in the USSR. I also have good relations with a number of
the leading authorities in my country. In our discussions, I explain
to them the danger of a nuclear confrontation. I must say that
they share these concerns; the problem is how to translate this
knowledge into active policy.

Another way to reach governments is to educate the public
which then becomes a pressure group to influence government to
abandon confrontation and start cooperation. We have to explore
every avenue to reach and to influence governments. This is valid
for my country too, although of course the ways in which it is
done are quite different. In my country, for example, the movement toward a nuclear freeze is supported both by the public and
by the government. That's why the confrontation between the
public and the government is not so big in my country as in
America. For example, the Soviet Union is against a first strike.

My government has proposed several times in the United Nations, and in bilateral discussions with the United States, that first nuclear strike be abandoned as an option. In your country the government supports the first-strike option while the public is against it. And recently several very important and knowledgeable people like [former Secretary of Defense Robert] McNamara, [former Undersecretary of State George F.] Kennan, [former presidential advisor McGeorge] Bundy,and [former presidential advisor Gerard] Smith also proposed this, but the current government still maintains the strategy of a right to first strike. The U.S. government claims that this is because of the supremacy of Soviet conventional forces in Europe; otherwise, they argue, they would have to spend too much money to strengthen conventional forces and would have to introduce the draft. What they are saying then is that a dead European is cheaper than a drafted American. I don't know; maybe this is a good *business* policy, but from the human point of view it is abhorrent. This merchant point of view is very dangerous and destructive. You can't make money out of complete destruction anyway—nobody would benefit from this.

I think that ignorance is the principal root of the fear between our two societies. We don't know each other. Just a few days ago I was in central Florida delivering some lectures in small Florida towns. My listeners were members of Kiwanis and Rotary clubs, and so on. During one of the question periods, someone asked me, "Mr. Sturua, you live in the United States and there is no harm done to you. Now you know that every American tourist who goes to the Soviet Union is shot by the government." I then asked, "Are you joking or are you serious?" He said, "I'm serious." I then asked, "Who told you this?" "Everyone says so," he said. We sometimes think that sophisticated people in New York or Washington represent the whole populace in the United States, but in the depths of the United States this ignorance about communism and about my country is enormous. Such ignorance leads to fear, and there are people who misuse this fear and explain the theory of communism as an aggressive philosophy which aims to conquer the whole world. But our history shows we are not conquerers; more than that, it shows that we were always the victims of outside aggression. Even more, any social change must be *internal*. No group can impose its own philosophy on another nation. Unfortunately this side of Communist theory is not well known in your country and is hidden from the public because it doesn't play into the hands of those who are trying to instigate this hatred of communism, socialism, and of the Soviet Union.

Of course, no one can deny that there *is* an ideological confrontation between the philosophy of private property and that of commonly held property. We believe that in the final analysis our system would work better to satisfy the physical and spiritual needs of people. At the same time we say that this dispute over which system is better must be fought peacefully. If you prove your system is better, you will be the winners; if we prove our system is better, then we will be the winners. But no one will lose. If *our* system proves itself to be better, then you can introduce into *your* system some parts of our system. And we will do the same with effective parts of *your* system. This is already happening: you have introduced some state planning into your system and we have introduced some financial incentives into our economy. But why destroy each other? If we destroy each other, afterward no one will find out who was right and who was wrong. This is another meaning of the word "fight": you can fight to improve and enrich human life.

Communism is a living theory, not a frozen one. We never regard the writings of Marx and Engel as a *Bible,* something carved in stone like the Ten Commandments. Even the founders of communism stated that the development of human civilization will change and correct the theories because theory is just the beginning of communism. Marxist writings date from the middle of the nineteenth century. When you try to prove from these writings that the Soviet Union wants to conquer the United States, that is just cheating. It is historically inaccurate and has nothing to do with contemporary communism and Soviet foreign policy. Our foreign policy is based on defending our internal security and our friends. We have to cooperate with the whole world—it doesn't matter if it is the socialist world or the capitalist world. We have to defend and promote peace, disarmament, and cooperation in all fields. More than that, nowadays we face such enormous problems—of ecology, energy, and development of outer space—that we need unity of the whole world to solve them. Neither the U.S. nor the USSR is strong enough or rich enough to solve these problems alone. These problems demand the unity of humanity because if we are to survive we must unite in order to solve them. This is the final and most important goal of our foreign policy and our Communist philosophy.

No ideal theory when implemented can be a hundred percent purely maintained. We live in a very unideal and turbulent world. Therefore there are mistakes and unforeseen difficulties, but the "main highway" of our movement is dictated by this theory. Although some people in your country might not believe this, they must study the historical record from the very beginning when the Soviet Union was established after the revolution in 1917. If you study the record very thoroughly and without prejudice you will see that this kind of criticism isn't valid at all. Of course, I would like to repeat that we have made mistakes, which is understandable because as the first socialist country in the world we had no experience and no examples to follow. We had to pave a whole new way. We never claim to be one hundred percent blameless or without mistakes. Of *course* we make mistakes, and sometimes they are even *grave* mistakes—but the point is that *we learn from them.* We try to draw conclusions from our mistakes and not to repeat them. I think this is a very positive approach, especially nowadays when some mistakes like nuclear war would be unforgivable and irreversible.

One tendency of human nature is to claim that you are right and not to admit your mistakes. When we talk about nations and about all of mankind we must develop a new yardstick, because a mistake made by a nation, especially a superpower, can be very destructive and dangerous. Some people in your country say that we do not criticize ourselves, but if you will remember how harshly we criticized the cult of personality and mistakes and even the crimes committed by Stalin, you will see that we are *very* self-critical. More than that, self-criticism is one of the most important parts of Communist theory. We say that in every society there are several driving forces which have no economic strength but a spiritual one. One of them is criticism and self-criticism. People in the United States are gravely mistaken when they think that there is no public opinion in my country, no criticism of the government. or the party, no self-criticism on the part of the government or the party, or that everybody is a "yes man" in the Soviet Union. That has nothing to do with the reality. But to be persuaded that this is really the case you must study Russia not as an *enemy* but as a *potential friend*. If you study Russia just as an enemy, of course you just try to find our weaknesses and use them. Your approach must be positive: let's find something that *unites* us, not divides us. It is very easy to find what divides us. If you build nuclear weapons instead of bridges, you will always be inclined to find also a theoretical justification of such behavior.

> *Huddle:* Some people I've interviewed believe the Soviet Union has nuclear superiority over the United States. They say that when we build our nuclear weapons, the Soviets also do, and that when we don't, they continue to build them.
> *Sturua:* The main point is that nowadays it's meaningless to say who has military superiority because we both have the capacity for overkill. I can give you hundreds of facts and figures which show there is a raw parity between our countries in military terms. More than that, your technology and industry are superior. You can always get into gear and overtake us because technologically and financially you are much stronger than us. This propaganda about the Soviet Union's "definite margin of superiority"—to use President Reagan's phrase—is just a justification for continuing the arms race. He is wrong. It is a raw parity, and you can read the real conclusions made by the Joint Chiefs of Staff and other American military authorities who don't support President Reagan's viewpoint. But even if we *were* militarily superior and could, for example, kill you twenty times over and you could only kill us nineteen times over, what is the difference? It doesn't matter how many bullets you shoot into a dead body. The potential of overkill destroys the meaning of "superiority." Nobody knows what will happen if there is a nuclear war. We have no right to experiment in such a destructive way. It doesn't make sense to talk about who is superior; it would be better to talk about arms freeze and then reduction and, maybe someday, elimination.
> *Huddle:* It seems that both governments want to be stronger before they start reducing.
> *Sturua:* Yes. It is a natural inclination to want to be stronger than your adversary. But nowadays our government says there is raw parity between our countries and there is no need to continue the arms race. The old philosophy that "war is the continuation of foreign policy" is now obsolete because how can you continue your foreign policy if you destroy everything? You say that some people think the Soviet Union wants to conquer the United States? If we destroy you and you destroy

us, who will be conquerer and who will be conquered? In the ancient world, when one country conquered another, it used people as slaves and it used the economy of the defeated nation. How could we "enslave" dead Americans? It is senseless.

Huddle: Some interviewees have expressed fear of a subtle subversive manipulation of people's minds by communists.

Sturua: Real sympathy toward another nation cannot be based on subversion. If you sympathize with me, it is not because I can subvert you but because you can believe in me. If I just brainwash you, your sympathy will be very superficial—it will evaporate immediately. And how can we brainwash two hundred thirty million Americans? It is impossible. Moreover you know that famous saying, "You can fool some of the people some of the time, but you can't fool all of the people all of the time." The same thing is true of subversion and brainwashing. It is childish to claim that subversion can change the mind of a nation; to change the mind of a nation, you have to deliver something *real*. You can't convince them with fairy tales.

Huddle: One thing that makes us uncomfortable in America is what we hear about the handling of dissidents in the Soviet Union.

Sturua: The population of the Soviet Union is two hundred seventy million. Even if all the people who claim they are dissidents really *were* dissidents, they still represent a miniscule portion of the population of my country. There is nothing strange that some one hundred or maybe one thousand people oppose our system. Why not? It is entirely up to them if they don't like it. But the American media exaggerate their influence in the Soviet Union and try to show that there is a great dissident movement that is destroying the Soviet Union from the inside. There are just a few of them in Moscow and other big cities. You can see the results in our elections. There are hundreds of thousands of people who vote against the Soviet representatives in our elections. It is difficult to talk about the dissidents in general terms because every case is different.

I don't know. There may be a better way of handling dissidence. I don't claim that is the perfect way. Again, there are many kinds of dissidents. Some are common criminals, but if they claim to be dissidents, they know someone from the West will come to defend them. Another question people have in the West is whether people declared insane by Soviet society really are insane. The fact is that almost everybody proclaimed insane by Soviet medical authorities who afterward went abroad either committed suicide or ended up in your mental institutions.

Huddle: What about Sakharov and Solzhenitsyn?

Sturua: I must say that in Sakharov's case my country goes against the law because according to law he must be prosecuted and jailed. But because of his great stature and accomplishments, we spared him his crime. We have a law which prohibits propaganda of hatred and of war. He tries to induce hatred among nations—he says that the United States and other Western nations must prepare to fight a war against the Soviet Union because, he says, the Soviet Union wants to do the same thing to you and so you must take a preemptive step. But we don't want to attack or invade the United States. It is a foolish idea. I don't know why he says such a thing. Maybe he is a bitter man. I don't know. I don't know him personally. Maybe he knows that this kind of accusation makes him popular with the Western media so he can bask in the sun of his popularity.

Solzhenitsyn is a very talented writer but unfortunately he sacrificed his talent as a writer to his political activities. Instead of writing things of real literary worth, he started to write big, fat, unfounded political pamphlets aimed against the Soviet Union. He is a bitter man and I can understand why. He spent some time in a jail in Siberia; he was gravely ill with cancer and his life wasn't very light. But you must understand that if you are a writer and if you want to be a leader in a nation, you must be above your personal bitterness. He couldn't do that. Moreover his philosophy is so reactionary that even Western liberal intellectuals abhor what he proposes for Russia and the world— which is to go back to the Middle Ages and to destroy contemporary civilization, to base the new civilization on the village communes, to abandon everything for a theological state. Even the Moral Majority rejects his theory. He is dissatisfied with everybody, even with God and the Bible. He says that the early Christians made some changes in the Bible to suit their own ideas. He says that the West became a consumer society and abandoned the Judeo-Christian philosophy completely, becoming obsessed with money. So he says that we have to go back to the pure sources of religion. It sounds very noble, but how can you go back to the first centuries of mankind? He is looking back, not ahead.

Huddle: Perhaps there is a kernel of truth in his ideas.

Sturua: If you remember what Hitler and Goebbels said, that was also true for Germany. But what happened afterward? Every lie, especially every big lie, has a grain of truth in it.

That's why these big lies are so dangerous and why they are swallowed by men. If there is no truth in it whatsoever then nobody will believe it.

Huddle: How do we find the truth? How do we build a society that reflects the truth? It seems there are some good things in your country and some in ours, and good things in every person. So how can we build a global society which reflects this?

Sturua: There is truth and there is truth. If you talk about truth in philosophical or religious terms I think we will never achieve it. We will always come near to it, but we will never achieve it. And this is perhaps the best incentive for the development and sharing of knowledge. Even the Communists don't claim that it is possible to capture the whole truth. But there are relative truths: peace is better than war, cooperation is better than confrontation, and we have to secure the lives of ourselves and of future generations. This is all truth and not debatable. But if you try to eliminate this kind of truth because you are a keeper of something that is above all these things, you are playing a very dangerous game.

Huddle: Perhaps there is an expression of truth which embodies the *essence* of all the things you have mentioned.

Sturua: It is very difficult to answer this question.

Huddle: For example, that the cosmos is a fundamental unity.

Sturua: The wisest men of our history failed to answer this question, beginning with Socrates and going to Wittgenstein. I don't know. Who can answer this? Who knows the whole truth? We have to translate this into practical terms so that we will survive. Truth begins with life and we have to preserve life. If we don't, we will never find truth. So this is the first step: preserve life. Another step is to create a meaningful life.

Huddle: Which is perhaps the only kind of life people are going to feel is worth preserving.

Sturua: Yes, yes, but don't play with words because sometimes people say, "Better dead than Red." I would say, "Better Red than dead." If you are Red but still alive and you feel that Red is not right, if you are alive you can correct this situation. You can make it become yellow or blue or white. But if you are dead, you have no chance to correct the mistake. I am thinking of the famous quote by Alexander Haig: "There are some things which are more important than life." He meant freedom and so on. It is just a game with words. If you are dead you have no freedom at all. A slave has a chance to become a free man; a dead man has no chance to become free.

Huddle: Some people have said that if we are really committed to preserving freedom, we leave a better chance to end up with both life *and* freedom, that death is preferable to sacrificing freedom.

Sturua: That's quite understandable, but this is also more my-thology than real life. Who now really threatens the freedom of the people in the United States so much that you would prefer to die? Is your freedom so threatened by the Soviet Union that you would prefer to die? To be annihilated in a nuclear holocaust?

Huddle: Some of the people I've interviewed genuinely seem to believe this.

Sturua: I've never seen an America enslaved by the Soviet Union. Did you ever see such a thing? Why die for such a thing?

Huddle: I understand what you're saying. What I'm saying is that this is the concept that some Americans have of your country.

Sturua: The concept is *wrong*. The most important thing is that you can live in your country and that you are free—well, I would have to say that you are not really so free; you have other chains. But what I want to say is that it is a contradiction in terms. You see, if we wanted to enslave you we would have to abandon nuclear war because if we start the war we would kill you, and how can we enslave dead bodies? So even if we were such evil people that we wanted to enslave you we would never use nuclear weapons. That is the point. That's why this confrontation between the idea of being alive and being free is artificial and introduced by ideologues in the United States to justify the arms race.

Huddle: Several interviewees have expressed the belief that the Soviet Union is on the verge of or has possibly made a break-through in weapons technology, creating weapons based on principles of electromagnetism [see Eldon Byrd, pp. 181–191].

Sturua: I am not an expert in this field but I know of no such breakthrough. This talk is maybe good reading for fiction, es-pecially for science fiction, but it is very dangerous when it is introduced into foreign policy. Maybe in the distant future mankind will invent something like that, but if we try to avoid or eliminate the difficulties between our two countries in some kind of meaningful way, we will never have any drive to pro-duce such a weapon. The point is to create the international atmosphere in which our technology can be used constructively and not destructively.

Huddle: How can we best do this?

Sturua: I think there is "two-way traffic." We have to develop trust and at the same time we have to make real steps toward disarmament. Developing trust will help disarmament, and each small step toward disarmament will increase trust between our nations. If we apply this simultaneous approach, perhaps we will make some breakthroughs. The point is that if you ask for complete disarmament tomorrow, you will fail. There is no trust for it. We must do it step by step. We must be very patient in developing trust.

Huddle: In practical terms, how can we develop trust?

Sturua: For example, if we had not only signed but ratified the SALT II agreement, we would have developed a small amount of trust on which we could have built another step—a discussion about SALT III, SALT IV, and so on. Every achievement in disarmament breeds trust; it makes nations relax and remember détente. They now claim there was no détente. How can you compare Soviet–American relations in the 1970s with relations in 1982? There is a great difference. Nowadays there is anti-Soviet hysteria in your country; in the 1970s there were cultural, technological, trade, and scientific exchanges. Your movies were shown there and our movies were shown here. This was helping to develop trust because at the same time we achieved the SALT I and other agreements during summit meetings. But afterward, especially during the Reagan administration, everything has changed and it is a great setback. This shows that the practical way is disarmament negotiations. That is sometimes very long and painful, but still they are negotiations.

Huddle: A couple of people I interviewed talked about the need for creating a global security system which safeguards the security of all nations. Could you comment?

Sturua: Yes, I agree. There is a good foundation for a global security system: the United Nations. If you read the charter of the United Nations thoroughly and the resolutions adopted by the U.N., you will find a very sound foundation for this global security and for global understanding. The point is that we now have to implement these notions because the very best wishes and hopes are nothing—are just trash—if you don't implement them. I think the implementation of the U.N. Charter may be the most important step in the process of developing global understanding and security. Who knows? Maybe this is a grain of future world government.

Huddle: One proposal being put forth in 1982 at the United Nations second Special Session on Disarmament calls for a sa-

tellite system, to be globally administered, which would monitor troop movements, weapons testing, and so on. What do
you think of that? (See Howard Kurtz, p. 165)

Sturua: I don't know if this proposition can solve all the problems, but I understand the idea of it. Maybe if a big brother
watches over the small brothers, the small brothers will behave, but I think the *real* big brother must not be a satellite—it
must be in our brains and hearts. Nobody can really solve this
problem just with technology. But as a method of verification,
a piece of the total mosaic, why not? Yes, because nowadays
trust isn't very developed and verification must play a very
substantial part in disarmament. And you know that SALT II
was also based on this sort of satellite verification which is very
extensive and dependable.

Huddle: As the Third World gains increasing power, how can
we improve relations with them?

Sturua: To begin with, huge amounts of resources are being
diverted to military production. Every second mankind is
spending seventeen thousand dollars for the arms race. The
Soviet Union proposed in the United Nations and during negotiations with the United States to decrease our military budget and to dedicate five percent of this to developing the Third
World. But the United States never accepted this proposal.
Moreover your government substantially increased your budget until now you are talking about trillions, not billions, of
dollars. We spend less than you on the military, which is quite
understandable because we are not so rich. As for the Third
World, our position is to help as much as possible. We would
like to do more than we do now, but as long as we are forced
to compete in the arms race, we can't give so much. If this
proposition is accepted by the United States and we can reduce
our military budget, it will help not only in our own development but also that of the Third World. After all, if the Third
World doesn't catch up in developing their modern civilization,
sooner or later it will be detrimental not only for them but for
both of us too. If the majority of the population of the world is
dying from hunger, is uneducated, who will gain from this?
How can we talk about developing the human race and how
can we be successful in developing a global approach when
two-thirds of the global population is in misery? Sooner or
later every ideal attitude gives you a practical bonus. And on
the contrary, if your practice is not humane it will destroy even
your practical aims. Because if you want to enrich yourself

through the arms race, the arms race will end up destroying you.

In the Soviet Union our major difficulties at this time are economic ones. We have some objective reasons like bad weather, a very harsh climate. There are also some subjective reasons like bad management and so on. But I think our main problem is to solve the economic problems, especially in the field of agriculture. There are also inherited difficulties. Our society is, after all, very young—only sixty-five years old. We inherited not only the backward economy of tsarist Russia but also a very backward social structure, alcoholism, superstition, and other things which haven't been completely eliminated. It is a very difficult goal to make the human being change from the backward Russian to the forward-looking Russian who is maybe in the first row of contemporary civilization. The transformation of our people is a major priority of our country. I should also say that women are the majority of our population. It is a very vocal and strong majority. They play a very substantial part in every phase of our life. You can't build any society without women, because if you exclude them, you fail.

Huddle: Do you think it would be possible for me to conduct interviews with a broad range of people inside the Soviet Union as I have done here in the United States?

Sturua: Yes, of course. Why not? I am an example. If we were in the Soviet Union I would say the same things to you. Maybe I would even say more if I had more time to think about these questions. Why not?

Gene La Rocque

Retired Rear Admiral Gene La Rocque is the director of the Center for Defense Information located in Washington, D.C. The Center publishes analyses of defense budgets and interpretations of government policy, as well as producing audiovisual materials for use in public education. Admiral La Rocque testifies frequently before the Congress.

I was born sixty-four years ago in Kankakee, Illinois. When World War II came along I volunteered very early, in 1940, to go into the navy. I never intended to make a career of the navy, but I enjoyed it so much that I stayed in until my retirement. Also, at that time I thought that if the United States stayed strong militarily we could preserve peace in the world.

World War II absolutely convinced me that war was probably the dumbest way you could find to settle international difficulties. I watched a lot of my friends killed and I spent four years of my life out on a destroyer, encased in a steel tube, with no women and very few associates. I didn't see the United States except for two brief periods when we came back for repairs.

One thing that distresses me about war is the way our feelings toward different peoples of different nations are turned on and off by our own political system and by the media. First the Japanese and the Germans are our friends; then war breaks out and they're our enemies; then we dehumanize them, which makes it possible for us to hate and kill them. During the war Japanese here in America, including second-generation Japanese (Nisei) born in America, were locked up in concentration camps on the West Coast just because they had slanted eyes and their ancestors came from Japan. And I must admit, I was at Pearl Harbor when the Japanese attacked in 1941 and I hated them for four years; now I love them again. The same was true with the Germans. When I was growing up in Illinois right after World War I there was still evidence of where the lovely people of Kankakee, Illinois, had painted yellow signs on the fences of Germans in our community who had immigrated to the United States. In Kankakee there was great hatred for the "Huns" during World War I, and now we love them again too; we even helped them rebuild their country. War is a crazy system. And meanwhile we kill a lot of people.

We could, of course, argue that World War II was a "just" war. After all that was why I joined up. Hitler was a pretty clearly dangerous enemy and we Americans saw we had to do something. Some people call it the "last good war," the last war we really knew what we were doing. When the Korean War came along, I became somewhat disenchanted with the United States' ability to maintain peace in the world. I was thoroughly disenchanted with our participation in Vietnam, because we never could find a reason for being there yet we still went around killing both our own and the Vietnamese people. In the meantime we'd sent troops to the Dominican Republic, into Lebanon, and elsewhere around the world. One Brookings Institution [a think tank in Washington, D.C.] study shows that since 1945 the United States has used military forces two hundred fifteen times in order to achieve international goals. If we look at our history just in this century, we have fought an average of one major war every sixteen years: the Spanish-American War, World War I, World War II, the Korean War, and the Vietnam War. And yet we somehow continue to pride ourselves on being a peace-loving nation!

We've come to think of war and military force as a natural way to achieve our national goals. In today's interdependent world that is an outmoded concept. For one thing the United States has only two hundred twenty-six million people and the world consists of over four billion people. Also, we depend on other countries for resources, and military force is of declining utility in its ability to influence international affairs. We can't "run the world" anymore. And yet we're still *trying* to do so with military force. My experience in the military has taught me the futility of that.

The other major element is the advent of nuclear weapons.

It's a whole new ball game. After every major war in history the nations that have lost have been able to pick themselves up from the rubble and start again. But after a major nuclear war you can forget it. A nuclear war would cause such devastation that it's doubtful that civilization will prevail. People with no experience in the military or in strategic planning are unaware of the devastation nuclear war can cause; consequently most of them are not concerned about it. There's a saying that "in nuclear war, the survivors would envy the dead." The United States is in fact preparing for nuclear war. We are training our troops, we are arming them with nuclear weapons, and we are making plans for a nuclear war. Our army divisions, our air wings, our navy warships are all being equipped with nuclear weapons. I consider all this to be very dangerous. Some groups like the Committee on the Present Danger emphatically state that the United States does not see nuclear war as a feasible option and that we are not in any way preparing for this, but that is merely uninformed speculation. We must look at *facts*. In 1964 when I was captain of a guided missile cruiser, the U.S.S. *Providence*, it carried nuclear weapons. The facts show that eighty percent of our navy combatant ships now carry nuclear weapons. In the next ten years nearly all of them will. Our army divisions have nuclear weapons, and the plans are there to use them. Anyone who doesn't think these facts are true should read Field Manual 100–5 of the United States Army. It goes into great detail about using nuclear weapons, and it describes nuclear weapons not as an adjunct but as a complementary integrated part of our fighting capability. People should also read the secretary of defense's annual report to the Congress; it says that the United States will not renounce its ability to use nuclear weapons first. To anybody who says we are not planning for a nuclear war, I would ask: "Why are we building all the nuclear weapons and why are we issuing them to the troops and training them on how to use them? If we don't plan to use them, why do we, through NATO, keep seven thousand nuclear weapons way up on the front lines in Europe? Why have we trained thousands of our allies how to use nuclear weapons?" All the evidence is there that we plan to use nuclear weapons to fight a nuclear war, partly because we think that the Russians may use nuclear weapons and we would need the capability to deal tit for tat on the same basis.

Anyone interested in national security also needs to get two books. The first one is the annual *Posture Statement* of the secretary of defense, which gives our whole atomic and war-fighting structure for the world. You can't really pursue this project without reading that. Second is the *Joint Chiefs of Staff Publication One,* which defines all the military terms. The facts are available if people just take the time to read them.

I am appalled at the ignorance around the issue of national security. We've done a film called *War Without Winners* in which one section shows a missile fired from a submarine coming out through the water and into the air. When he saw that part, one very prominent congressman, knowledgeable in the field of national security, said, "My goodness, I didn't know we could fire nuclear weapons from submarines underwater; I thought they had to come to the surface." And *he* was relatively well informed! Most people haven't the vaguest notion about how big the Russian navy is compared to the navies of the U.S. and her allies. People speculate out of ignorance and make all sorts of ridiculous statements. Just deal with the facts.

I got the idea for setting up the Center for Defense Information from Eisenhower's comment "Beware of the military–industrial complex." I knew John Eisenhower when he was on the army staff and I was on the navy staff. We were working on Joint Staff matters, which gave me the opportunity to talk a good bit with him. In Gettysburg I listened to his father, whom I felt knew the military better than anybody else. He said that this was the first time in our peacetime history that we've had a huge standing military force. After every other war we cut back our military forces to a very minimal size and went on with our civilian pursuits. But after World War II, Eisenhower said, we found it necessary to create a huge military-industrial establishment in peacetime for the first time in our history. That's very dangerous for this nation, first of all because it's a very large establishment. We have thirty million living veterans in the United States—half our adult male population. Most of those people felt very kindly disposed toward their wonderful days in the military. In many cases the experience in the service may have shaped the man and done him a lot of good, but they've forgotten that the primary purpose of the military is not to mold the character of young men—it is to kill and destroy. Second, we now have some five million people who get a paycheck from the Pentagon every month: two million on active duty, nearly a million drill-paid reserves, a million civilians, and a million retirees. By and large those five million people are very supportive of the military, particularly the retirees. It now costs about fifteen billion dollars a year to pay us retirees. You can't cut our pay, and we get an automatic cost-of-living increase every year. We don't even have to ask or fight for it; even when people on active duty don't get it, we get ours.

The industrial portion of the military-industrial complex is highly centralized. An extremely small number of very powerful companies like McDonnell-Douglas, which is the biggest arms contractor in the world, get the biggest contracts from the United States government. They're only interested in making whatever gives them a profit. They don't care if it kills and destroys. Our government really owns many of those plants and the people are in them simply as managers in a sense, and make money through weapons sales. They make about seven percent on military hardware sales to our government and armed forces; they make fourteen percent on the sales of military equipment to foreign governments and armed forces. Now, sales to foreign governments are really sales to the United States government, which in turn sells the armaments to the foreign governments. To take a specific case, Litton Industries in Pascagoula, Mississippi, agreed to build some destroyers for the Iranians. They then entered into a contract with the United States government, so Litton was covered. As far as they were concerned the political overthrow in Iran didn't matter because our government would at least pay them for the work they had done to date. So it's an ideal situation for them.

What we've created in this country is an entire industry that supports the military which, in my opinion, is far more opprobrious than the Krupps, who were the major weapons manufacturers in Europe from the period prior to World War I through World War II. They were a private industry which became wealthy by selling weapons all over the world. Today we've dignified sales of weapons to foreign powers by putting it all under the aegis of the American flag. America sells weapons all over the world, but it's really our government that sells the weapons and handles the contracts, and it is our government and our industries that send salesmen overseas to *push* weapons sales. Why? We sell weapons to compensate for the oil that we have to buy in various parts of the world. In other words, because our oil imports are so high, we need to export weapons in order to improve our balance of payments. Most people think we can't give up the oil and that the weapons-trade situation is a "necessary evil." I disagree. Besides our very wasteful use of oil, we are setting up an extremely dangerous situation: *How can we guarantee that nations we're arming today won't turn against us tomorrow, using the very weapons we've sold them?* It has happened before and it can happen again. Another very bad result of this military–industrial complex is that we have concentrated a very high percentage of Americans involved in research and development in some form of military R&D; I've seen figures as high as eighty percent. Because we've put our talent into building weapons, we're falling behind Germany and Japan, our former enemies, in developing commercial products.

There's no question that our overemphasis on weapons research and development has provided us with the best weapons in the world. We can also change to whole new generations of weapons with increasing rapidity, which is another problem in itself. In the old days military forces were small, had little money, and it took twenty or thirty years to introduce a new cannon, a new ship, or a new airplane. Nowadays ships and airplanes come in four or five years and are increasingly expensive. This creates a constant instability in the balance of power. As a result people feel the whole question of national security is out of their hands and they have become more and more trusting of their government. An attack on this country is only thirty minutes away, and we have no defense against incoming missiles. There's no way a person in Chicago can defend himself against Soviet missiles, so he has to assume that the Pentagon can. So if the Pentagon wants another billion dollars, he assumes that if we give it to them maybe they can defend me against Soviet missiles. The really tragic and ironic thing is that our military is actually unable to defend them. We have no defense against Soviet missiles. When the government, particularly the military, *implies* that it can defend those people and takes their tax money, *it's like a giant con game.* When I go out around the country and talk to people, they are *amazed* when I tell them *that we have no defense against Soviet missiles and that the Soviets have no defense against our missiles.* That understanding is *fundamental* to any discussion of national security. In fact *there is no such thing as national security;* you're chasing after the Holy Grail if you think you can *find* national security. That's like saying you're going to be safe all your life. Forget it; we live in a very dangerous world.

Really, I don't know that anyone can ever really feel secure because at any time you can get squashed by an automobile or stung by a bee. Life is a series of challenges and responses. When I go out in my boat I'm not secure. I'm in an environment that I have to constantly confront. Just as life is a challenge for the individual, life for the nation is also a challenge. If you want to be "secure" you'll have to lock yourself up in a room somewhere and never walk out onto the street.

I think the term "security" is greatly overused because no one is secure except someone who is insane. Once, when I was a young fellow, I was working on a construction crew building a road through Manteno State Hospital for the Insane. As we worked, I watched this man on a grassy strip pitching ball all day long. But he didn't have a ball and he didn't have anybody to throw it to. One day I stopped and talked to him, and I asked him about his pitching. He said to me, "You think I'm crazy, don't you?" I said, somewhat embarrassed, "Well, uh, not really." He said, "Let me give you the facts: Ty Cobb, one of the greatest pitchers in the world, pitched ball and got twenty thousand dollars a year; I pitch ball every day of my life and I get a hundred thousand dollars a year." Now that man was very secure and happy. And I think that if people want to reach the stage where there's no real challenge left, and reach that kind of security, they're either going to have to do it with drugs or with some mental breakdown. Little old ladies can't be secure with their inheritances; some charlatan will come along and take it away from them. The day you feel secure is the day you're in danger.

Thomas Jefferson said, "The price of freedom is eternal vigilance." If you're vigilant, you're on your toes, alert, looking to see what's out there. That's the challenge of being alive. At the opposite end of the spectrum from the *insanely secure* are the *insanely frightened*. So rather than talking about what's going to "make America secure," I think we need to ask ourselves "What is going to make this country confident and healthy?" And that means figuring out how to make the *individuals* in this country confident and healthy.

Lester Brown

Founder and director of Worldwatch Institute in Washington, D.C., Lester Brown has written voluminously on issues of global concern including food, population, environment, energy, and redefining national security. Two of his most recent books are The Twenty-ninth Day *and* Building a Sustainable Society. *This interview took place in the spring of 1981.*

I grew up on a farm in southern New Jersey, so my roots are in agriculture. When they married, my father was a hired hand and my mother a domestic. There is not much formal education in my family; neither of my parents graduated from grade school, and they've never read any of the books I've written because they're just a bit difficult for them. I have a brother three years younger and a sister twelve years younger. Between 1933 and 1945 our family went through a traditional transition, with my father going from being a hired hand to a tenant farmer and a sharecropper, to eventually coming to own his own small farm by the end of the war. My parents still live on the family farm.

As my younger brother and I were growing up we were in 4-H and FFA [Future Farmers of America] and had all sorts of new ideas. As long as we did the chores, Pop gave us a certain amount of freedom to do the things we wanted to do. We had twenty cows to milk and other things which kept us busy, but when I was fourteen my brother and I bought and overhauled a junked tractor, got it running, rented a couple of fields and started growing tomatoes. We kept expanding until by the time I was twenty-four we were marketing a million and a half pounds of tomatoes a year. I farmed all the way through high school and college; in fact a combination of growing tomatoes and scholarships put me through school.

About then my brother and I split up. He took part of the business and went off on his own. I continued growing tomatoes, and at that time my personal goal was to become the world's largest tomato grower. We were already among the top two percent in terms of size on the East Coast. But then I went to India on a national 4-H Club Foundation exchange program and lived in Indian villages for almost a year; my brother took over the tomato growing. When I came back I grew tomatoes for a couple more years and decided it just wouldn't be all that satisfying to continue that for the next forty years. I wanted to get involved in international agriculture, so I got a master's degree in agricultural economics and joined the Foreign Agriculture Service in 1950.

My first assignment was handling affairs for the rice-bowl countries of Asia. Then I got another master's degree in public administration, and after returning to D.C., I was asked to project food supply and demand in the Asian region. I suggested that it would be difficult to do *regional* projections without a *global* framework in which to set those projections. This led to my writing *Man, Land and Food: Looking Ahead to World Food Needs,* the first systematic projection to the end of the century of world food, population, land, and other resources. *U.S. News* did a cover story on it which was read by Secretary of Agriculture Orville Freeman. One thing led to another, and in about six months I was on his staff. During that period I grew to appreciate very deeply the need for someone to understand the big picture against which we view day-to-day decisions. The seeds were being sown for Worldwatch Institute.

During the last part of the Johnson administration, Orville Freeman asked me to head a newly established agency coordinating U.S. agricultural technical assistance programs in some forty countries. I also did a lot with our food aid programs. In 1969 I helped start the Overseas Development Council and was there for five years, writing a number of books on food, population, and interdependence. During my last year there we began to sense the need for an organization to deal with problems strictly in global and interdisciplinary terms. William Dedo, then executive vice-president of the Rockefeller Brothers Fund, and I developed a long memo outlining the structure and role of such an organization. He presented it to their board of trustees who approved a start-up grant.

Perhaps because it was around the time of the Bicentennial, we explained the role of Worldwatch Institute with a historical analogy: when the wagon trains headed west from St. Louis or Independence, they hired a scout—the Kit Carsons and Jim Bridgers—to go out in front and gather information useful to the decision-makers in the wagon train, things like the location of fresh water, game, safe campsites, or where the Indians were likely to be. The scouts had no operational responsibilities; their job was to be out in front, peering over the horizon to see what was ahead, but not getting so far ahead that they broke contact with the train. We see Worldwatch Institute as a scout. We have no operational responsibilities—no programs to manage, classes to teach, or six o'clock deadlines. We're free to wander out in front and gather information to feed back to decision-makers—members of parliaments, planning commissions, or individuals trying to decide whether to have another child.

Some of our Worldwatch papers have been widely translated. One is in nine languages now, and about four have more than a hundred thousand copies in print. For our first four books, we now have fifty-six signed contracts for publication in various languages; we even have the Russians paying us dollars for Russian-language rights. We're getting feedback that what we're doing is being used, and that makes it worthwhile. Our staff analysts are both rigorous and literate. We look for people who can make a difference on issues. In a number of instances our reports have led to changes in policies and priorities. Perhaps the most dramatic was Eric Eckholm's study on the Third World firewood crisis. Another area in which we've had impact is solar energy. Dennis Hayes wrote *Rays of Hope: A Transition to the Post-Petroleum World*, as well as two Worldwatch papers which deal in great detail with solar energy. These have had wide distribution and impact.

One Worldwatch paper is precisely on the topic of redefining national security. It notes that in most of the modern era the principal threat to human beings has come from *man-to-man* relationships, but as more pressure is put on the earth's resources, threats to our future well-being will increasingly flow from the *man-to-nature* relationship. To illustrate, some countries in Africa consider encroaching deserts to be a far greater threat to their long-term viability as a civilization than invading armies. Or for the United States, new renewable energy systems might be far more essential to our long-term security than new weapons systems. In the modern era, particularly between 1940 and 1970, we have been living in a world of highly refined economic data and enormous confidence in technology. We have lost sight of the biological underpinnings on which our civilization depends. We've overgrazed, deforested, overplowed, and overfished. Today these biological systems are beginning to deteriorate. Unfortunately we have not yet grasped the *enormous* significance of this, particularly the fact that our survival and well-being directly depend on basic biological systems. If they deteriorate, our economic system will also deteriorate. Bits and pieces of this are beginning to surface in public policy, but it is still far from being a prime factor shaping future policies. It eventually will; if not, we'll be in deep trouble and there will be no security.

We need more analyses of the nature of emerging threats and how these relate to each other. We need to communicate these findings broadly. We must increase our understanding of these new threats until we reach some sort of critical point and make almost a quantum jump. Historically I would point to the behavior of the United States immediately after World War II. We did something that no other victor in war had done before, which was systematically to assist in rebuilding the defeated countries. Until that time the prevailing approach was to plunder, pillage, and rape. Our actions constituted a sudden and major shift in the world. It even became the basis of a movie, *The Mouse That Roared,* whose plot was based on the notion that the way for a small country to get ahead was to declare war on the United States, surrender, and then wait for foreign aid to pour in.

One morning we will wake up and realize how silly it is to devote enormous resources to fighting each other while we face such imminent and real common threats. It is almost like a family with youngsters who fight each other until someone from down the block threatens them, and then they quickly coalesce. Someone called it "the Martian response"; if we thought we were being invaded from outer space we'd quickly pull together, forgetting we were Americans or Russians or whatever, and concentrate on defending our planet. Hopefully we will quickly realize the *real* threats to our national and global security: the need to develop renewable energy sources, increase food supplies, get inflation under control, stabilize population size, and so on.

The next step will be to incorporate our new knowledge into new attitudes and values which can be translated into policies, priorities, and lifestyle changes. I have a feeling that things will reach a critical point and then something will trigger massive changes. It's hard to say exactly how this will come about or what will be the triggering event. I've toyed a bit with the notion that the Russian invasion into Afghanistan was such an event. My own feeling is that the Soviet invasion was a serious miscalculation on their part, a sign of weakness rather than of strength.

One thing that changed behavior after World War II was the realization that war, with its invasion and plundering, was an expensive way to improve one's nation's physical well-being. Before the modern era, about the only way to get more resources was to enslave defeated peoples and take away theirs. With modern economics and technology, another far cheaper avenue suddenly opened: it is much more efficient to build new factories and generate new resources through exploration and development than to fight a long and costly war to take something from somone else. Looking at the Afghanistan situation, I think the Soviets have realized that whoever made the decision to invade Afghanistan now has to face the consequences—for example, as a direct result they may be refused access to some of the technology they very much need in an economy which I believe is in real trouble.

The Soviets depend increasingly on imported grain. In 1980 they were planning to import thirty-four million tons of grain. No country in history has ever imported that much. The Soviets are steadily losing the capacity to feed themselves, and I see no easy way for them to solve that problem without substantially restructuring and redesigning their agricultural system. I summed up some of these problems in a short article entitled "Marx Was a City Boy."

I think the Soviets will eventually realize that in order to satisfy their people's aspirations they have to depend on the rest of the world for food and technology. Also, that much of their system is probably not very viable. Any system which practices so much repression stifles initiative and innovation, reducing the quality of human resources in a way that will be very costly for their society in the long run. This fact will, I think, force them to change their relationship with the rest of the world.

The Soviet leaders have tended to shut their eyes to some of their internal problems. For example, in the field of agriculture they have so muted the relationship between effort and reward that there is very little motivation. Ties to the soil are almost nonexistent in the sense that we know them. American farmers can expect to pass their farms to their families, giving them a certain attitude for the soil which does not exist on the Soviet state farm. Gustafson, a scholar at Harvard in the field of Soviet affairs, says that the Soviets now have a half-century legacy of soil neglect and deterioration to deal with.

After the grain embargo President Carter announced an accelerated alcohol-fuels program, a move perhaps not unrelated to the Iowa primaries. Anyway, three years from now, if the Soviets need grain in a major way, they may see a lot of that grain going into storage to produce fuel for American cars. So alienating Americans is a very risky thing for them in the long run. I don't think they understand that.

During the 1980s we will be busy redesigning our economic system, which was designed to run on oil at two dollars a barrel, so that it can continue to run if oil reaches forty dollars a barrel. This is a very simplistic economic way of putting it, but our economic system simply has to be redesigned. We've started, but we have a lot more to do and not much time to do it in. The world will probably be doing this systems redesigning while trying to avoid runaway inflation, breakdown of the monetary system, wholesale starvation, and so on. We will have an abundance of issues to bring the new world view into sharp focus.

Worldwatch Paper number thirty-five, entitled "Food or Fuel: The New Competition of the World's Cropland," looks at the extent to which governments are beginning to encourage conversion of sugar, grains, and other agricultural commodities into automotive fuel. As that process continues in Brazil, South Africa, Australia, the Philippines, Austria, and the United States, farmers will have a choice between producing food crops or energy crops. And they will produce whichever is most profitable. This new development will underline the disparities in income throughout the world as nothing has done within our lifetimes.

These issues underscore the need for creating new institutions and practices. Besides increasing the competition between rich and poor, these agriculturally based fuel initiatives will put enormous additional pressures on croplands. We are already faced with a need to double food output in the next generation. If we add energy crops to that, it creates an almost impossible pressure on croplands. In a food-exporting country like ours there is a very strong constituency which supports converting part of that food into alcohol to run cars. Although this is politically popular in the United States, it has profound implications for population policy in food-importing countries around the world.

The world economic system will have to be transformed in a way that is sustainable over a long term. The question is not "Will we adjust?" Nor is the question "Will we cut back on oil consumption?" One of these days we *will*. The issue is not "Will we stop overfishing?" We *will*—for one reason: the oil and the fish will be gone. That is not the issue. The real issue is "Will we make the adjustment as a result of exercising foresight, and will we do it cooperatively and collectively? Or will we do it belatedly, chaotically, competitively, and perhaps catastrophically?" *That* is the real choice. I'm hopeful that if we do enough careful research and analysis and information dissemination we will choose the former path rather than the latter. But the important thing to keep in mind is that you don't transform the system without changing the values and attitudes that underlie that system. We're talking about an economic transformation that is on the scale of an entire social transformation: everything from what we eat to how we travel. You do not get these transformations without a very basic change in values. Thus what appears to be a resource shift becomes an economic transformation, becomes a social transformation, becomes a philosophical transformation.

At a very practical level I think that once again we must acquire the understanding our ancestors had about our dependence on nature. By this I mean an understanding of what is happening to the world's forests, croplands, soils, water, and so forth. We must then translate that understanding into changes in diet, family size, the way we manage soils, cultural practices, cropping patterns, and so on. We simply must get away from human arrogance, from thinking we dominate nature; instead we must realize that we are *part* of the whole complex natural system of our planet and that we are *dependent* on it.

Rob Caughlan

Rob Caughlan is co-founder of the Roanoke Company, a small public relations firm with an active ecological concern. He lives with his wife and two children in the San Mateo area of northern California. We did this interview in the fall of 1980.

I was born in Alliance, Ohio, and moved to California when I was five. My dad and grandfather died when I was young, and my mom and grandmother raised me. I have one brother, who is a yoga teacher. He's into ecology and teaches eagles how to fly; he helped get me interested in ecology originally. I was also inspired by my surfing; the "Save the Coast" battle to stop development along the beach was the first big environmental campaign I got involved in. In college I studied political science, but school was just something to get out of the way so that I could go on to what I was interested in doing—which was politics.

Immediately after college I went to work for a very hot California campaign management firm, doing press and propaganda. We did the first campaigns for [U.S. Congressman] Pete McCloskey, Dianne Feinstein [mayor of San Francisco], and [U.S. Senator] Alan Cranston, as well as a bunch of other campaigns for congressional and state offices. That was my first nitty-gritty training. Later I had my first confrontation with ethics in politics, where you have to make a decision on how to use your talents: I did not want to use my talents to help elect Joe Alioto over Feinstein, so I lost my job.

Then I went to work for California Assemblyman Leo Ryan as his field representative and administrative assistant. Part of the reason he always got seventy to eighty percent of the vote was that he had an active district office and took good care of his people. I ran his campaign for Congress, but when he won I didn't want to move to Washington. At that time I bumped into my partner, David, who was interested in making some money as an entrepreneur, and we got together to figure out how to set things up so that we could just do what we wanted to do. We didn't want to do anything or work for anybody that we didn't like personally and philosophically.

Our first project was to start the National Sam Ervin Fan Club. At that time Nixon was still strong and everybody was putting down politicians for doing the Watergate investigation. I had written to Sam asking for a button for my political button collection. When I found out that he had no political buttons, I got a friend of mine to draw a picture of him and we made up some buttons. Then we thought, "Instead of just buttons, why don't we have a whole fan club with membership cards and everything?" So we had a press conference on the Fourth of July. I wore a white suit and a stars-and-stripes necktie and had a bust of Abraham Lincoln there and a picture of my family, just like the Nixon press conferences where he always had all this patriotic stuff in the background. The women made homemade chocolate-chip cookies, we had this whole fanfare, and the media just went nuts. We were in the *National Enquirer* and the London Sunday *Times,* and Barbara Walters interviewed me.

We started out on the project with a hundred T-shirts and five hundred buttons, and we thought, "We'll just give them away to our friends and try not to lose too much money on it." The thing turned into such an overwhelming success that we almost went bankrupt, because for five dollars we would send you a membership card, a button, a T-shirt, and a poster. We weren't trying to make money on it, and we'd said that we'd donate the proceeds to the ACLU [American Civil Liberties Union] or to the impeachment campaign, which hadn't started yet, but which we were encouraging. The day after the press conference we had five hundred letters in our mailbox, and it never stopped that whole summer. We had created a Frankenstein and had to hire nine people just to process mail. We ended up with seventy-five thousand members in the Sam Ervin Fan Club.

Since then we've run a lot of other political campaigns. One, which led to my working for the Carter administration, was a campaign to stop the Army Corps of Engineers from building a dam on the Stanislaus River in northern California. I read how Carter, as governor, had stopped a dam in Georgia, and thought maybe we could get him to come out and do a fundraiser for us in Hollywood. I was really impressed with him because I'd never heard a high public official really take the gloves off on the Army Corps of Engineers and their whole pork-barrel mentality. It was a thankless task for him because these congressmen get a lot of power from those big dams, no pun intended. They like to give that money out to their district, and in a way that's what they're supposed to do. It goes back to what I said about Ryan's taking good care of folks at home. But I don't think it's good to waste money, even for your friends. That's one of the things the liberals have to learn. As long as we progressives and liberals, no matter how compassionate we see ourselves, allow the stupid wasteful- ness that goes on with public works projects, we will keep seeing people like Ronald Reagan and Howard Jarvis [who pushed Proposition 13, which mandated state tax cuts] cutting the bud- gets—except they won't cut the *military* budget or subsidies to oil companies. They'll cut school lunch programs and welfare pro- grams. Remember, if you're going to beat up on somebody, pick somebody small and weak. That's what Reagan did when he was governor here in California. He went after the students because they had no power, and he went after the welfare women and mothers with dependent children because they can't fight back. And he went after the mentally ill. So he cut welfare programs, closed mental hospitals, and tear-gased the schools. But he always picked his targets carefully and picked really weak ones. If you're going to scapegoat a group, make sure they can't fight back.

As Carter kept winning, I ended up as the chairman of the "Environmentalists for Carter" group in California during the primaries. After he won the election they offered me a job in Washington, and I said no, but if they ever get to San Francisco to look me up. Barbara Blum, director of the transition team, did so, and eventually she persuaded me to work with her at the Environ- mental Protection Agency. I told EPA that I'd do two years mini- mum and my wife Diana would do three years maximum, and that's what we did; I worked three years to the day.

It will take me years to figure out what I learned there. For one thing I found it's sure a lot easier to tell the government how it *should* be run than it is to *run* it. I also learned that anybody waiting for the federal government to solve their problems had better not hold their breath. That's one reason I favor small-scale decentralized approaches to big problems. I like the idea of "think globally, act locally." Obviously some situations require a national or international approach, such as when Ohio refuses to solve its pollution problem and begins wrecking the lakes in New England. In those cases you need the national government to step in and say, "Wait a minute, Ohio, you're not only fouling your own nest, you're fouling your neighbor's nest as well, and that can't be tolerated." But on the whole I think it's best to solve problems locally wherever possible.

Another lesson is that it's really important for do-gooders and reformers to be strong, because there are some real hard poker players out there. There's a difference between being strong and mean. Teddy Roosevelt put it real nicely. He always railed against people he called the "timid-good"—good people who get pushed over all the time. He also called for "gritty idealism" which I think is in contrast to the airy-fairy, peaceloving "tie-dye" idealism that characterizes many liberal groups. I have found it's much easier to work with Democrats than with environmentalists, and much easier to work with Republicans than with Democrats. Republicans understand the importance of organization, efficiency, timelines, charts, and getting things done better than the Democrats do. Environmentalists and other good-cause movements are horrible to work with because they're always quibbling with each other. We have to expand and broaden our coalitions to include a lot of people not usually involved, which is real hard to do because everybody's got their own priorities.

Did you ever read Gibbon's *Decline and Fall of the Roman Empire?* For the first seven hundred years the Romans did great, mainly because they were real good at keeping the barbarians at each other's throats. They'd bribe one here or whisper in somebody's ear there. But finally, after seven hundred years, the barbarians finally went [*taps head*], "Duh, we get it! Look what they're doing!" And some of the barbarian leaders started saying, "*Wait a minute.* If all us barbarian tribes get together and go at it in a unified, organized way, we might be able to get down there and get some of that good Italian wine!" I think all of us do-gooder types are in somewhat the same position. We're quarreling with each other, and at some point we're going to have to tap ourselves on the heads and go, "Hey, we get it! You know what's happening here?" *Because we've obviously got the numbers.* If you take any poll "Are you in favor of protecting the environment and having a healthy quality of life?" everyone will go, "Yeah, sure, that's good." Then how come we're not getting it? The problem is that in a democracy you need the vast majority of people on your side, especially if you're challenging fundamental principles or status quo situations where the status quo has the most power, money, and therefore the most to lose.

I don't know if we'll solve our problems or not. I'm not particularly hopeful about the future of mankind. Studies like the "Global 2000" report or the Club of Rome's *Limits to Growth* are all basically saying that there's big trouble on the horizon, but if you look carefully at what's being done to avert it you see that the responses are so timid compared to what really needs to be done. I really don't know if we'll solve them. It's a real shame to think that the human species may never get to realize its incredible potential. To me, that would be the ultimate tragedy.

When I get philosophical about it, though, my attitude is that the worst we can do is turn this place into a moon; if we wipe out all life on earth and turn it into another glob of dirt circling around another star, the universe probably won't miss us all that much. It's a kind of nickel-dime planet and a nickel-dime sun and a nickel-dime part of a Big Place—and so what? So we wipe ourselves out. Well, it may not all be that important anyway. But from a *personal* perspective and from a *father's* perspective I find it very sad to think that our kids will be the last generation or the next-to-the-last generation, or even the next-to-the-next-to-the-last generation. Jacques Cousteau has been criticized for saying that the oceans have only forty years left. People say, "Don't you think that's a little extreme, captain?" His response to this is, "Look, if I'm a hundred years off, do you get the point?" *That's* the point.

To me, our national security is going to depend on how we resolve gigantic problems like population, resources, and economic distribution. It depends far more on our approaches to solving those problems than on how many missiles we happen to have in Nevada this month. Continued reliance on weapons won't

solve our basic problems and only absorbs more precious resources and human attention. There's no lack of solutions out
there; there's a lack of *will* to use the solutions. We know what to
do. We could do plenty of things to help solve, say, the firewood
crisis in Third World countries, but instead we continue to spend
a lot more money sending guns to keep some sleazy Third World
dictator in power and keep the peasants under control. Our thinking is terribly narrow and shortsighted.

It's not that I favor the Communists either. I think they're real
thugs, and I'm a big pro-American type. I really love America and
believe in the American approach to things. I'm an American history buff and have been accused of being an ultimate cornball when
I talk about America. It boils down to Winston Churchill's comment that democracy is a very poor form of government, but all
the others are so much worse. I don't like government as a whole. I
like Jefferson's idea that the government that governs best governs
least. Politically I'm a leftie in a lot of areas, but in others I'm a real
frothing right-winger. For example, I like efficiency in government. You'd never get a nickel from me for one nuclear power
plant because I think they're a waste of money. I wouldn't argue
against them on the grounds that it hurts the environment and the
little bunnies; I'm done with that. I'm just going to argue straight
economics and say "These plants are an economic disaster; if you
people are dumb enough to allow your tax money to be sunk in
these, you guys'd buy the Brooklyn Bridge."

It may be a long time before we achieve the idealistic goals
our country has chosen—human rights, equality, and justice for
all. But Carl Schurz, a U.S. senator who lived in Lincoln's time,
once said: "Ideals are like stars. You will never succeed in touching them with your hands, but like the seafaring man on the
desert of waters, you choose them as your guides, and following
them you will reach your destiny." That's the way I feel about the
American ideals. If we just keep pointing in that direction we'll be
on the right track.

Cynicism is certainly rampant today, and that's one reason
we lose sight of our ideals. I'm real cynical about cynics, though. I
think cynicism is just an intellectual's rationalization for not doing
something. Washington is one of the most cynical cities there is.
So many bitter, cynical bureaucrats say, "It doesn't matter
whether it's Reagan or Carter or whoever; things are going to be

the same because we really run the show here." I'm not in favor of scapegoating the bureaucrats as much as I used to be, however, although I do think lots of reforms need to be made. I met many really dedicated, sincere people who work long hours in the various bureaucracies, trying to solve these problems and not getting much support from the people outside, because every bar and barbershop in America is filled with experts on the economy and on the international situation. It isn't easy to serve the people these days, partly because politicans have used the bureaucracy as a whipping boy for a long time now and bureaucrats have become demoralized to the point where it's hard for them to function with any kind of idealism. I was considered a Boy Scout in Washington, walking around with my eagle bracelet and Abraham Lincoln belt buckle, and people would say, "Talk about bumpkins from the boonies. . . ." I would say, "Oh, yeah, I believe in America!" and everybody was rolling their eyes, going, "Right, right."

The attitude on college campuses these days is "Nuke Khomeini and smoke dope!" I'm really sorry about that. I hate to see college campuses drop back into teenybopper lethargy with no social activism. From what I hear, the kids who are graduating are all motivated by greed; they want to be corporate bigwigs when they grow up. I hate to think that panty raids are the biggest thing around campuses these days. What will help? I don't know. Like I say, I'm not particularly optimistic. I guess we just keep plugging away at it. And some trends are actually fairly positive, such as toward decentralization and appropriate technology. These will be developed anyway because of economic considerations and diminishing resources. So some good things will happen, probably in spite of us rather than because of us.

There's a macho attitude in the United States right now: "We're tired of being pushed around and considered a second-rate nation." Actually I think the Russians are really freaking out right now because Brezhnev won't live much longer and they're going through a transition of power. They don't have any mechanism to cope with that gracefully, which is one of the crucial differences between our system and their system. I think the United States' long-run approach to the Russians should be that of [former U.N. Ambassador] Andrew Young rather than of [Zbigniew] Brzezinski [former presidential national security advisor] or [Henry] Kissinger [former secretary of state]. Andy's approach is basically that if the Cubans go into Africa we shouldn't get upset because ultimately the Africans would kick them out. There's a fundamental desire in all human beings to be free; it's a major motivating force for humanity and always has been. The Africans would maybe use the Cubans' technology and get some money from them, but just like the Egyptians did they would ultimately say, "Thanks a lot, chump. Now beat it!" The same thing has happened with a lot of our own foreign aid programs.

Andy Young is saying to Third World countries, "Look, compare the United States with Russia; talk to people in the countries we deal with and talk to people in Afghanistan. See who you'd rather go with, us or them." I think the United States comes out stronger. Our principal source of strength is our freedom. I really believe that freedom is one of the most important goals I have as an individual, and that you can't be free unless you're being responsible. They have to go together. That's important on the individual as well as on the national and international level. We have to be really responsible with what we have or otherwise we will lose our freedom. Everyone has to use their powers as well as they can in order to restore a general sense of responsibility. In Washington I saw lots of people trying to get more power, while they weren't using what they had very well. I think we should do as well as we can with what we've got.

To do that we've got to be aware of who we are. Me? I'm a little surfer in California. Who am I to tell everybody what to think or do? I've got a cartoon of three hippies sitting around the coffee table in an espresso shop. One of the guys is leaning back in his chair, saying, "I think that I can safely say that I speak for the vast majority of the American public." That's the way I felt in Washington: Who the hell am I to be sitting there saying, "You know what you ought to do? You ought to do this and you ought to do that." I have no monopoly on wisdom and I haven't met anybody who does. So where are we? We're left with this big confused mass of people who are all trying to figure out what to do.

I want to do more media to educate people about social issues. If people knew what the problems are, they'd be more willing to solve them, especially if they see that these are basically survival issues. They really don't understand that yet. But if they realized that we're all interconnected, that what happens in Africa is relevant to what happens here in the United States, and that what happens in Harlem is relevant to what happens in suburban California, then we have a chance to solve our problems together.

Ultimately our security depends on everybody else's security. When everyone else feels more secure, we will be. That may sound pie-in-the-sky, but it goes back to my belief that you've got to shoot in the direction of your ideals. And I think we ought to be shooting farther and faster than we have been.

In the United States we're going to have to wise up to the fact that we're really a minority group on this planet. It ain't going to be all that long before a lot of other folks start looking at us and saying, "Hey, you guys, clean up your act." And for that matter, the whole southern part of the planet below the equator may soon say real loud to the whole northern part, "It's time you guys share some of the spoils, because you're pretty spoiled." Ultimately happy people don't fight, so it's in our national interest to see that other people are fed, clothed, and sheltered properly, and have a chance for a decent life. All the people I've ever met have basically the same motivations. They want to have a happy, healthy life; they want their kids to be okay; they don't want to worry about how to live out their lives in old age or what to do when they're sick; and they don't want to be hungry. I can empathize because I've been as poor as I ever plan on being; being poor ain't fun. *Can you imagine anything more horrible than having your kids starve to death in front of you and not being able to do anything about it?* Just the thought of that rocks me. And yet how many hundreds of millions of parents on the planet tonight are in that situation?

We can't let that kind of thing go on without dealing with the ramifications at some point. We've got it real easy in this country. Even our depressed areas are in good shape compared to most places in the world. If we take our responsibility to be in the vanguard of solving these problems, a lot of people will still probably die between now and the solutions, but I think we'll come out of it okay. If we don't, then authoritarian ideologies will ultimately take over. I'd really hate for that to happen.

I think it's really important to be able to have a sense of humor about whatever you're doing. I think even Jesus had a sense of humor, because in order to be that big you have to understand how small you are; and if you understand how small you are, then you can laugh about it. You can also try to set an example. You can't preach about not being greedy for power or wealth; you've got to live it. You can put out the concepts with parables, stories, and so on, but setting a personal example is still the best way, whether you're in a position of leadership or just among your friends and acquaintances.

It's essential to run the Pentagon more economically and make the military lean, but I don't think weapons are the main way to achieve security. Real security lies in having a harmoniously running planet. Marshall McLuhan said, "There're no passengers on Spaceship Earth, only crew." There's a lot of the crew that ain't being well taken care of, and we ought to change that. Real security will come from solving those problems. Some people may call this pie-in-the-sky idealism, but to me environmental and human welfare issues refer to nothing less than the survival of our species. And it's *very* pragmatic to be concerned about survival. To talk about peace is not idealistic either; it means talking about how to keep from destroying ourselves. The old military types who think the only way to guarantee survival is by building more weapons certainly have a point of view that's hard to rebut in some areas. They can look back at the Hitlers and say, "Look, if it hadn't been for us, you guys would all be marching around with swastikas on your arms these days." My main point, though, is that environmental concerns are not airy-fairy things. They're very pragmatic, survival-oriented, national security issues, and we ought to raise them as such.

Patriotism doesn't have to be a jingoistic "my country, right or wrong" wrap-yourself-in-the-flag kind of thing. It can be patriotism in the best sense of the word: love for your country. I've always felt that environmental protection was the healthiest form of patriotism. When people care about their country, they want to cherish it and make sure it'll be around for their kids. And it doesn't take a great leap of consciousness to understand that you can't be concerned about the nation without being concerned about the tectonic plates' skidding around on top of the magma too. Thomas Paine, one of our great patriots, once said, "First, I'm a citizen of the world." So it is a really basic American concept to be concerned about the rest of the world.

Russell Means

Russell Means is a leader in the American Indian Movement. The interview took place in New York City in the fall of 1980.

The only thing that will make the United States of America secure as a nation, as a society, and as a military power is a fundamental redefinition of their worldview. And this is true for any industrialized country. In other words, we have to go back to the philosophy of life held in the twelfth and thirteenth centuries. Or even back further. What I'm saying is that industrial society is totally based on the theme of colonizing, exploiting, and manipulating our sacred Mother Earth and all her children. But it is very evident that our Mother has only so much to give.

The philosophy of the industrial society is one of continuing this colonization until there is nothing left to colonize, except *oneself*. We can see this already happening in the centralization of government, of economics, and in multinational corporations. This has been a fact everywhere in the history of human beings: from the Greeks to the Romans to the Egyptians to the Mayans to the Incas to the Aztecs to the various Chinese dynasties, and to the subcontinent of Hindustan. When a society began to centralize its economics and therefore its politics and government, they were beginning to slide downhill, going toward their destruction as functioning societies and civilizations.

I think that it is in the best interest of the United States of America and every industrial country, and nonindustrial country, to take this new worldview, which is actually the oldest view on earth: respect for our Mother Earth and *all* her children. People talk about human rights and civil rights in this country, but no one talks about natural rights and natural law. Natural law is learning to live within the sacred cycle of life.

National security is *natural* security. When you can swim in Lake Erie, then you'll know we're on the right track. Every alleged civilization has to use energy to produce energy. Within the cycle of life, of course, one does not misuse things and waste energy. If we look at the lessons of the twelfth and thirteenth centuries of Europe we can see that developing and using renewable resources is the only hope for the natural security of anyone. At that time everyone used wood, which is a renewable resource, for energy. Then when they started extracting coal for energy, people removed themselves a little bit further from the natural cycle of life. Next they went to oil and now to uranium. Each process represented not progress but a regression; each process for extracting energy has become more difficult, takes more technology and energy. The red people and the aboriginal people around the world understand this—from the aborigines in Australia to the mountain people of Vietnam and Taiwan to the indigenous Ainu people of the northern islands of Japan, to the Saumese of Norway and Sweden and the Soviet Union, to the Eskimos, to the American Indians.

When the land is free and regarded as sacred, then the human race will be free.

If we can change around three to four hundred years of backward thinking and of looking at the universe upside down, then we are on the right track. And it is happening. The American Indian has always been in the forefront of attempting to teach respect for our relatives' vision. With the antinuclear movement, it is the first time in the last four hundred years that the white man is beginning to look at his relatives that surround him.

Where do we begin? *No nukes!* We have to organize. We are not going to convince David Rockefeller or Rio Tinto Zinc. We have to organize, to build an infrastructure of respect, not only in the United States of America but in all the countries of the world. It is a long, slow process, and one of the major things about this new worldview is that one has to realize that time is not of the essence. That only became of the essence when Isaac Newton reduced the spirituality of the universe to a linear mathematical equation. And then [Karl] Marx and the rest of the clowns followed him in reducing all of life to a linear mathematical equation. This is seen in both the capitalist society and the Marxist society. *Both ideologies are based on a linear worldview and on colonizing all our relatives and our Mother in order to run their societies.*

One has to recognize the cycle of life. Industrial society sees the hunters and gatherers who lived and are living within the sacred cycle of life as "living in a harsh environment" with "wild animals." But when one sees oneself living within that sacred cycle, all of a sudden the wilderness becomes your "home" and the wild animals become your "relatives." Nothing is wild and there isn't any wilderness. A Lutheran historian once told me, "You take a square foot of ground and look at it, and you see that life is unbearable. It is harsh. It is murderous." I said, "Wait a minute. The Indian looks at that square foot of ground, with all the insects and what-have-you, as an exercise in sharing and generosity." So you see, industrialized society is actually the epitome of pessimism and the natural way of life is the epitome of optimism. We believe that all things are good. The Christian believes that you are born a liar and he spends the rest of his life attempting to prove it—we have treaties that attest to that fact. Whereas the red people and aboriginal people of the world believe that everything is born innocent, sacred, and good. We believe that human beings were *cursed,* not blessed, with the power of reason because common sense will tell you that every living thing on this earth is born with a direction and a role in life to play, except for the human. Because of this common sense we came to the conclusion that we were cursed with the power of reason and could only build our civilizations on what we could learn from our superior relatives who have the capacity to share their complete beings. The white man's philosophy is that he is *blessed* with the power of reason. Thus he gives himself the license to exploit, manipulate, and colonize all that is sacred and holy and good, because he has made himself a god, superior to all the "dumb animals." If you believe you're superior you go around trying to prove it, and that is just what the white man has been doing. When you recognize that you are cursed with the power of reason, then you realize your existence on earth is actually dictated by spiritual beliefs which arise from all that surrounds you. Those spiritual beliefs can only be learned by listening. It takes generations to listen.

The animosity between the United States of America and the Soviet Union is nothing but superficial politics. Both countries are doing the same thing. In fact the Soviet Union is doing a little bit better than the U.S. in the sense of colonization, genocide, and murder of our Mother Earth. After all, the Soviet Union only took about sixty years to accomplish what took capitalism three hundred and fifty years.

You know, I couldn't begin to list all the violations by the United States of America of its treaties with the Indian people. Article VI of the Constitution of the United States says those treaties, ratified by Congress and proclaimed by the president, are on a par with and equal to the Constitution of the United States and therefore are the law of the land. Daily, since the United States' existence, these have been violated. Now it has come full circle because the government is violating the decent rights of *every* human being in this country, led by the multinational corporations. Everyone is beginning to suffer what the Indian people have already gone through, except it is taking a much more insidious path than the blatant colonization and genocide of the American Indian. Industrial society, which is a parasite, eventually ends up feeding on itself and on its colonies. And that is exactly what is happening because the only safe place for multinational corporations to continue their pillage, murder, and rape is in nation-states with stable governments. This leads to the support of dictatorships and massive exploitation of people in many countries. You can see this. You know what I mean.

To turn around the whole viewpoint of industrial society you have to go back and start cleansing the idea of what Isaac Newton got hit with. In other words, you have to reteach industrial society how it became an industrial society and the reasons why it is against common sense to continue. Responsible people throughout the entire world are looking for a new worldview and there isn't any *new* worldview. It is the *oldest* view, and that's why the American Indian is still a functioning member of the oldest civilization on earth, because we still maintain a lifestyle that goes by the instructions that the Great Mystery gave to us at the beginning of time. Just as the hawk, just as the winged things of the air, the four-leggeds, the things that crawl and swim, the green things of the earth, just as they maintain their lifestyle and spirituality by continuing with the instruction given to them at the beginning of time by the Great Mystery, so should the two-leggeds. It is very simple. You don't have to go into any long dissertation.

People in industrialized society have removed themselves further and further from the realities of the world. We can see that in modern-day architecture, where they have made the outside so ugly that they are attempting to move the outside inside. It's laughable. It's pathetic to go into these buildings and see them trying to grow trees and bushes. Unreality. They are confining themselves to their own prisons. It blows my mind! Then you see them down at some art museum, marveling at Gauguin and Van Gogh paintings that depict the natural lifestyle. *They are willing to pay tens of thousands of dollars, and it is all right outside the door!*

I'll tell you a true story about an old man back home who couldn't speak English. He came to New York City once on a visit. When he got back home, he was telling a bunch of young Indians, "Do you know what the white man does in New York City?" They said, "What's that?" He said, "They will go down and buy a little bitty plant for twelve dollars!" and then he just busted up laughing and slapping his leg and just couldn't get over it. And that is all he said. Do you understand where he comes from? He is surrounded by plants, by nature. He has an outdoor toilet, that type of thing. Materially he has nothing, but spiritually he has everything. He is surrounded with wealth. I just love that story.

When you are part of the natural cycle you know your role and don't worry about it. Only those who do not know their role or direction live in confusion and cause even more confusion. Industrial society is the one without any roles in life, totally confused, running around looking for a direction. That is why industrial society is so unhappy. Any society that is happy does not want change. Industrial society continually wants change—"progress" is what they call it. Happy people don't make history. They don't want to change a good thing. Only unhappy people want to change things.

One of our prayers is that we have to recognize that our presence in this life is but a blink of the eye in the lifetime of the Ancient Ones, the rocks. You see, we know that. Our human lifetime on this earth is but a blink of the eye in the lifetime of a rock, so who cares about time? Man is worried about destroying the earth. You can't destroy our Mother. You might destroy life on her, but she has billions of years to get well. She has all the time in the world, literally. She will still be here after the disappearance of the arrogant racist who believes he can destroy our Mother. Who knows, maybe this is part of a very large cycle, and a couple of billion years from now it will be you and me sitting across a desk discussing the same horrendous problems. Who is to say?

In 1973, when [the Native American Movement rebellion at] Wounded Knee was going on in South Dakota, an anthropologist in Arizona was talking to an old Hopi man in one of the pueblos. He asked the old man, "What do you think of these young militant Indians talking about liberation and freedom?" The Hopi thought for a while and then he looked at that white man and said, "Listen, the Spaniards were here for four hundred years and they are gone, and you have only been here for two hundred years."

The Indian people tried to join the civil rights movement, and they slammed the door and shut us out. We tried to join the antiwar movement, and they kicked us out of that. Now, finally, the cycle has come around and we are joining the antinuclear movement. It is fantastic! I was at the International Gathering for Survival outside of Rapid City. It's one of the most fantastic things I have been involved in, outside of Indian ceremonies in my own lifestyle. It was a heavy experience. I learned so much. You saw all those sacred colors—white, black, yellow, and red—getting along together, and everything was clean. Even the Indian people coming up from the reservation couldn't believe it. It was a beautiful happening. Everyone I heard, from all over the world, was talking about "Mother Earth." They weren't saying "ecology" or "environment"; they were saying "Mother Earth." That is a key, you know, that little accomplishment right there. It was the first time I ever heard white people constantly say "Mother Earth." It was a great feeling.

Richard Falk

An internationally recognized spokesman for the global humanist perspective on world affairs, Richard Falk is a prolific writer and lecturer. Some recent titles include This Endangered Planet: Prospects and Proposals for Human Survival, A Study of Future Worlds, *and* A Global Approach to National Policy. *In addition, he has written several volumes on international law and war crimes. He lives with his wife in Princeton, New Jersey, where he is Alfred G. Milbank Professor of International Law and Practice at Princeton University. We did this interview in the fall of 1980.*

I grew up in New York City and lived most of my late childhood and adolescence with my father, a lawyer with quite a conservative worldview. I was a rather marginal student who excelled, if in anything, in athletics; my high school yearbook is filled with things like "To the future Dodger pitcher." The Brooklyn Dodgers were my favorite team, while the Yankees represented the establishment. I guess my first political commitment was to like the Dodgers as an underdog that achieved success by grit and determination rather than by power, money, and professionalism. "Third World baseball" versus "First World baseball."

As an undergraduate at the University of Pennsylvania I was very apolitical; my father's conservative influence on me was considerable. He was the lawyer for many leading anti-Communists, a number of whom I have known from my childhood, and my outlook during the late 1940s and early 1950s was largely shaped by that view of the world. I went on to Yale Law School, becoming a pretty good student although I wasn't very interested in law.

I studied Sanskrit and became interested in non-Western legal traditions. Two professors, F. S. C. Northrop, who wrote a book called *The Meeting of East and West,* and Myers McDougall, an international law professor who was rethinking the meaning of law in the world community, had a major influence on me.

I then taught at Ohio State law school for six years, and in that period my orientation toward social and political reality took shape. For the first time I lived directly in an atmosphere that challenged the minimal moral premises I had taken for granted. There was a great deal of explicit racism, and I got involved in helping some black students obtain the right to live in off-campus housing owned by members of the board of trustees. Their position was outrageous. There wasn't enough on-campus housing for the black students, who had to live far away in this very inconvenient housing. Since their landlords knew they had no choice, the rents were much higher than in the better, convenient housing. That experience, and friendships with young faculty and graduate students, helped me develop a more progressive worldview. Also, reactionary ideas of the John Birch Society, very active in Columbus, created in me an opposite response.

Prior to the American involvement in Vietnam I started writing about intervention in the internal affairs of foreign countries. In the late 1960s I went to North Vietnam to observe the consequences of war from the perspective of international law. I was very moved by that experience. I saw what it meant to live in an agrarian society being subjected to high-technology warfare. The people and leaders were very different from my image of Communist leadership, which was based on slight contact with bureaucrats from the Soviet Union and Eastern Europe. Seeing firsthand this kind of encounter between Third World people and people of my own country was critical in teaching me to listen to the *victims* of existing cultural, economic, and military structures of oppression.

I came here, to Princeton, in 1961. Although in some ways it represents a bastion of privilege, I find it a suitable place to work and teach. During my time at Princeton I have come to focus less on law and more on understanding the fundamentals of politics and culture in order to transform things. This reflects a gathering skepticism on my part about law in that it tends to be a force for maintaining the existing order rather than for promoting positive change. My teaching and writing have shifted toward "world order study," an attempt to understand present trends and their future implications, as well as possibilities for developing a world society congenial to realizing a series of desirable goals. For over ten years I have worked with a group of scholars from different countries on the "World Order Models Project." We consider politics from the perspective of the oppressed, envisioning nonutopian transformations that are obviously connected with real social forces emerging in the world. I concentrate on interpreting these trends in order to understand what might be possible in the future, combining this with the belief that it is also appropriate to make commitments in the present. Concrete encounters between different civilizations, social classes, and national societies are necessary in order to test the vision one has of the future.

The question of security may be *the* central issue for people in advanced civilizations to consider at this time. We think of ourselves as more secure to the extent that we are militarily more powerful, and in a quantitative society like ours that translates in a very mechanical way into numbers of missiles and planes, size of armies, and the like. Such an assessment is exceedingly misguided; in many ways we become less secure as we rely on more unstable kinds of strategic doctrines and weapons systems. We somehow have to separate our understanding of security from our preoccupation with violence and prowess. In some profound cultural way this confusion arises from the patriarchal control of the instruments of violence. The institution of war has been a male preserve, evolving out of the male role in hunting societies and as warriors. This male role, which gradually became fused with innovative technology, involved a lot of unexamined attitudes that were possibly relevant in an early period of human evolution where it may have helped to be stronger and run faster. This was translated mythically to glorify macho behavior—thrusting out from the group in a situation of danger, using violence to protect the whole. We still have the "cowboy image" in American society. Remember Kissinger's famous identification of himself as being a "cowboy riding alone at night into a town." He thought of himself as that kind of romantic and heroic figure; he didn't want to be thought of as merely some sort of academic statesman.

Women too have been socialized to accept this ethos through hero worship and the like. The kind of nurturing earth-connectedness generally associated with the "feminine" has been lost in Western civilization's relentless quest for material progress and domination over others. To restore health to the body politic we need to achieve a much more harmonious balance between these masculine and feminine tendencies. The beginning of movement is *understanding*. In other words, if you understand—not just with your head but in a more total way—then you change. There is a saying, "Seeing is movement"; if you are walking and a tree falls across your path, seeing the tree and moving out of its way are inseparable. If we really come to see and understand that in the name of the state and national security we are destroying our planet and our prospects for a positive kind of survival and evolution, we will transform things. This requires that we rediscover our dependence on nature, remembering that the earth is the ultimate nurturing basis for human existence.

We also need a better sense of appropriate human limits, such as not relying on technologies which, if they fail, inflict irreversible catastrophes. For example, I think we are the wrong species for nuclear technology. Perhaps in the universe there are planets with more evolved species, beings capable of handling this sort of technology. But given our fallibility and nature's instability with earthquakes, we should recognize that we human beings shouldn't try to do certain things within our biosphere. Remember the nine-megaton Titan II missile which almost exploded recently in Arkansas because a wrench was dropped? The government said, "Well, it was only a matter of human error." *Nine megatons is somewhere between four hundred fifty and nine hundred times the explosive magnitude of the Hiroshima bomb!* Right in our own territory, all around us, we have bombs that are supposedly protecting us, put there by institutions that are supposedly representing us. Most of us have no direct say in where these weapons are located. There is a loss of connectedness between our people and our authority structures; there is a kind of gut-sense that political leadership is not associated with human welfare. We see this in the lack of interest in elections: "It doesn't really matter." And yet people feel helpless to know what to do. This loss of connectedness is one of the fundamental problems we face.

My main point, however, is that these technologies presuppose human and social infallibility. The only way we can do this is to pretend to be God, which exemplifies the sin of pride—

perhaps the most dangerous flaw of modern civilization. This worldview is a kind of materialism shared by both Marxism and non-Marxist liberalism. Both are strategies for organizing society's productive capacities to achieve maximum material output. They have different ideologies that provide justifications for doing this: the capitalist form stresses individual incentive and individual reward, whereas the socialist and Soviet form stresses societal ownership, centralized planning, and bureaucratic management. But what they share is the view that unlimited progress comes from applying human ingenuity to develop the economic life of society. Both systems are based on the notions that you can constantly innovate through technology, that nature provides an inexhaustible neutral terrain that can be indefinitely exploited, and that human capability has no limits. Everything is measured in *materialist* terms; whether these are defined by a state socialist system of accounts or by a Western capitalist system of accounts is really a *trivial distinction*.

That doesn't mean that there are not important differences in the quality of life in the two societies. I have no question that state socialism's bureaucratic centralism and the role of the police in Soviet society create a very repressive relationship between the government and the people. People have little creative space to develop in a satisfying way. That's very sterile and stultifying. On the fiftieth anniversary of the Russian Revolution a famous Soviet mathematician, Kapitsa, said that he thought Russia's greatest tragedy was that the the young people have forgotten how to think. Ideological rigidity discourages positive and creative use of the mind. Our society has much more creative space and more possibility for innovation. In America, on the other hand, we are victims of a deep set of confusions that arise from the fact that our cult of materialism hasn't produced genuine fulfillment and satisfaction. In many ways our signs of societal distress are at least as serious as they are in the Soviet Union. For example, the failure of social forms like the family to sustain themselves, widespread use of tranquilizers and harder drugs, violence-drenched popular entertainment, and the way pornography and sexuality are handled within our society all suggest an attitude that is very destructive toward others. Which suggests that the system isn't working.

It is very difficult to figure out political reality, because what is *said* and what is *done* are so often in contradiction. If you are in the Soviet Union, when you read *Pravda,* despite the title which means "Truth," you know that you can't believe what you read. You may read it to see what the party officials *want* you to believe, but you know that isn't where you get the *real* news. In the United States we read newspapers in a much more trusting way; yet in many fundamental respects our news has the same distortions. But we're more vulnerable to it because the very atmosphere of formal freedom makes us more trusting. Ironically it may be harder to learn to see reality in a Western liberal society than in a totalitarian society.

Does the Soviet Union pose a threat to the security of the United States? Like us, Russia is a very powerful state in which the military exerts a lot of influence. And like us they have opted for security through power. Yet they are much more preoccupied with the danger they think they face from their neighbors than with us. The Soviet Union has been very frightened by our establishing diplomatic relations with China, with which the Soviets share a very long border. On the other side, Europe is becoming more powerful. Next, the problems they had in Afghanistan led them to their invasion there. And finally there is restiveness in Poland and Eastern Europe. If you look out at the world from the Kremlin it's a pretty grim place. They feel encircled, as they did in the early stages of the Russian Revolution; they want to convey to the rest of the world that if too much pressure is put on them, it could be dangerous: "Don't mess with us or you won't mess again!" I think that U.S. militarist elements have misinterpreted and exaggerated this posture to enhance their relative power and to overcome their loss of prestige after the Vietnam defeat. Another motivation for exaggerating the Soviet threat comes from political leaders in both parties who have no answers to our society's economic problems. They find it much easier to emphasize the Soviet challenge—it is something external, it is congressionally popular, and it has powerful interests behind it.

What really endangers America's security, however, is our deteriorating economy and an energy policy that depends on external supplies from politically unstable parts of the world. Those two sets of issues are very difficult to solve because they threaten the distribution of wealth among different social classes in the United States and perhaps to some degree the material lifestyle of all Americans. It is much easier to suggest that *everything* that threatens us is associated with "the enemy out there," so that we believe we must mobilize all our resources to respond to the "Soviet challenge." Social scientists call this a "displacement activity." Since you can't do the thing that *really* needs to be done, you do something else, creating the illusion that you're responding to the threat. But our current response is *terribly* dangerous and fails to address the real challenges in any serious way.

The first step in addressing these problems is to start suggesting that we face them. We must begin to take energy conservation as seriously as we take Soviet missiles. We could easily put resources into mass transportation and also work to create a more holistic and satisfying concept of the relationship between work and residence that doesn't require moving around so much. We could deconcentrate industry and make a real effort to create livable cities. These are not new ideas, but if they were given top social priority we would make far more rapid progress.

We must also move in the direction of making genuine efforts to stop and reverse the arms race. We must help the public understand that genuine security doesn't come from the numbers of weapons but from creating a situation where the weapons that exist are not likely to be used. Also, until the U.S. and the Soviet Union begin denuclearizing the world we are being naïve to believe that we can arrest the spread of these weapons to additional countries. We have to look at it from the position of the Third World countries: if the most powerful and wealthy countries believe their security requires increasingly sophisticated nuclear weapons, why shouldn't weaker and poorer countries acquire these weapons also? In that sense the U.S. government's whole emphasis on nuclear nonproliferation is another "displacement" activity: it is easier to worry about preventing nonnuclear countries from acquiring weapons than to do something about those *with* weapons. I think this has some racist elements in it: we propagate the illusion that the "real" way disaster could happen to the world is for some "irresponsible nonwhite government" to get hold of these weapons and provoke tragedy. We seem to forget that Western governments too are capable of terribly irrational and barbaric behavior. One only has to look at Nazism, at Stalinism, and at the bombings of Hiroshima and Nagasaki to prove this point. I think these attitudes are part of our "collective amnesia," a kind of "semi-conscious conscious conspiracy."

I have little confidence in what governments and official institutions are likely to do to enhance national and global security. Possibly, religious institutions could play a major role in raising these issues as a moral concern. One great failure of religious institutions has been to turn over to the state the questions of security and power. But if the state misuses power and wealth, that's a profoundly immoral way of existing—particularly in the Nuclear Age with its potential for catastrophe. The churches are beginning to awaken, to recognize their failure to raise questions about our civilization's drift in this destructive direction.

Real social growth will entail moving in the direction of some kind of social ownership, perhaps an antibureaucratic kind of socialism. In America we can be more imaginative about this than socialist societies have been so far, and be very wary of concentrating power and bureaucracy. We can also combine economic ideas with some cultural ideas about what constitutes a more satisfying lifestyle, better diet, and what really enables people to fulfill themselves. In other words, we can introduce a less materialist definition of human well-being.

This next decade is a very crucial one. The contradictions of the old order are likely to become most acute. Very likely we shall see an increased struggle for control of oil in the Middle East. That will be going on at the same time that these new spiritual and humanitarian forces are struggling to be born and groping toward developing a kind of leadership and a whole new understanding of reality. We're living in an era of transition. On the one hand the old order is dying but is still very powerful and has the instruments of physical power and violence at its disposal; and on the other hand something new is taking shape and trying to articulate itself and become an effective foundation for the future.

Politically the most important thing people can do is to recover their sense of responsibility and of their power as citizens. But probably not much will happen on a large scale without our receiving some pretty severe shocks, like Three Mile Island. We are so complacent as a civilization that reality may have to inflict a lot of pain and punishment before enough of us wake up. Yet each of us does have a great deal of power to choose our values and the way in which we live our own lives. The most important statement we can make in creating a new world order is what we each do with our own lives. That also has a contagious effect.

Hazel Henderson

A writer and lecturer, Hazel Henderson lives in Gainesville, Florida. Her recent books include The Politics of the Solar Age: Alternatives to Economics *and* The Reconceptualization of Politics. *Recently she has been working with people from Third World countries on new concepts of development. This interview was conducted by phone in the winter of 1981.*

I've just come back from England, which to me is sort of symbolic because the crisis the world is going through is one of industrialism, whether of the capitalist or of the socialist variety, and industrialism started in Britain only two hundred years ago. England now seems to be the first example of where it's ending. While there I made a trip to Iron Bridge, a tiny valley in central England where the River Severn rises. That's where James Robertson, the author of *The Sane Alternative,* lives, and where he and Alison Pritchard now run the Turning Point Network. The whole idea of rounding out the industrial era was very clear there because they've turned the entire town into a museum of industrial culture. The town is dotted with tiny old factories where they first learned to smelt iron, using the coal mined in that valley. It's quite poignant to see all those early cast-iron artifacts. The great English painter Turner went there and painted the veritable hell that beautiful green valley was turned into by those early smelters and blast furnaces, which lit up the whole sky with fire, smoke, and sulfur put off by this process.

Those early industrialists of course had no thought for anything other than maximizing production. You could see the way in which that whole mind-set began in that little valley. There are all of these letters back and forth between these good Quaker gentlemen, who really believed in this industrial process which maximized the efficiency of producing these iron products, the household equipment and all the things we now take for granted but which were the *miracles* of that age. They all thought this would bring about the Millennium and truly believed they were doing God's work; they were going to create a secular *paradise* with those incredible blast furnaces. I don't know how they could ignore the human suffering going on right under their noses, however. Children were sent down to mine the coal; there are pictures of women crawling on their hands and knees through those coal mines because they couldn't stand up, with harnesses on, pulling coal trucks just like draft animals. Yet all of this was clothed with optimism and religious fervor.

It was fascinating to see how a whole era which we've normally considered "human progress" got started. And now in that valley-turned-into-museum it is coming to its logical conclusion. And with it, all the ideas which brought about the Industrial Revolution, ideas which got propagated in North America too and created our industrial system, and in the Soviet Union and Eastern Europe, and so on. And everybody bought the whole package. Industrialism, whether capitalistic or socialistic or communistic, was sort of a cargo cult: it promised to deliver the goods.

In Britain today one is looking for how the political system and the people will wake up to the decline that's happening. Britain is a perfect example of this lag in people's perceptions, particularly the perceptions of politicians. Like Ronald Reagan here, [Prime Minister] Margaret Thatcher is obviously still caught up with redoubling her efforts to do the thing that we all see is failing, trying to get one more last turn of the wheel to hype up the production process. Basically that's what supply-side economics is: "Let's fuel the fires and gobble up the resources a little faster, cannibalize the environment and the social fabric in order to make the funny-money GNP numbers look better." In Britain the chickens are clearly coming home to roost, in unemployment, riots, and so on. There is no possibility of hiding those social costs anymore; recently in the U.S. many people have been seeing the social costs of the same sorts of policies as even more people are thrown out of work.

The most positive interpretation we can make is to call this a "social learning experience." Those of us in the social change movements can use this as an opportunity to educate others by pointing out that there is a tremendous transformation going on and that there is no possibility of revising the dead industrial order. It was based on conditions which no longer exist.

There is only one game in town: to devise productive systems and economies that fit with the new ecological realities. These must be based on recycling everything and on managing resources over the long term. None of the politicians can admit that the old game is up. So it falls on the shoulders of the people who are talking about new and conserving lifestyles, renewable resources and solar energy, to carry out the education process that the politicians and the education establishments seem unable or unwilling to do. When you have this kind of rapid change, you don't expect it to be fostered by the ruling establishments and the people who benefited during the height of the old system. This is going on both in the East and in the West. It's all part of what's happening in Poland and in the Soviet Union where minority populations are getting restive. There is enormous potential right now in social change voices and activities—the antinuclear movement, the cooperative movement, the new communities movement, the voluntary simplicity movement, and all of that. In particular the movements of ethnic and racial minorities and the rise of women are entering a new period of importance.

There is a particularly urgent need for these people to come forward now with radically alternative ideas by means of which they can critique the old industrial order from outside the system. It is perfectly clear that the whole system was never designed for us anyway. For example, the productive contributions of women were not even recognized and rewarded with cash, which of course has been the almighty measuring rod, whether in dollars, rubles, yen, or francs. So women have this extraordinary perspective which enables them to make the most vigorous critiques of industrialism.

A French Marxist tells me that the feminist critiques of Marx's writings are the most devastating. Carolyn Berg, who wrote *The Two Paycheck Marriage* (1978), is a good example. She has collected an enormous array of statistics to support the case that market-oriented economists, socialists, and Marxists, have consistently underestimated the unpaid activity of homemakers, the part of the economy which makes it possible for the cash-based part of the economy, measured in GNP, to look "successful." For example, the figure now used to put value on the housewife's contribution is twenty-eight thousand dollars a year [1978 dollars]. An awful lot of husbands don't bring home that much money from the paying job. New legislation is now in Congress which would specifically recognize marriage as an economic partnership: any cash income just gets split down the middle and it doesn't matter which partner does the "house-spouse" thing.

This kind of development is giving the Marxists a terrible time because Marx was completely patriarchal and had exactly the same shortcomings in this line as any other economist. The work done in the community by women, rural subsistence farmers, and volunteers running the hospitals and all sorts of other things, *just didn't count*. In fact I think Marx sort of despised peasants and rural life; he thought anyone who didn't get in there and maximize production was basically backward. So what women are saying (and many of them are in the trade union movement) is, "Are you interested in the issue of oppression and human rights per se or are you just interested in the oppression of factory workers? If you are just interested in the oppression of workers, well, forget it! You're never going to form a majority coalition to change things." The feminists are also saying, "Look, do you want us to join your revolution so you can win it, or do you want to keep us out and always be a minority?" They're like little boys in their clubhouse and we're really sticking it to them, saying, "Do you have a problem? Are you afraid of women?"

This area is exactly where the dissident voices are going to have to break through. In the last play to restore the dying system our industrial leaders are calling for "reindustrialization," which is really a "rearview mirror" term, and even worse, as a last gasp, for remilitarization. Many people have pointed out for a long time that sometimes the only way to keep the system running is to increase arms production and try to foment a war somewhere. We're seeing this happen very clearly now in U.S. foreign policy. Instead of trying to conserve energy we're preparing to fight a war, whether it's in the Middle East or wherever. You see the type of reprehensible advertising by the electric utilities which more or less says that nuclear power is the only way to escape dependency on Middle East oil. They are suggesting, "Do you want a war in the Middle East over oil, or do you want nuclear power?" As if those were the only two choices!

I think the crisis will emerge very, very rapidly because the attempt now is to hype up military budgets in this country. Reagan is doing this now, and Congress is just rolling over and playing dead in terms of this enormous arms buildup, the greatest one proposed since the Vietnam War. All the chickens will very rapidly come home to roost in inflation. These generals want their expensive toys, and production of that hardware will probably get bogged down in enormously accelerated inflation rates long before it yields to common sense. People like Seymour Melman have pointed out for years that military spending depletes the economy and destroys jobs; in the next few years we'll see the graphic illustration of that in all the countries increasing their military budgets. With it you'll see increasingly divisive domestic turmoil resulting from the denial of social programs and destruction of the kind of political consensus necessary for domestic tranquility—all in order to feed the military monster. This will drive the crisis even further, increasing rates of inflation. We must make that connection more and more clear to people: that we're not buying one penny's more security and we're making the world a lot more dangerous. Even if we avoid an accidental nuclear war we will decimate our own economy with inflation.

We also have to understand that the Russian economy is probably under even worse stress than ours in trying to set up military production. They have to starve their civilian sector even more than is done here or in Germany and Britain. This will cause similar unrest in the Soviet Union. The Polish situation is quite predictable, really, and I think what's happening there is not overlooked by the Russian people. I mean, that *is* reported in the Russian press, and the Russian people are envious of the Poles: "By golly, they have it a lot better than we do. They're getting all these concessions." We need to develop more people-to-people exchanges and more networks like Amnesty International to facilitate our developing a better picture of what's going on and to share ideas.

I'm wondering if we, both in this country and in the Soviet

Union, aren't overly impressed with the power of the party hier-
archy and the "leaders." Just realize how brittle and fragile that
leadership is in all of the industrialized countries. It is being under-
mined by the withdrawal of cheap energy. As the energy situation
gets more and more critical they cannot do all the things they used
to do to keep central control. One thing we have to remember is
that in all of these countries, one of the symptoms of the decline is
the aging, palsied leadership. Does it really make much sense to
try to proselytize those leaders? They're all two steps from the
grave. I think we psych ourselves out because they "have their
fingers on the button." All through history some small elite group
has held the power and the ability to get society into a war. We
just have to stare that reality in the face and realize that, yes, it is
possible that the human race on this planet may commit some sort
of species suicide. Yes, we have to accept the fact that these old
palsied men in charge of all these patriarchal societies all over the
planet, yes, they *have* got their palsied fingers on that button. But
if we give too much psychic energy to that system or focus on all
the incredibly awful possible scenarios of global destruction, then
we will have less energy to develop positive alternatives. My
sense is that we should be very respectful of the fact that these
blithering old idiots could indeed destroy the planet, but what we
all have to do is work harder in a totally different dimension to
surround the planet with this new network of consciousness and
grassroots political action.

I think we will see many collapses, though I don't think it'll
be like it was in the 1930s where the whole thing just went to hell
in a handbasket. There was no social underpinning back then with
the kind of legislation we have now, which transfers income and
keeps people's purchasing power at a reasonable level. What I
think will happen is that an enormous amount of this bubble of
debt will get written down in a very orderly fashion, for example,
the last three or four days the stock market has plunged and
billions of dollars of paper money have disappeared overnight. Yet
there hasn't been a riot and nobody has jumped out of a window.
The same thing with the bond markets; those holding bonds will
be absolutely decimated and yet they won't know whom to be
angry with. There'll be a lot of hand-wringing and general nasti-
ness, cities will go bankrupt, and there will be chaos in the school
system. I thing the best way to visualize it is like a great big

inflated dome over the whole society which is slowly billowing down and deflating. Since it isn't happening in any immediate or catastrophic way, nobody will quite recognize the dimensions of our monetary crisis.

Meanwhile we are shifting over to a new type of economic structure that is being built right now, although there is very little recognition of that either. When you look at which industries are doing the best and are growing, they are largely in the area of conservation and renewable resources. If they had any chance to compete at all in the free market (rather than having to compete with the giant subsidies given to nuclear power, oil, and all of the old industries), these new industries based on solar, windpower, and bioconversion would already be romping away with the economy. They're being suppressed because we are bailing out all the dead and dying industries through this old system of subsidies. As this is the Oil Age, the symbol of this is the automobile industry. So if we take off that pair of spectacles and take a fresh look at the economy, we would see how the new economy is already competing and growing like a weed. Really, the big political task of the Solar Age is to bring about the transition, fighting for federal dollars and trying to get the subsidies on nuclear oil and coal removed. We absolutely have to argue every single dollar of budget priorities, and that is the oldest argument in the world: the priorities of whose ox gets gored.

Money is being created in a whole number of ways right now, so that economic theory simply cannot keep up with the reality. The monetarist economists had their theory that you could keep the economy running well by allowing a very orderly and slow growth in the money supply to just match the productivity of the system. They would say that to prevent inflation you just control the money supply, yet no one knows how to *measure* the money supply anymore because we have all these new kinds of checking accounts and people can switch their balances from checking to savings to interest-bearing accounts. We also have the new money-market funds. And now these people are putting out new indicators and new measures for how you ought to be able to calculate the money supply almost every other month! The Federal Reserve Board itself does not know how to control the money supply; how can you control something if you can't even measure it?

Another level of inflation came from the Vietnam War, which we never paid for and which Reagan is about to make even worse. Johnson gave us his "guns and butter" budget to fight the war without raising taxes; the basic inflation rate at the time was only two percent. Now, however, when Reagan tries to do the same thing the basic inflation rate is much more like *eight* percent. So there is another enormous contribution to inflation. In addition we have to recycle more and more money in order to get lower grade and more inaccessible resources. That means a declining productivity of our capital investments. This is not, incidentally, a declining productivity of workers. You see, the way politicians define it it is worker productivity that has declined. The politics that flow from that kind of interpretation is that we have to cut back on black-lung benefits, turn up the Muzak and make the production lines go faster, and "get these lazy workers off their butts." The kind of productivity that is declining much more rapidly is that of capital investment. Fifty years ago if you wanted oil you just hammered a pipe into the ground in Texas and oil came out; nowadays you spend billions constructing pipelines from the Alaska oilfields.

The other kind of productivity I see declining drastically is management productivity. Take the incredible mismanagement of the American automobile industry. Those weren't *workers'* mistakes; those were basic strategic *management* mistakes. They did not notice the Japanese competition or foresee that Americans would want smaller and smaller cars because of fuel cost increases. The electrical utility industry is another case. Management has sunk *enormous* quantities of capital into constructing nuclear power plants which should never have been built because the demand they were intended to meet is never going to materialize.

As the decline of the system of industrialization becomes increasingly obvious I think more and more attention will focus on the Federal Reserve Board. People will begin to understand that the free-market, monetary, and price systems were not derived from God. That it was simply a certain political form of resource allocation designed by someone to benefit someone. This will naturally politicize the Fed, and already has. People can now see clearly that the Fed's decisions can throw people out of work, employ them, cut the housing market, or cut access to credit. So what we'll get are basic legislative proposals to focus on the political role that money performs in our society. In *The Reconceptualization of Politics* I outlined what happens when a society places all of the burdens of its policy-making on the price system. In other countries if they want to adopt a certain policy, for example, to conserve energy, they'll simply mandate that cars be smaller and more fuel-efficient. In America we try to use the price system to effect all of our policy goals, setting up incentives and subsidies and crazy quilts of rationing by price. Eventually you blow out the ability of the price system to make all those changes. A few years ago, for example, our Congress rejected the idea of rationing the *commodity,* energy, by mandating fuel efficiency; so we rationed by price, forgetting the effect that would have on the poor. That allows the rich to go on driving but kicks the poor people off the roads. The next thing we've done, through the Federal Reserve Board, is rationing *credit* by price, in other words, raising the interest rates. That doesn't work because the big boys, the rich companies, can go right on paying the prime rate, which is now up to nineteen percent [in 1981]. All you do is drive all the small businesses and the little people to the wall. It means that consumers and homeowners can't afford mortgages; it means that little companies, small businesses, go bankrupt by droves, and the *Fortune* Five Hundred and all those big boys can just go right on borrowing, and what do they care if the price of borrowing money is eighteen or nineteen percent?

What has happened, of course, is that the U.S. economy no longer bears any relationship to the free market; it's now a crazy quilt of administered, rigged markets, incentives, subsidies, and rationing by price. There's no relationship to a free market. Basically what the Reagan people are doing is *pretending* that they're going back to the free market and the "invisible hand," whereas the invisible hand is actually *our own* and always has been. There is no free market derived from God; the market system, as a way of allocating resources in a society, was a very brilliant human invention. It was invented in Britain about three hundred years ago. If people had a cosmic time and space perspective and could assess the long-term good of the whole biosphere and all people of all times, and if *that* were the definition of value and were equated with the "invisible hand," then that would be the "cosmic economy" or "cosmic accounting system." The moment we switch over to the cosmic accounting system, then communism would work and capitalism would work and anything else would work.

What I would like to say to people is that we forget how much power each one of us has to make daily choices of what to buy and consume. We should each try to keep in tune with the cosmic accounting system and think about the long-term and planetary consequences of our actions. How will what I am doing affect my grandchildren or great-grandchildren? If each one of us can remember our great-grandchildren in every decision we make, and remember the interconnectedness of the whole planet now, that will really help. Are we buying meat in the supermarket? That's a high-energy-consuming food that's frozen, wrapped in plastic, shipped across the country. Or do we shop locally where possible, at the cooperative? The next stage is to organize a farmers' market in your area so you can really help the local producers. Shorten the links in your life between you and the producer of things you consume so that it becomes clearer and clearer what those interdependencies are. The life choice of becoming a vegetarian is a way of awakening that cosmic accounting in yourself.

The next step is to take these values into political activity where you *do* make that call today to your political representative and say that you don't want money spent on the Clinch River Breeder Reactor and that you support [Rhode Island Congresswoman] Claudine Schneider's amendment which would transfer those moneys to solar and conservation budgets. All I can say, and I really harp a lot on this, is that we really must "think globally and act locally."

Edgar Mitchell

Astronaut on the Apollo 14 Mission, founder of the Institute of Noetic Sciences, and currently a business consultant to major corporations, Ed Mitchell lives in Jupiter, Florida. This interview was done at the end of 1981.

My background includes twenty years as a naval officer, a doctorate in aeronautics and astronautics and twelve years as a navy test pilot. Avocationally, however, since childhood my interest has been in the study of comparative religion, philosophies, and social systems.

I grew up in a family with a western pioneer heritage; my family came to Texas following the Civil War as part of the great westward migration. I was reared on the family farms and ranches in the Southern Baptist tradition. At one point in my young adult life I became agnostic. I had to reject the religious tradition I was trained in because it was impossibly dogmatic, with a worldview totally out of touch with modern knowledge.

Early in life I arrived at the conclusion that the two great bodies of knowledge, science and religion, seemed to be proclaiming mutually exclusive worldviews. In my mind this duality was unacceptable and needed to be resolved, if possible. I could not conceive of "truth" as being compartmentalized in such a fashion.

Scientific methodology has led us to materialistic, reductionist concepts descended from Aristotelian logic. The religious point of view has led us to believe that the universe is not only matter, but was created with purpose, intelligence, and harmony. I never believed these two ways of thinking had to be mutually exclusive, although as formal bodies of knowledge they seemed to take that position. I have spent forty years trying to resolve these issues to my own satisfaction.

When I had the chance to fly Apollo 14, an experience on the flight allowed me to gain the insight that there are ways to integrate materialist thinking with an acceptable metaphysical philosophy. As I looked at Planet Earth from the distance of the moon, I had an explosion of awareness. I sensed the universe in a different way. I knew, at a very deep level, that the universe is orderly, harmonious and intelligent, that the direction or thrust of evolution is discernible through that intelligence. ("Intelligent" is used here to mean the ability to retain, assimilate and propagate information.) The universe is not ordered only from random, stochastic, unaware processes but contains the means for orderly experiential growth. It's very difficult to put the experience into words except to say that it was extremely joyful. I sensed that the universe is completely connected, that everything is a part of an undifferentiated whole. It is not just a mass of molecules floating around randomly colliding with each other and building ever more imposing molecular structures. It does build structures, of course, but not randomly and not without direction.

Consciousness seems to be the underlying, unifying factor, not an effect of the universe. That insight helped to give direction to my search. I seemed to have stumbled upon experientially what philosophers have been proclaiming for centuries. From that point on I set about making that insight more meaningful. What are the details? How do you bring together the knowledge gained through science with that gained through the subjective experience of many individuals? How does one appropriately view the dualities and paradoxes with which life seems to be filled? In this process of gaining understanding, each body of knowledge from human experience has something important to contribute.

The major thing I discovered from this experience is that we are not accidents, nor victims of the universe. We have the intelligence, capability and creativity to shape our own reality. We are more than our physical selves; we can sense our own consciousness and create our own environment. Once we humans reach a certain level of perception of the true nature of our own reality, we realize that we have been unaware as to the meaning of being human. We're not really earthbound beings confined to a physical body; we have within us the seeds of the creativity of the universe. As long as we continue to perceive ourselves in a limited, provincial way, that is, as limited to the earth and as victims of our environment, we will continue to live in fear. We will undoubtedly also continue to behave in limiting ways and to commit atrocities against each other and the environment as we have done for thousands of years.

But when we start to see each other as fully aware conscious beings, and see our intelligence as a part of the very foundation of the universe, then we will begin to behave very differently. We will begin using our potential for our mutual benefit. It is precisely this sort of shift in perception that will create greater security and greater prosperity for each of us and for the earth.

The universe seems to have been evolving toward this point from the beginning of time, perfecting the "software" of our consciousness. We seem to be organizing the information of our existence in ever more complex ways. And we seem to have reached a significant juncture in our evolutionary development: we have created a technology which has served us very well in the material sense, but we haven't grown spiritually, psychologically, and emotionally to the point where we are wise enough to handle that technology very well. We need and want technology to benefit us but none of us wants the mass annihilation that will result from its use if we continue to think in the hostile and fearful ways that were the pattern of the past. Our challenge at the moment, therefore, is to change our thinking about ourselves. We must gain better awareness of our unlimited potential and learn to direct our lives individually and collectively toward the kind of future we can agree that we want. In essence, we need to take conscious control of our evolution. But conscious control can only be effective after we discover within ourselves, experientially and individually, our true nature.

My positive vision of the future is one in which humans explore together their common needs for survival, resolving their conflicts through discussion and empathy with other people or other nations. We must work toward a cooperative rather than a competitive model. The battle to the death, when applied to societies and nations, is an obsolete concept held over from primitive times. We cannot survive on this earth unless we begin to recognize that fact and begin to behave differently. We need to promote a sharing of resources and responsibility, respect for individuals, and to take complete responsibility for ourselves as individuals.

We must see the universe as ultimately abundant. The limitations we currently perceive are simply limitations of our beliefs and perceptions. We have trained ourselves over thousands of years to hold a worldview of scarcity. Certain elements may be scarce, but the universe is not scarce. It appears that all we need is available to us; we just need to exercise creativity to find the patterns and the new ideas to solve the problems we encounter. Our lack of creativity is simply our lack of belief in ourselves and lack of knowledge about our role.

Let's take energy as an example. Petroleum is clearly becoming a more scarce item and it costs more to procure it. However, energy is not scarce. We can find other sources of energy that will be increasingly competitive with petroleum; but discovering and utilizing these requires creativity. I suspect that we may have the wrong slant on the very nature of matter itself and that matter itself may yield us unending sources of energy when we learn to view it differently. A number of very well-educated and creative people, for example, believe in so-called "free energy."

A more personal example of human potential for creativity is the notion that the creative part of our mental machinery presents us with optimum solutions for any particular problem whenever we "tune in" to that creative or higher sense of self. We are so used to thinking in terms of controlling and manipulating people and resources because of our notions of scarcity that we become frightened to turn loose to our higher selves. Only when we are in the most dire circumstances and have exhausted all of our own thinking do we turn problems over to a higher sense of self. Then, generally, solutions appear. Time and time again, I have found in my own life that when I stop thinking about a problem in a stereotyped, programmed way and turn it over to my creative mind, that is when I get a solution. And, quite often, the solution initially looks ridiculous. When examined a bit more closely, it appears clearly viable. Some techniques enhance this; for example, sleeping on a problem after we have done a lot of thinking about it. That's one way to get the "aha!" experience. If we continue to block our creative impulses it becomes increasingly difficult to receive them. Just like a muscle, you have to use it.

One of our great problems in dealing with other cultures is our belief that they think as we do. One must have a deep understanding of how the cultural subconscious influences thinking before you can model their behavior. The Soviet leadership, for example, sees nothing wrong in manipulation, lying, and changing direction if it suits their perceived interest to do so. (Of course, the West is not particularly clean in that department, either.) They believe the greater good is served by submission to the will of the state, whatever that will is. It is a part of their value system. With our penchant for individual freedom, we have great difficulty understanding their system and as a result, we categorize them as "bad" or "treacherous" people. That is clearly not a smart thing to do if we want to coexist. Moreover, such attitudes demonstrate that the people who hold these judgmental points of view understand very little about the role of belief systems in human functioning. We have to understand that cultural behavior, like human behavior, is determined by the subconscious belief system, not by rationality. Other cultures have their own value systems and they are programmed to use them in their own way. We have to understand that value system, not necessarily adopt it, but simply understand it. We must deeply understand that the Eastern bloc truly views us as suspiciously as we view them.

The Soviets believe that the world will only be secure when it conforms to their system and their political philosophy. We believe differently. We believe it will only be secure when it conforms to our political philosophy. Clearly there has to be something that appeals to both camps, something that is a higher form of thinking than that of either camp. Even though we also have our rigid materialistic leaning, our system permits diverse ideas to emerge and to be tested politically and economically more readily than theirs. We have attempted to separate our church and state and allow them to function independently. In the Soviet Union the spiritual or consciousness realizations seem to be buried at very deep levels. These realizations are likely to take some time to emerge in the official leadership of that society. But in due course they will emerge.

A long range way to address the problem of evolving social systems is continuous training in philosophy and modern psychology for people who are not currently in leadership. It seems that when people assume positions of power, they quit learning and their leadership takes on a new character. They adopt a consciousness and value system that is different from the personal values of the individuals in that system. In other words, a bureaucracy tends to operate on values that are different than the personal values of individuals. The bureaucratic values lag behind personal values and are self-perpetuating. Immersed in the bureaucratic system, people become captured. Regardless of country, this seems to happen. Furthermore, bureaucratic structures change very slowly, much more slowly than people change.

I think the breakthrough will come when new people with this new consciousness move into the various bureaucratic structures. It is a truism that any kind of government will work when people of goodwill are trying to make it work. Some forms are more highly evolved in that they recognize intrinsic human values and develop ways of synergizing these into a collective governmental form that works.

Our own form of government is an advanced, social experiment that has endured for two hundred years. At this point we are seeing some weaknesses in the way we operate in a dynamic world environment. We need to find new forms that go beyond and modernize our capitalistic democracy in order to go successfully into the future preserving democratic principles and individual freedom.

Clearly some aspects of socialism have merit, particularly in the underdeveloped countries where people lack the educational base and evolved social thinking to make democracy work. But the manner in which a society can peacefully evolve from primitive to more sophisticated social and political organizations has yet to emerge. I believe strongly that we will find answers when we learn to tap into our creative potential in more effective ways. Judging from the past, this will probably be done by fits and starts: two steps forward and one step backward.

The major crisis we have to avoid in the current decades is self-destruction on a global scale. I don't know how we are going to do that, except by doing more and better of what we're already doing. We can't change our institutions over night. We must, however, get people involved, to recognize the folly of standing poised with overwhelming weapons of destruction pointing at each other; sooner or later we will make the mistake of using them. However, until we can find ways to reduce the fear and paranoia of the world, we are not going to find an easy solution. I firmly believe that people who promote destructive forms of competitive adversary relationships are doing so from a position of fear and ignorance within themselves. They try to model in society what they are experiencing in their own lives and this is fear and anger at a deep subconscious level. When we see ourselves and understand the nature of the universe better, we put away fear.

The battle against ignorance has been going on for thousands of years. As we become more knowledgeable about the nature of the universe we live in and our place in it, this should reduce the fear we feel on a personal level. That will reflect into the national and international levels. Our challenge is to review our cultural history and traditions in light of ever-increasing new knowledge of what we are and what the universe is. We will see a lot of old ideas we need to discard and perhaps rediscover many that serve us very well such as honesty, integrity, truth, caring, and love. All of those are very positive values which I am sure we will address even more in the future. Things like adversary relationships, manipulation, and deceit are forms of inhuman behavior that will decrease when we begin to see ourselves correctly. Disregard for the planet, for our environmental dependency and for our own higher selves must fade into the past because such behavior will not serve us well in the years ahead. Individuals must realize this in greater numbers and indeed this seems to be happening all over the world as crisis grows. When it reaches a critical mass, things will change even faster. Right now, we are in a very risky transition period and I suppose things could go either way. Whatever we decide, however, it's our own human creation.

The ultimate moral philosophy is "love God and do what you want to." The presumption is that being truly in tune with the universe is all that is necessary. The appropriate moral system seems to emerge. Presumably one will do the right things and operate in a moral way. But until we're all tuned into that value system, we have to structure our morality, our behavior toward each other, and our social rules in a much more rigid way. As we grow more consciously aware it would seem to me that we will be undoing laws rather than adding more. We keep trying to legislate morality; impose it by fear of punishment. It never has worked and never will. Fear is anathema to love and morality.

We have to undertake the study of how human beings learn and are programmed. Our conscious thinking is only a fraction of what governs behavior. As we come to understand what the subconscious is, what the creative consciousness is, and how we learn, store, and retrieve information from our mind/brain, many of our concepts of dealing with each other will change. I am amazed at how little official research is done on consciousness. We need maps of inner reality, just as we have maps of outer reality. In terms of creating greater security, that is some of the major work we need to do in the next couple of decades.

Edward Teller

Dr. Teller, famous for having been instrumental in the development of the hydrogen bomb, works at Lawrence Livermore National Laboratories and the Hoover Institute. He lives with his wife in Stanford, California.

For me, it is not possible to separate the ideas of security and freedom. To enhance security and freedom requires unity and a common defense established among free nations, as well as applying technology to the arts of warfare to make ourselves sufficiently strong so that attack on the Free World will never appear rewarding to the Russians. We have become more and more refined in the technology of warfare, but this holds for Russia more than it holds for the Western world. If this trend continues, then it is completely unavoidable that we shall lose our freedom, except possibly at the cost of our lives. If we want to both be free and live for the foreseeable future, more technology in warfare on our side will be needed.

You ask where I think this arms race will end. It is a very peculiar state of mind where people want to know what is the end. Human conditions change from age to age, and more recently from generation to generation, and even from decade to decade. To try to predict under these conditions what will be the end of the arms race is not reasonable. There is now an unavoidable process in the world whereby the industrial or scientific revolution will embrace the globe. This will certainly happen in your lifetime if not in mine. People who already interact strongly will be drawn more closely together. For example, if people are to be fed, life in the oceans will have to be systematically exploited; the art of weather prediction, and subsequently of its modification, is coming closer very rapidly. These factors make it increasingly more difficult for each individual nation to make effective decisions; in the end that will become impossible. I firmly believe that eventually we will have to have some form of world order.

Now the classical way, or the usual way, would be to establish world order by conquest. The Russians have prepared for just this situation. They clearly proclaim that it is in the interest of all people to enjoy the blessings of Soviet leadership. The Kremlin is looking for accomplishing this—peacefully if possible and by force if necessary. They make no bones about the fact that this is what they plan.

In the Free World we are trying to do something very different. Or at least I should say we *could try* to do something very different. This is to arrive at some form of world order by agreement. If it should happen, this would be unprecedented, and therefore exceedingly difficult to accomplish. It would be a *miracle* if it were to succeed. In fact it is *above* a miracle, because not only is it difficult in itself but we do not even have a reasonable plan or a reasonable discussion going on about how to accomplish it. And if we are to accomplish it, we certainly will not be able to do so in a haphazard manner.

Meanwhile the Russians are not waiting for the peaceful reorganization of the world. They impose their rule wherever they can, wherever they find a vacuum of power—the Middle East, Africa, or even in the Caribbean. When those who want peace do not have enough power to assure protection to those who want to cooperate, it is impossible to create a world order by mutual consent. In my opinion such protection cannot be unilateral or done with a paternalistic attitude. It has to be done by common consent and cooperation. We must not impose our system on anyone. In all, this makes the goal of world order, which is obviously what I want, even more difficult to achieve.

If we add to this task the condition that we must shy away from the continuing refinement of weapons technology then we will make it unavoidable that the totalitarian system will spread over the face of the world in your lifetime. If we are to avoid that, a counterforce to the Soviets has to be established, not only to protect the United States but to protect freedom everywhere. If under the protection of sufficiently strong arms we have a goal to move toward a reasonable world order, we will have a second chance—a chance to make a next step. But how will the arms race end? I do not know. In each new situation there can only be a next step.

I only see a choice between either giving up and forgetting about freedom, or being prepared to defend it and to extend it to everyone who wants to participate in its mutual application and in its mutual defense. If this can happen in a manner that does not justify arms, that requires political conceptions which today as yet are not much used. If all these things—maintaining a strong military defense while moving toward a reasonable world order—should happen, then we may have a chance to develop new ways of resolving political conflicts. But to go further than that and predict what will happen beyond that point, this is too much to ask for. You know, to predict death under certain conditions is always easy; to predict life is much more difficult.

I used to argue for world order in more concrete terms than I'm doing now. I've found it increasingly difficult to define it or bring it down to a level of reality. I still believe that one should seek conditions under which the world order may evolve, but I do not find it particularly useful to define that world order ahead of the time when concrete steps can be taken toward its execution.

At this time I see most clearly a couple of needs. One is the need for the free democracies to maintain a common and technologically advanced defense on a much more imaginative level than we have it today. The second is realistic economic policy to enable the developing countries to develop. On this, I can give you one example which might put me in conflict with some of the antinuclear activists you have been interviewing. I am convinced we should build nuclear reactors to replace as much oil as possible and thereby make oil more available to the developing world. And that is the reason why I call the nuclear activists "elitists." They think only about their highly pampered way of life and manage to repress any thoughts about the more than three billion human beings who live outside the United States in poverty such as is nowhere found within the boundaries of this country.

Huddle: In trying to protect our freedoms in the United States, do you think it is possible that we may end up losing them?
Teller: It is possible but extremely unlikely. You know, I heard

the same argument before the Second World War: "We cannot resist Hitler because if we try to resist Hitler, it would have to be by armed force, and if we use armed force we will lose our freedom." We defeated Hitler and we retained our freedom. As you well know, and as everybody except the Communists, the totalitarians, realize, freedom is not something that will perpetuate itself. For freedom you have to work at every turn, in different ways according to the conditions. Whatever the external conditions, I think freedom can be defended. But the means by which freedom needs to be defended will vary according to conditions. And if you ask the question whether in defending freedom you may lose freedom, my answer is *of course*. Under *any* condition you may lose your freedom if you do not look out. I can give you a very interesting example. We had a free speech movement at our universities. They called themselves advocates of free speech. They talked of freedom. It became clear very rapidly, however, that they meant freedom for their *own* speech and no freedom for *anybody else's* speech. A movement for freedom which has no other stated purpose except freedom can very easily be the end of freedom if you are not careful. And no matter what the conditions are, you will have to be careful in order to protect freedom.

I see no way to improve relations between the United States and the Soviet Union at present. To have palatable relations with the Soviet Union we have to have more strength. As long as the Soviet Union considers us as essentially inferior there is no possibility of better relations. We need better relations within the Free World, with our allies, many of whom we have deserted. We have to postpone better relations with the Soviet Union until such a time in which they will have to respect us. Now this does not mean that I advocate *no* relations and no *good* relations with the Soviets. In some scientific fields we are collaborating. For instance, in the controlled use of nuclear fusion I saw a situation where collaboration was possible. I had to bring it about. It exists now. And I have no reason to regret that. However, as the life of the nations goes this is a very minor point; in this case free collaboration was tolerated in Russia precisely because it was, on the whole, of no great importance. Wherever we tried to establish better relations the Russians exploited it, distorting it into a change of the power balance and into a further endangering of freedom. So far we have an expansion of communism into Eastern Europe where freedom was simply repressed, and recently into Cuba and into

Africa. Now at this moment communism is expanding into Afghanistan. The limits to this expansion are not to be seen. As the power balance shifts, the opportunity for the Russians to introduce their system increases. We ought to learn the lesson that freedom is indivisible, and we should respect it in other places as we respect it at home.

Huddle: If you were the president and there were a nuclear attack by the Soviet Union on the United States, would you strike back?

Teller: The question is both horrible and incomplete. The purpose of military strength is to prevent such a situation from ever arising. The Russians will not attack us unless they are very certain that they can wipe us out. If we behave *reasonably,* nuclear attack will never happen. If we behave *unreasonably,* then we will have a choice to surrender or to die. And which we choose will be a matter of taste. I would choose dying. I can even tell you why—for two reasons: first, I was not born in this country, and I have a clearer conception than most Americans of what *lack* of freedom means; and the second, if you are determined to die rather than to lose your freedom, you are more apt in the end both to survive and to remain free. The more you are prepared with arms, the less the risk. I did not tell you what kind of arms, and I won't. We have neglected to refine our arms, and we have neglected civil defense—a most horrible neglect. We have neglected active defense against incoming missiles, and also our retaliatory power although we have neglected that less than the others. If the Russians attack and we have no other choice except to surrender or to shoot back, I would shoot back. But I would like to behave in such a reasonable manner that this choice never arises. And it is on account of thoughtless people who talk about disarmament in a crudely considered and illogical manner that this question can arise at all.

Huddle: You used the word "reasonable.". . .

Teller: A very dangerous word.

Huddle: I want to understand something here. Although what *you* may do may seem reasonable to *you,* or what *I* may do may seem reasonable to *me,* how can we be sure that the *Soviet Union* will perceive *our* actions as reasonable?

Teller: They don't. They have a completely different set of values which goes back to the age of Genghis Khan, who conquered Russia, who was ejected from Russia, but indeed erected a government as absolute as his own. The whole Russian political tradition is something in which the concepts of freedom don't exist. For them, freedom of the citizen is as unreasonable as it would be for us to say that if you let go of your microphone it would fall toward the ceiling. They haven't experienced freedom. They are convinced that when we talk about our kind of freedom we are hypocrites. Yes, *hypocrites!* They don't believe that such a kind of freedom can exist. After all, it is hard to imagine something you have not experienced in your surroundings or in your history. Furthermore if you are a Russian with opinions different from the Soviet official position, then you are set apart in a somewhat disagreeable manner. Under these conditions those Russians who consider reasonable what we in America consider reasonable, those people are put into asylums and are treated by rather radical methods for their mental disease of having some strange conceptions of freedom. If you are a Russian it is a very dangerous business to be "reasonable" in the Western sense.

You know, there are some puzzles, some questions that you'd better postpone until some other questions have been solved first. And if you don't take my advice, and you probably will not, you will find yourself in a very deep and horrible trap. Like the trap of agreeing with Russians about what is reasonable while shunting aside the "little problems" of their concentration camps, their mental asylums, and their treatment of Solzhenitsyn and Sakharov.

Huddle: Given that the Russians lost some twenty million people in World War II and that they perceive themselves surrounded by hostile regimes, it seems to me that they would be very defensive about protecting their way of life.

Teller: Solzhenitsyn is very sensitive about Russia's dreadful experience in the two world wars and yet he managed to maintain this "mental disease" which we call freedom. I do not think that if I were to be a Russian citizen I would have had his fortitude, his vision or his vitality. Probably, had I been born and grown up in Russia, I would never have reached the age of seventy-two. And I know of many friends in Russia who didn't. The hope of a thawing or changing in the attitude in the Soviet Union is premature.

Shigetoshi Iwamatsu

Dr. Iwamatsu is a survivor of the nuclear bombing of Nagasaki. Today he is a professor of sociology at Nagasaki University and lives in Nagasaki with his wife. This interview was conducted (in Japanese) in November 1980.

I was born in Nagasaki in 1928. Not long after, my family moved to Sasebo, a military port. Just about all our neighbors were military people. My father was in the lowest rank of the navy; by the time he was promoted to the next level he was discharged. Later as a civilian he took care of the port's engineering facilities. I was the oldest child, and have a sister and three brothers.

What I remember about my early childhood is that I liked chocolate a whole lot. I used to go into town, buy some chocolate with my little bit of money, and walk home, talking with my friends and eating chocolate. When the war started there was no more chocolate. For some reason that sticks in my mind!

In school a strong emphasis was placed on national celebrations, especially ones having to do with the Emperor. We spent a lot of time learning about the Emperor and his power. On certain days we didn't have regular classes but had to go to school anyway. There the principal would assemble us, prostrate himself before a small shrine, open the doors, and pull out a wrapped portrait of the Emperor. Next he pulled out a polonia wood box, which in Japanese tradition is how you store very precious objects. He placed both of these, one at a time, on the raised platform on which the teachers stood. Then he unwrapped the portrait and opened the wooden box, taking out a scroll on which was written the Emperor's statement about the purpose of education. This was all rolled up, tied with a cord, wrapped in a purple silk cloth (purple is the Emperor's color). After unwrapping the scroll with the greatest reverence, he read the Emperor's words aloud to us: "This is what I think: To rule the country is a very noble task. Our ancestors began our country a long time ago and achieved great virtue. . . ." And so on. The gist of the statement was that the first Emperor, who was descended from the Sun Goddess, had established the structure of morality and a teaching worthy of the greatest respect. "And so, young people, too, must obey these great teachings and devote yourselves to the Emperor. If there is a war, you must serve the Emperor by completely giving your life to the cause. For people to devote themselves to the Emperor by giving their lives is the same thing as for children in their homes to obey their parents." Thus the government applied the concept of the family to include the entire country. The Emperor was like the father and mother of the whole country. So the idea of giving your life for the Emperor was a very natural thing.

As a child that was the only way we were taught, so I had no idea that there could be another way of looking at things. I received this instruction from the time I was six until I was twelve. Even after that, when I entered junior high school, the principal went through the same ceremony. This kind of thing went on in schools all over Japan, from elementary school through the university. There are true stories about how school principals went inside burning school buildings to rescue the Emperor's picture and the scroll from the shrine. Someone who failed, who allowed the picture and scroll to burn, had to commit suicide. He either had to cut his throat or hang himself. Unless he did this he was not fulfilling his responsibility as principal. It wasn't even that they were *ordered* to do this; it was just that it was their own sense of duty according to what they knew were the expectations of society. You can see what an absolute kind of thing the Emperor system was. If you even criticized the Emperor, you would be put in prison.

We moved back to Nagasaki and I entered junior high school. Not long after I started high school a national law was passed ordering students to work in military-related factories. In my school we would study a few months and then work at a shipbuilding factory for forty days. Around the beginning of 1945 we started working in a factory which built mines. By then Japan was growing very weak. Almost the entire navy had been crushed. At the time, however, we didn't know that. From what we were told, we thought that Japan was still doing well in the war and would win. In fact we were convinced that we *had* to win. Since Japan was God's country, there was no possibility of losing. So we had to go to the factory and do our part, making the weapons. We were all doing our best for the Emperor.

We also had the idea that we could repel all foreigners from our country. For over two hundred years, from 1639 till the mid-1800s, Japan had been pretty much isolated from the West. When the Russians came in the 1800s, wanting to establish trade relations, we agreed to supply them with water and food at the port but refused to trade with them. Even though that period of isolation ended in the early 1850s with Commodore Perry's arrival, there was something of that same notion of "being able to keep out the foreigners." Some of the more progressive students wanted to open Japan up, but the upper classes were afraid the whole feudal structure would crumble if they opened the country to the "barbarians." Some people developed the idea of making the Emperor the center of Japan's government in order to assist the transition. They considered the foreigners "barbarians" and felt we had to discriminate and consider ourselves superior. So even though trade relations were set up with the West, we were still very separated from the rest of the world's people.

That feeling of being superior to foreigners continued until 1945, when we lost the war. It was a pretty natural concept: the Emperor had descended from God and the Japanese people had descended from the Emperor, so it seemed only reasonable to us that other people should be considered lower than the Japanese people. Our idea was that when all the other countries recognized where they stood in relation to Japan, it would be a peaceful world. There was no concept of democracy—none at all. Since war was for the noble Imperial cause, it was considered proper. That's also why the Japanese troops did some terrible things to the people of Korea, China, and Southeast Asia without thinking they were particularly bad things to do. Those things, incidentally, were not published in Japanese papers or reported on the news; we heard that "so many Chinese have been killed," but there were no details of *how* they had been killed. Not only were atrocities—cutting off people's heads, burning houses, killing women and children—not reported in the news, but the soldiers over there were ordered not to talk about such things, not even with their families. The military leaders told them that if word got out to the general public it would have a bad influence; they ordered the soldiers to keep it to themselves. Even after the soldiers returned from China we still didn't hear about such things. All we heard was "We're winning, we're winning." And of course we concluded that Japan was really strong because it was the Emperor's army.

Before the atomic bomb was dropped on Nagasaki there were a number of other bombings, but no very large damage had been inflicted. By this time we students were on two rotating shifts. For one week I'd sleep at night, get up early, go down to the factory, come home, and take a nap. The next week I worked at night, returning home in the morning and sleeping during the day. Because it was noisy I couldn't sleep. So my body would get very tired when I had the night shift. There wasn't much energy to think about anything; about the only enjoyable thing to do was to eat. Most people in Nagasaki had very little food, but we were staying with my mother's family, who were farmers, so we were very blessed by comparison. At the same time most amenities of daily life were scarce and my clothes were quite tattered. Life was pretty hard in a lot of ways. But of course we were fighting for the Emperor, and no matter how poor we were or how hard things became, there could be no talk of luxuries until we won the war. Everyone just tightened their belts.

This went on until August 9, 1945, the day the atomic bomb was dropped on Nagasaki. Early that day there was an air raid. Usually this meant the Americans would fly overhead, drop a few bombs, and it was over. This time when the planes flew overhead, nothing was dropped. I had a brief thought, "That's odd," but nothing more. It occurred to me that maybe they were checking things out. Anyway it was a really hot day, and after the plane headed toward the north and the air raid was over, we came out and started to work again. Not long after that there was a *brilliant* flash outside the window, and I wondered for an instant if a lightbulb had burst. But even as that thought crossed my mind, the building began to shake and the roof and walls collapsed. I covered my ears and fell to the ground. All this took place in just a few moments.

I had no idea what had happened. I thought a bomb must have fallen right on us and that we had been badly hit. Things were flying all over the place. I remember thinking, "Why didn't the people responsible for our air raid warning sound the siren?" All around there was utter chaos. Then almost immediately I thought, "Maybe the Americans are going to drop another bomb!" and I got up and fled. Most of my friends were covered in rubble. One friend called my name and we escaped together. I didn't see if any of our companions were killed, although my friend said there were. I guess I was the only one who wasn't hurt at all. My friend was fairly lightly wounded, but everyone else I could see was bleeding badly and had deep wounds.

We ran out the back of the factory. The whole thing was twisted and mangled; everything was in ruins. Whatever was flammable was burning, and smoke was pouring out. Almost immediately the structure collapsed and burst into flames. Behind the factory there had been a concrete wall; now it was completely gone. A house behind it was completely gone too. Further beyond were terraced rice paddies. Debris thrown up by the bomb covered the sun, turning the whole world around us a dark red. It was like you imagine hell to be. We clambered over the rubble, up into the terraced paddies. Nearby many other people, bleeding and tattered, were also running. Blood and dirt had all gotten mixed together, so they looked like bloody clay dolls, running away. I had a distinct feeling that maybe I was the only one who still looked normal. I learned later that our factory was only *eight-tenths of a mile* from the epicenter of the blast!

People who could still move fled up into the terraced fields, just trying to get away. I think we all had the same thought: it was dangerous to remain where we were, near the place the bomb had been dropped. On a flat area up on the hillside there was a house. People gathered around the well; they were thirsty and were drinking water, my schoolmate too. Even though I was thirsty, for some reason it didn't feel good to drink here, so I put up with my thirst; I was the only one who didn't drink. Later I learned that radioactive fallout had poisoned that water, but at the time I didn't know that. No one did.

Up in the mountain we hid in a tunnel for quite a while. Then we left and climbed higher into the hills, coming at length to a field where a doctor's house stood. A lot of atomic bomb victims had gathered there. Those who made it that far were relatively fortunate; more serious or fatally wounded ones were lying in the rubble down below. Since it was wartime, the doctor had practically no medical supplies, only some tincture of iodine, which he applied. He couldn't do much else for them. And of course there was also the radiation. I imagine that most of them died within a few months.

We left the doctor's house to return to Nagasaki. By the time we got back to the factory ruins soldiers had arrived and told us we weren't allowed inside. [Laughs] I had wanted to get my hat and schoolbag! So my friend and I wandered along the railroad tracks. All around fires were burning. We sat on the tracks for a while. I thought, "I guess Japan can't win the war anymore." Maybe a week earlier, during an air raid, it had first occurred to me that Japan might lose, but now I knew that there was no way we could win. But part of me still hadn't completely given up hope for Japan to win. Maybe it was just that in Nagasaki we couldn't help with the war effort anymore.

Many people were wandering around, bleeding, their clothes torn and covered with mud. Others lay dead and dying on the sides of the roads and by the rails. Those who were still able to call out were crying "Help! Save me! Won't someone please help? It hurts so!" Most of them were so badly wounded that they could no longer call out. Finally, a train came into Nagasaki and, as luck would have it, stopped very close to my friend and me. The people in charge said that only wounded people could board, and since I wasn't hurt I couldn't get on. But since my friend was wounded, we asked them if I couldn't please accompany him; and so they let me on. The car we were in was a baggage car with no seats. It was filled now with terribly wounded people who were wailing and crying. When I looked around me I had the impression of being with squealing, crying pigs on their way to be slaughtered. It was now evening as the train pulled slowly out from the city. When we stopped at the next station, people cried out desperately for water, but the station people wouldn't give them any and the train just continued until we reached the town of Isohaya, quite a way from Nagasaki. There, those who could still walk got off the train. When the women who had gathered to help saw all the people covered with blood, they began to cry very loudly. We all went to a military hospital across the way. The badly wounded ones stayed there; the lightly wounded were taken to a nearby elementary school by truck. My friend and I went with them. We ran into a teacher there from school, who told us that Nagasaki had been badly bombed, that America was really terrible, bestial. . . . He went on and on like that. Then my friend and I were put in a small room and told to sleep, so we stayed overnight there. In the morning, quite early, we headed back; we had begun to worry about our families. We got on a train and headed to a station near Nagasaki and walked from there. Around the station there were still many victims covered with blood and dirt. We returned to the area where our factory had stood; most of the fires were out, though here and there smoke still curled up from the smoldering rubble. We ran into my friend's father and sister, so we parted company.

I went back alone, passing through the center of the bomb blast area. [*Laughs*] I had no idea about radiation at that time, and I was simply heading back to where my family was. They were so relieved to see me; they thought that I was dead since I hadn't returned the night before.

When I first learned that Japan had lost the war it was a terrible shock. To tell you the truth, that was even a greater shock than the bomb itself. On August 15, at noon, the Emperor made an announcement on the radio. I had no idea that the announcement was going to tell us that the war was over and that we had lost. Actually I couldn't understand the radio very well that day, so I wasn't sure what he was saying. I understood something to the effect that Japan was losing badly, but I really thought he was saying something like "Keep doing your best until the very end." Later, walking along the street, some people told me that the Emperor had said we had lost the war, but when I heard that, I thought they were mistaken. For about three days my family and I didn't believe it, even though all those people were telling us that Japan had lost the war. It wasn't until it appeared, written clearly in the newspaper, that we finally had to acknowledge it as a fact. As I said, *that* was far more of a shock to me than the atomic bomb. After all, with the Emperor, Japan was *God's* country. There was *no way* we could lose, and yet . . . we had lost. It was so incredible and *so* sad. I immediately felt as if I wanted to commit suicide. I even had a razor blade and was thinking of cutting my throat. . . . But [*laughs*] my family was trying to gather its possessions together in order to flee, because we knew the American troops were going to come into Japan now, just as the Japanese troops had gone into China and Southeast Asia. So I had to help my family get packed and didn't have time to kill myself. But, you know, I really had it in my mind to kill myself. After all, that was the way we had been taught in school, that you gave your life for the Emperor . . . and that Japan *could not lose*. And so if Japan had lost, then everybody had to die because we had failed the Emperor. I really felt that, and I really believed I absolutely had to kill myself. I felt it was wrong to live.

Gradually, however, I began to think that my life was more important than the fact that I had failed the Emperor. That was a new feeling for me. You must realize that for eleven years I had been completely steeped in the ideology of the Emperor system; it was in me to the very core, in my heart. It took more than ten years for me to really change my thinking completely. There were so many little ways that the thinking of the Emperor system lingered; it took a long time to reflect on everything and unlearn all the things that had been so deeply instilled in me. To become utterly convinced that there must never be war again. To tell the truth, it was only after that ten-year period of reflection that I really began to come out in opposition to nuclear bombs. Up until then I struggled inside myself: Is war good or bad? I still had doubts. But then for the first time I came to the realization that the advent of nuclear weapons meant we must never have wars again. Actually it took fifteen or sixteen years after the end of the war before I entered the antinuclear movement. I watched the United States and the Soviet Union going back and forth, building up their nuclear weapons, testing . . . seeing where it was going. . . . Finally I joined the antinuclear movement.

On the one hand I wanted to be a scholar. Of course you don't make a lot of money, but I really was most interested in learning about the truth of things. So I decided to remain at the university and become a professor. I couldn't really even begin to think about any other kind of work. At first I had no idea at all of ever participating in the antinuclear movement, not a notion. But seeing the terrible and rapid development of nuclear weapons, and having had the experience of being in the nuclear bombing of Nagasaki, I put those two things together and thought about the future and the meaning of those things for our survival. I realized that I could no longer stay silent and ignore the desperate need for a social movement that would oppose nuclear weapons and war. Maybe, too, I felt that it was a miracle that I had not been hurt and that perhaps God had a purpose for me to fulfill in telling people what I had witnessed.

I joined the Nagasaki chapter of People Against Nuclear Weapons. No one else at the university was involved in that movement so I was asked to provide information to the group. I began to think actively about what kinds of things the Nagasaki chapter could do. First, we could oppose the actions of countries developing nuclear weapons; then we could join hands with other people in the world movement for peace; finally, we could let the world know, by newspaper and radio and so on, what our concerns were. When America exploded a bomb I wrote President Kennedy; when France exploded one I wrote their president; when the Soviet Union exploded one I wrote Khrushchev the same sort of letter. And gradually I collected letters from people around the world who were involved in the peace movement and wrote them letters. I corresponded for a number of years with Bertrand Russell. And I exchanged information with reporters and journalists, in Japan and elsewhere in the world, on the nuclear issue. In particular the *Toronto Daily News,* the *Washington Post,* and the *Los Angeles Times* printed several articles. From the readers of those articles I received a lot of letters, and because I really wanted them to understand why we opposed war and nuclear weapons so absolutely I responded to all of them.

As for what will make the whole world more secure, I think we can look at history and see that fighting has been a human activity since the beginning; yet with nuclear weapons, war would mean the death of all of us. Here in Japan we strongly oppose nuclear weapons because we have an idea of what they can do. In other parts of the world many people still do not realize what nuclear weapons mean, and so we feel it is urgent to tell them about the experiences of Hiroshima and Nagasaki. We have to tell them the terrible dangers of the nuclear arms race. We also must tell them that together we must find the roots of war and eliminate them. Those roots begin in the heart of each person and within the structure of society, where prejudice, greed, and aggression begin and are nurtured. We must change the situation which enables the strong to bully the weak, and we have to develop a real sense of equality among people, where people appreciate their differences.

The most fundamental place to implement these changes is in the educational process. For example, until I was seventeen I received my education under the Emperor system and the military system, and that deeply affected my entire life. The education of children, then, is most important. It is important to put the ideas we are talking about—of equality and appreciation of human differences—into the education of young children. We have to eliminate things that develop greed and aggression and all the other things which lead to war. We need cultural exchanges and interactions between people of different cultures so we can see that each country, each culture, and each person has its own expression which has value.

We also have to encourage all countries and all people to realize that weapons are not necessary, and to look for what contributions each country and each person can make to spreading that awareness. We have to teach that if we can get rid of the weapons, we will create a much better way of living in the world. This will of course take time, but even so we must do it, a little at a time. Most people now think that "since the other countries aren't doing it, this is too difficult and the road is too long," or "we don't see other people working on this." We must start somewhere and do what we can.

At this time we have a very narrow way of looking at things. We think of the earth as being very big, with lots of resources; but in reality within the universe we are a very tiny little point in space. We have to realize how limited our resources are on this planet. I used to think, looking at the oceans, that there was limitless water, and that air too was without limit. This notion is structured into our economic system; water and air were always available, and pretty much free. That was the major premise on which our whole economic system was based. We have slowly come to realize that there are limits to our resources, to the number of people the earth can sustain, and to the number of things we can produce. The basic premise on which our economic system is based is crumbling, so I can no longer believe in the economists. As quickly as possible we must develop new principles and new economics that fit our understanding of reality. One thing we must incorporate into that new set of principles is the value of people—not just of people living now, but also of people who will live in the future and inherit the earth. We must leave them adequate resources. So we should only use what we need;

after that we should leave all that we can for future generations. We need to think about what we are producing and why, to stop making things we don't need, and to fix things that are broken.

As for the Soviet Union, I know very little about them. And it bothers me that I know so little. Once, several years ago, flying back from Europe to Japan, I stopped over briefly in Moscow and, along with others on the plane, was led into a room and had to wait there for several hours. That was troublesome to me; it created a bad impression. Also, one hears that the people there cannot criticize things and that they will get put in jail if they do, and that the Soviets are responsible for a number of terrorist acts in the world. I think the Soviet political system has a lot of problems. Marx, I believe, did some very good thinking and had a pretty good understanding of many of the things wrong with the capitalist economic structure, but what has developed in the Soviet Union is quite far removed from what he wrote that Communist society could be. From what I understand, I think things in Russia are structured very badly.

In comparison I find that America is much freer. You can speak your mind pretty freely, and you are not limited in where you can travel. However, I was surprised to see how poorly developed the public transportation systems are; this is a society that is very unkind to people without cars. Maybe it doesn't bother Americans, but I find it very difficult to figure out the bus routes and schedules. In Japan, schedules are posted at each bus stop.

I think each country should be honest about its shortcomings and mistakes. For example, as a Japanese I feel very critical of the activities of Japanese soldiers during the Second World War. It is my responsibility not just to criticize the atrocities of other nations' soldiers but to recognize that these have been committed by *my* country too.

The United Nations can play an important leadership role in bringing about these changes, but perhaps more emphasis should be placed on developing the fundamental *spirit* of the United Nations. Now it is largely devoted to technical matters, and although those are very important, there is a fundamental sense of quality which needs to be developed more. Hopefully this will happen in the coming years.

Joanna Macy

Joanna Macy is probably best known for her workshops on "Despair and Empowerment" and for her research on the role of religion in social change. She lives with her husband in Washington, D.C., and travels widely, lecturing and conducting workshops. She is the author of Dharma and Development, Religion as Resource in the Sarvodaya Self-Help Movement, *and* Despair and Personal Power in the Nuclear Age. *This interview took place in the fall of 1981.*

I grew up in New York City and have two brothers, one older and one younger. I went to a French school and idn't study English until I went to college. To live a life that sn't on the edge always seemed boring to me, and I've always fascinated by the courage and service of people who da ien I was young, I met Albert Schweitzer and we corresp wanted to be a missionary like him when I grew up. In ajored in religion, which at that time meant Christian ultimate questions on the nature of reality and m me the most. But I felt that Christian answers cu neck all it was all very judgmental: God was bre n with the time. Also, I was supposed to disre dove my body, with the earth, and with fe but I into the French existentialists and even found the atheists boring. rch

I went to France on a Fulbrigh on on the French Communist party. I in theoretical Marxism, its passion bution. Intellectually there were ship of the proletariat is to come about inevitably, but we must work so hard for it) and I was very frightened by the denial of human conscience that I saw happening in Soviet-dominated Europe. I found that particularly frightening because my childhood heroes were people who dared to stand alone and speak the truth, like Joan of Arc or Father Damien. The Soviet system seemed to have little or no respect for this ultimate source of creativity and power in the inner reaches of the heart through which we are interconnected.

I worked in the State Department for a while and then there was a period of about twenty years in which I was having babies, traveling, living in Germany with my family, working with Hungarian Freedom Fighters at the time of the Budapest uprising, teaching, and doing work for the Urban League. I ghostwrote a book, taught French in Lagos and German in Delhi, published a newsletter in Tunis when I was in the Peace Corps, and was active the peace movement. It was a wonderful life, but it was hard me to take it seriously because it didn't seem to be neatly ized and integrated like other peoples' lives.

While in the Peace Corps in India I encountered Buddhism. I ting a volunteer who was helping a Tibetan community foothills of the Himalayas. Those people moved me very y are bearers of a very rich tradition in dance, music, d weaving. I just loved being around them because of nary way in which they were human. At first I didn't er them by asking them for teachings, but when I ere to leave India in another month I went to them. I efore receiving the teachings you first have to empty u can't come full of thirty or forty years' worth of it me on top of a mountain in a hermitage for a me scour my mind. After that I received a lot of ing and study. I realized I wanted to go further tually went to graduate school in comparative

oint in my life came in 1977 when I went to a event with two of my children and was over- ormation—everything from the horrors of nu- lubbing of baby seals. Afterward, on the train bridge, I had my first full realization that we lly do ourselves in and destroy all life with us.

For months thereafter I focused on trying to understand how you could live with that knowledge. You could go numb again or you could somehow learn to embrace despair, hold it like Persephone going down into hell. You have to go into those dark places, stare at the monster, and be able to hold it.

The following year, I chaired a seminar on planetary survival issues at Notre Dame University. Rather than read papers, we each talked about how we personally felt about survival. Before the scientists and humanists who attended read the papers they had prepared, I invited them to express their personal feelings about these matters. That led me to write an article, "How to Deal with Despair," for the June 1979 issue of *New Age*. The response to that article was extraordinary. Apparently it spoke to people's condition; their letters have been very moving, saying, "Thank you for helping me to see that I am not crazy." It gave them such strength to know that their anxiety and despair were a normal response born of their caring, of their recognition of our unity and interconnectedness as a species.

That article appeared just as I was leaving for Sri Lanka to study Sarvodaya, a Buddhistic grassroots development started in 1958 by A. T. Ariyaratne, a high school science teacher. Today it has reached over five thousand villages in Sri Lanka and touches the lives of several million people in the country. There are almost a hundred thousand full-time volunteers. Only six percent of them receive any kind of allowance.

It seems obvious that "development" of a country means not only economic but also spiritual and psychological development. "Sarvodaya" means "everybody wakes up," a term borrowed from Gandhi. "Waking up" is what the Buddha did under the Buddha tree. To be enlightened, we are called upon to wake up from all the fear and anger with which we burden ourselves when we believe ourselves to be separate egos. When we wake up, we realize our fundamental unity.

Waking up means living in the four abodes of the Buddha: loving kindness, compassion, the joy of others, and equanimity. These virtues are not abstract, but made very concrete; for example, "loving kindness" means that every time you speak, recognizing and acting on your desire that other beings be free from fear, greed, hatred, and sorrow, you deliberately phrase things in the kindest way possible. "Compassion" means to work with others to see that the village water tank is clean or that literacy classes are available. "Taking joy in the joy of others" is having town meetings and work projects in which everybody participates and contributes, including children and old people.

I traveled all over Sri Lanka to visit villages doing Shramadana, "Sharing Energy," which is the central organizing strategy of the movement. I was fascinated by the way it helped transform the village and the people. I feel they have developed something which is as applicable to the First World as it is to the Third World. The Shramadana lasts a specific period of time—a week, several weeks, or a series of weekends—during which you work on a project. At this time you share your food, make all your decisions in common, and work together with others giving your energy and time. The organizers are not asking villagers to change forever, but only to act in this cooperative way for a finite period in carrying out a specific task. These villages tend to be fragmented and divided by caste, class, educational, and economic boundaries—and particularly by partisan political ideology. But during the Shramadana all that feuding is forgotten. Everybody really does act like a brother and sister, working together and sharing. Because it is for a limited time, people are ready to join in. But again and again I heard people say, "Doing Shramadana changed my life."

More recently I have come to see the important connection between what I've learned in doing Despair and Empowerment Workshops and in studying the Sarvodaya movement. Many of us are numbed by our despair over the dangers posed by nuclear weapons, environmental deterioration, and by our sense of being unable to make any difference. We can transform our isolation and despair into a sense of interconnectedness and empowerment. Indeed I've found that in the despair workshops people spontaneously begin to use the metaphor of "waking up." They find it such a relief to be able to express their grief: "Here is a place I can cry about this and not have to cover it up." It is like shedding a falsehood you've been living with, the pretense that life is "business as usual."

For centuries people have believed that to be strong you must be feared, to be secure you must threaten the security of the other guy. In the age of nuclear weapons this is no longer a rational position. The more frightened our opponent, the more he feels driven into a corner and the shakier our future is. There is no "win–lose" anymore in the global situation. There may soon be thirty-five nuclear powers. That makes archaic the old assumptions of winning by force or by trickery. Either we all make it or nobody does. Nuclear weapons fundamentally change the very notion of what constitutes power and security as well as the nature of power relationships. We have to wake up to this fact: power just doesn't work from the top down anymore. It is something we can work to change at any level. It has to do with what we say to our kids when they go out and play in the Little Leagues. It has to do with our attitudes toward every aspect of life. Everybody has something different to contribute to this transformation.

We have given our leaders power and we can withdraw it. It tries my faith in the electoral system to see how unresponsive it is to the will of the people. To turn the situation around, we need to try everything from economic pressures and boycotts to massive expressions of popular will through delegations and demonstrations and people-to-people work. We can't wait for the government. It's too unresponsive, too limited, and too archaic an instrument to entrust with our future. People-to-people exchanges can, for instance, help bring Soviets and Americans together.

We also need to make major changes in our educational system if we are to make the transition from war to peace, not just for schoolchildren and college students, but also for the general population. Studies show that many of us are basically illiterate about international conditions and about our relations with other countries. There is gross ignorance of the fact that the Third World, which constitutes four-fifths of humanity, is in an angry and deprived condition. Even if we manage to avoid a nuclear exchange with the Soviet Union, we will be like an armed fortress surrounded by a sea of suffering. That's not very attractive; it breeds a quality of life that is primitive and ugly. We must each ask ourselves honestly how we can help change this.

I see the real revolution as a conceptual one. It starts with our self-concept going beyond that of the immediate ego to embrace other beings, other species, and our planet itself. This is inherently the most rewarding thing we can do. A separate ego is a prison in which we feel our loneliness, our frustration, and the terrible pain of separation. We gain a tremendous reward in extending the notion of what and who we are. Anything that helps us move in that direction is positive, such as games and activities in which nobody is put down or beaten, in which everybody enjoys teamwork.

Through proliferating cooperative interactions, we are in the process of evolving a more effective planetary mode of self-regulation. Up until now we have been regulating ourselves through separate nation-states that essentially see themselves as competing. Development of a world government will require a more fundamental transformation than simply building a new structure on top of national politics. Recently scientists have been recognizing that the planetary biosphere is itself a living system. That system can become self-conscious as we shift our sense of identity to the whole social collective. Issues of food, population, governance, and the environment cannot be resolved until we begin to act as if we are one organism. This does not mean we will relinquish our individuality and succumb to "group-think"; in fact the opposite is true. As a system integrates, its parts become more differentiated in order to handle specific functions.

I see us in a race between our suicidal instincts—the bomb, our depredations on the biosphere, the oppression of our fellow humans—and the development of collective intelligence. That is the real transformation, and actually this is nothing new. Saints and religious teachers of all times have said, "It's love or hell." Learn to love each other or live in hell. Somehow we never took it seriously. Maybe we thought it was just true for the saints. Sometimes when I'm feeling that life is horrible or unfair, I can hear the voices saying, "Did you think we were kidding all this time? You gotta learn to love each other or it's curtains." And that's really the message. There's nothing new about this except that we have to learn it together fast.

One thing that's important to understand is that transformation is not incremental. The pace at which we see things changing now is no indication of what is to come, no more than cells in the caterpillar tell you about the butterfly that's going to come forth. A river freezes all at once, not bit by bit.

Harvey Cox

Harvey Cox, a theologian at the Harvard Divinity School, Cambridge, Massachusetts, has been an active critic of U.S. nuclear weapons policy. We conducted this interview in October 1980.

I was born and grew up in southeastern Pennsylvania, coming from a long line of Quakers on the one side and Rhineland pietists on the other. On some level I was raised with deep suspicions about war and the military. These feelings were less an explicit than a natural part of what I grew up with. It came to the surface when I entered the Merchant Marine at age seventeen, right after the Second World War. As I arrived in Europe, the first place we landed was the Polish port of Gdansk, where the recent movement of workers started. I was young and impressionable, and it was a very rude and radical introduction to what war can do to a country: it was shelled and bombed and burned and then shelled again. In addition to enormous *physical* damages, however, I was as much impressed by the *human* damages: hunger, children reduced to beggars, and women to prostitutes. At seventeen I was pretty idealistic and it was tough for me to take.

I came back and went to the university after that, and ever since I have been involved in various kinds of peace and justice activities. I taught for a while at Oberlin College, and then at Temple University in Philadelphia, where I got very involved in the black churches. I've had a continuing interest and involvement with black churches over the years. I lived during most of the 1960s in Roxbury, which is a black district here in Boston, except for 1962 and 1963, when I lived in Berlin working for the World

Council of Churches. I was rather active at that point in something called the Christian Peace Conference, which is an Eastern European–based, church-related peace movement.

My involvement has intensified over the last couple of years, in part because of a visit to Hiroshima in the summer of 1978. I hand't expected it to be quite as overwhelming as it was. First, I went to the site almost entirely with Japanese people. I had the powerful feeling that *nothing will ever be the same*. Also an overwhelming recognition that this is not something that one can fully grasp intellectually or conceptually. I had something like a temporary paralysis while I was standing at the site. It was a little embarrassing; it was time to go, the bus was ready, and I couldn't move. I was still absorbing what I had known all along: in Hiroshima we had entered a new and critical phase of the whole history of our species and possibly of our planet.

So the last two years I've been working an awful lot against nuclear weapons. I do a lot of speaking. Almost every other weekend I go somewhere. Around here I helped found the Traprock Peace Action Center in Deerfield, western Massachusetts. We hit on a new strategy for antinuclear activism: putting the issue on the ballot. Three senatorial districts in western Massachusetts included on their ballots a referendum calling on the state legislature to petition the Congress to initiate negotiating with the Soviet Union for an immediate bilateral moratorium on further nuclear weapons production or deployment. Although the big problem is getting people to know that it's on there and what it means, it legitimates the issue in political circles. There it is, it's on the ballot, and it has to be discussed; arguments for it have to be advanced.

Among my other activities I'm one of the directors of the Center for Defense and Disarmament Studies, a nuclear disarmament think tank and information center. I also have helped to teach an undergraduate course here called "Issues in Peace, Justice, and Social Change." It's a team-taught course. Then I give a course here at the divinity school called "Theology, Peace, and Justice." We also are organizing a major conference on nuclear disarmament here next spring [1981], sponsored by the divinity school.

When we talk about national security, we need a fundamental redefinition of what makes people secure. We've come to a point where the more nuclear weapons you have, the less secure you are. People have the impression that any kind of a nuclear disarmament move is going to increase their insecurity. We must give people a sense of what an alternative security system would be. The starting point is to get rid of the notion that the more insecure we can make the Russians or somebody else, the more secure we are. That's the fundamental flawed premise of the whole thing. We also need to change the thinking patterns that have been introduced in the history of weaponry and warfare up until now; these suggest that the more weapons you had, the more secure you were. That idea may have had some validity in the era of tanks, Maginot lines, and antiaircraft guns, but it's not true with nuclear weapons. People have not distinguished these things.

I think the best strategy is the referendum concept, because it makes everybody think about the issue. You can begin to make the case to people that a nuclear weapons moratorium would contribute to their security, not only by halting weapons production but also by diverting money into human-needs programs. I think the biggest obstacle to all of this is the widespread sense of fatalism. I was in Utah, which is a politically conservative state. People are very patriotic, very strongly influenced by the history of the Mormon church, which still occupies a rather powerful position in Utah. The decision of the air force to put the MX system there has really caused an enormous crisis, a spiritual crisis, on the part of the people. The government is proposing to take a piece of land which is about the size of Massachusetts, Vermont, and New Hampshire put together. The idea is to build forty-six hundred stations or silos. A little train carrying two hundred missiles travels around to each one, and alternately places missiles in the stations, which are placed far enough apart so that a direct hit would presumably not destroy another one. The air force calls it the "Big Sponge" theory; these stations would absorb any first strike. You can imagine how people who live there feel about being designated as "the sponge."

It's hard to find anyone in Utah who's for it. All the polls indicate that around eighty to eighty-five percent of the people are either against it or strongly against it. But I talked with both Senators Garn and Hatch, with people in state government, with people in the Mormon and other churches, and with the newspapers, and there's the sense that *there's nothing you can do*. Even though everyone is against it, "They're going to put it here anyway, and there's not one thing you can do about it." The senators are for it because they reluctantly believe it is necessary. Both of them said, "Look, I'm not for this, but national security requires it, and it would be a cheap shot to say, 'Well, put it somewhere else rather than in our state.' That would be real unpatriotic."

I felt that my job out there was to help counter all of this fatalism. One thing I did was to encourage a vigil in downtown Salt Lake, so the people actually got out, moved their legs and arms, and did something. At least they could get up, go out once a day, stand in downtown Salt Lake City, and say "This is a bad idea." Once they do that they don't feel completely powerless.

We now have a Sunday vigil in Cambridge organized by most of the churches. Every Sunday, right after the church hour, people from the various churches stand for one hour in silence in the Cambridge Common. As it turns out we're standing right on the spot where Washington assumed command of the Continental Army. Since buses of tourists come by, we're going to prepare a pamphlet that says "This is where the first war started, and this is where it ends, because we can't have any more."

As for the Russians, they sort of come and go, depending on who needs them at the moment. I think there are two distinct things about the Russians. One is who they *really* are and what they *really* want, which is a problem that has to be dealt with. We can't ignore the real world. The other is the use of the Russian image of threat for various purposes, which I think is what predominates now in official policy. We have to understand the relationship between the United States and the Soviet Union on a very long historical scale, recognizing the differences between our two societies. Since about 1947 or 1948, or even earlier, we've primarily thought of the relationship strictly in the military sense, which has greatly inhibited our ability to think about the relationship of our two peoples with their own national histories and their own problems. It's important to start right out questioning the idea that what we're dealing with in the Soviet Union is a completely new and absolutely unprecedented kind of enemy, one that's implacably driven to world conquest and that cannot be dealt with rationally. I know too much history not to recognize that the same was said about the Turks, the Muslims, the Huns, and the Yellow Horde. It's just too familiar, and I think any intelligent person recognizes this as "satanizing" of the other side.

Western religious institutions and thinking have contributed to the demonizing of the Russians. They have made "godless communism" appear to be the worst possible thing that's ever happened. By depicting Russian society as dangerously expansionist because it is atheistic, religious organizations have contributed to a lack of realism about the Soviet Union. Since people are restless and angry and bewildered about lots of things happening in their own lives here in this country, it is always tempting and useful to have somebody to blame that on. One of the presidential candidates or one of their advisors said that if it weren't for the Russians there wouldn't be any tensions anywhere in the world today. That is completely absurd. But it is nice to be able to simplify it and have a "devil." We know that from the history of religion and theology. If you personify evil, you can locate it in a person or country and then "do something" about it. So that's all too familiar.

One of the most urgent things is to get a moratorium on nuclear weapons. If we don't get one within the next few years, the chances of avoiding a nuclear war will get smaller and smaller. We have very good possibilities in the next few years of reversing this part of the arms race. One of the reasons is that both countries share a common interest in preventing the proliferation of nuclear weapons to other countries. We also share economic and other kinds of common interests. We also must get rid of the idea that it's possible to fight and win a nuclear war, which I think has crept into the military thinking of both countries. Our peoples have a mutual interest in survival.

I would like to see a very large program on the part of the churches of person-to-person, institution-to-institution visits and exchanges, at all levels, between the Soviet Union and the United States. This is not happening. In fact it's been cut back, in part due to the Soviet intervention in Afghanistan. Such exchanges really must be encouraged. I'd like to see both the Protestants and the Catholics do something along that line. It could be done if enough people get into it. It isn't everything but it would help a lot. At the same time we shouldn't delude ourselves; we do have some real problems. I'm not in favor of unilateral disarmament, although sometimes I think that would be better than no disarmament at all. But I don't think that's the thing that you go around advocating. I don't think it's wise or prudent to do that.

I very much agree with Paul Warnke that one of the principal factors— probably the main one—determining the behavior of the Soviet Union is *our* behavior. Although other internal and external things influence them, what *we* do is very, very important. Yet there are a lot of people who don't believe that; they think that no matter what we do, it doesn't make any difference. A careful look at the history of the relationship between the two countries has been one of responding to each other. In college I majored in modern European history and did my senior work on modern Russian history, so I do know a little about the pattern of U.S.–Soviet relations and have tried to keep up with that field. I'm just stunned by the ignorance, the stereotypical and ahistorical thinking about the U.S.–USSR that so many people fall into.

I think we're also at a point in history where basing our economy on profit and accumulation is no longer possible because of the ecological menace that we now face. The capitalist form of organizing our economic life is slated to disappear. I just don't think it's going to work anymore. The problem is that we have no viable alternative model. For a long time some people thought the Soviet model would be that great alternative, but it turns out not to be a good model at all. I'm very much in favor of some of the things that are going on in southern Europe. In Spain, Portugal, and Italy we're first going to see a form of democratic Western postcapitalist social organization emerge. They have strong, well-organized parties of the Left, even in Portugal where they recently lost some ground, and also a tradition of democratic and liberal ways of organizing their Communist and Socialist parties. In Spain and in Italy they are very close to being in power. We need a model for reorganizing our society—I call it "social-democratic"; I mean, all these terms get eroded, but I'm referring to a way which isn't based on accumulation, expansion, profit, or commodity mentality. We need a new model desperately, and we need it in a part of the world where things that we value as democratic freedoms—assembly, press, and all the rest—are also valued and would be not only preserved but enhanced by that kind of change.

We also need a clearer understanding of the reality of the

Soviet Union. It is interesting to see how the reputations of countries rise and fall in the United States. I distinctly remember twenty years ago when the Chinese were considered *much* worse than the Russians. Recently surveys show that most Americans feel rather friendly toward the Chinese; it is very popular now to go on a tour of China. But the Russians have gone down in popularity. I think much of this is manipulated. Yet what is lost sight of in discussions about the Soviet Union is that things don't look very good from their point of view at this time. They have the Chinese on one side, resurgent Islam on the south, and labor upheavals in Poland. The Russians cannot possibly feel very secure. If I were living there and were in charge in some way, it would be pretty high on my agenda to come to some kind of agreement with the United States so that we could begin to deal with these other problems.

For the United States, I think what's happening is the end of the "empire." I don't think most Americans have ever been all that into empire. We're at the end of a phase which started right after World War I, when the United States became a world power and international corporate enterprise based in the United States began to be a competitor on the world scene. What's happening is the reemergence of a much more normal situation: the United States again becomes one among many nations, although still very strong in many ways. Seeing the whole world as a market and resource for our own corporate enterprise will not be seen as identical with the interests of ordinary Americans. That's the transition we have to make; we're moving slowly, by fits and starts.

We have to see this process historically. Until a couple of hundred years ago the idea of nation-states having this kind of "destiny thing" to play out in history was a relatively new idea. Even in the Western world people thought of themselves as Tuscans or Milanese or Bretons. The emergence of the national state as the vehicle of destiny or political organization of the world seems not to have worked out very well. I'm not talking about a one-world government; I'm talking much more about people really getting into their neighborhoods and regions. One small example of this might illustrate my point. Three or four years ago I went to the graduation exercise in my child's small junior high school here in Cambridge. Although one-third of the fifteen graduates were from other countries, the theme of the exercise was heavily patriotic: "Oh, to be an American!" They all recited this poem of what it means to be an American. There were Gambian, Japanese, and Chilean children, stumbling with their foreign accents, talking about what it means to be an American. The kids were cynical about the whole thing. Later I talked to the principal. I didn't complain. I said, "That was really a wonderful graduation; the kids worked very hard on it. You know, it is a little strange that kids who come from other countries go through this. Next year why don't you have a graduation based on the history and all the wonderful qualities we have right here in the neighborhood?" She said, "Oh, that's really wonderful." Instead of a complaint I made a positive suggestion. They took that up and the next year the graduation was completely different, without any chauvinistic quality at all. I didn't have a son or daughter graduating but I went anyway. The kids liked it much better.

We have to offer people something to take the place of this displaced loyalty and sense of identification with a national state. I find the notion that *the state is something you die for* is one of the really most dangerous heresies which has developed over the last couple of hundred years.

I believe people are capable of change. My writings and work strongly oppose theories of fatalism or determinism, whether it's karma or kismet or behaviorism. I object to anything that erodes the concept that human beings are responsible for what they do, individually and corporately. It's just a philosophical or spiritual choice you make, because the evidence is always mixed every day. Sometimes it's good, sometimes it's bad. But I remain hopeful. And even though most people in, say, Utah are gloomy about the possibility of stopping the MX, some people aren't. And those people are making a difference. When the discouraged people see other people who think something can be done, that communicates something very important to them.*

---

*Since this interview Utah did stop the MX.

B. F. Skinner

World-renowned as a pioneer and expert in the field of behavioral psychology, B. F. Skinner continues to conduct highly sophisticated research in his laboratory at Harvard University. Among his best-known books are Walden Two *and* Beyond Freedom and Dignity.

Huddle: From your perspective as a behavioral psychologist, what do you think we need to do to make America and the world more secure?

Skinner: We need to understand human behavior much better than we do. The reason we are not doing so well is that we are explaining our behavior in terms of things which are supposed to go on inside every person; my research and philosophy on behavior redirects the inquiry to the environment. People do what they do because of their genetic endowment, because of what has happened to them in the past, and because of what the situation is right now. The general practice in talking about human behavior is to look at the human organism as something where the behavior—traits of character and so on—comes from inside, from something out of reach. In our work, my colleagues and I point to something which can be gotten at and changed. We select those few facts which demonstrate relations between a person's current behavior and his past experiences.

Huddle: Before relating this more directly to national security, can you give one or two examples of how this works on the personal level?

Skinner: One example is sibling rivalry. Let's say a small boy is punished severely by his father for beating up his brother. As a result of that punishment, he may not act openly with respect to his brother or to other people. Some would say, "He feels *anx-*

ious about it," or something of that sort. Many years later, he goes to a psychiatrist because he is uneasy in the presence of other people; he doesn't adjust properly. A Freudian would say, "Well, he has anxiety and that's what's *causing* the trouble." Where does the anxiety come from? From sibling rivalry. I just drop the anxiety right out. I would say that punishment as a child is altering his behavior in similar situations today.

For someone behaving ineffectively because of punishment, one thing you can do is to get the behavior to come out and then not punish it. For example, a psychoanalyst usually establishes himself as a nonpunitive audience: "Go ahead and call people names. I won't care." Or, "Talk about sex: it doesn't matter to me," and so on. If you don't punish people for the things they have been punished for, this stuff slowly begins to come out.

I've often used the example of *confidence:* "What America needs is more confidence." Several years ago, *Newsweek* published an article by a man who'd been involved in the Tennessee Valley project back in the 1930s. He pointed out that the TVA farms weren't productive and that people were very poor, unemployed and discouraged. Then they put in dams which gave them electricity for the first time, enabling them to produce fertilizer. Farm productivity improved and everyone was fine. What made the difference? Confidence? No, the *dam* made the difference. You say, people now feel more confident because they can do things they couldn't do before without the fertilizer and electricity. The dam and electricity and fertilizer produced confidence, and confidence produced better farms.

It isn't that America needs more confidence. *America needs better conditions so people can do things and get results.* The *environment* has to be changed, not states of mind. Changing the environment will change "states of mind."

Huddle: Could you please give some examples of how you think the environment should be changed to create greater confidence or security in people?

Skinner: Right down the line, you can find all manner of things which could be changed to improve conditions. To take one example, few Americans like their jobs. Jobs are not designed to reinforce productive behavior. A good deal is being done elsewhere in the world, but not in the United States, to make mass production lines and so forth more reinforcing of productivity. A weekly wage is actually not a reward at all; it establishes a standard of living from which you can be cut off. You are not working on Monday morning for the money you'll receive on Friday; you are working to avoid being fired and losing that money. It tends to be a kind of slavery. The old form of slavery was, "You work or else I'll beat you," and this kind is, "You work or else I'll fire you." It's still the "or else" motive and that leads to a lot of trouble.

We also don't do very much to make leisure-time activities rewarding. We watch the tube or bet in a lottery or get drunk or take drugs. These are not behaviors which contribute to the security, well-being, or development of our country, yet when the work week is cut down to forty, thirty-five, or thirty hours, those are the behaviors which people engage in.

Welfare is another very bad thing in our national environment. People needing help should be helped. But if you are capable of doing work, then you should work because if you get something for nothing you are destroyed. Instead of passing out welfare checks to people who could work, we could somehow create useful jobs that they can do. But it is hard to do that in America because some people start saying, "That's creeping socialism," or something like that.

Huddle: How would you suggest we implement some of these changes, based on the insights you've gotten from your research?

Skinner: It isn't easy to make changes, because people feel threatened by change. Things can be done much better than they are now being done, but it does require that someone do them—and there is always a threat that the person in power will misuse that power. That was the point of my book, *Beyond Freedom and Dignity*. If you make a scientific analysis of behavior, you seem to be depriving the individual of his contribution to that behavior, so you are robbing him of credit due to him. People are very glad to pass on the credit for behaving badly (the juvenile delinquent is from a bad environment and "that's why he's got into trouble"), but when you, say, become a famous baseball pitcher, you want credit for that. We want credit for the good things and want to get out of responsibility for the bad. I simply want to eliminate the whole notion of responsibility and find out *under what conditions people work well.* I want people to do what they do because they receive positive consequences which makes them want to continue. I would like to see a complete absence of coercion, aversive controls or threats of any kind. This can be done anywhere, in any field.

Huddle: Could you give some specific examples of how this would look?

Skinner: Take schools, for an example. You can certainly get children to enjoy their work, to learn well, and to get along with each other without any violence. If you want them to learn more in school, you can't work on their attention span, their creativity or their intelligence. What you *can* do is to create very good conditions for learning. It's shocking to realize what could be done in American schools today that's not being done. I've just received a two hundred page booklet put out by the National Science Foundation on the condition of education in America and how to improve it. But there's not a thing in there about how to improve *teaching*. It's all about the curriculum and the materials teachers can use, but not *how* to use them. They believe that you can't teach teachers how to teach. Well, you *can* teach that kind of thing very well with program instruction. In 1960, in Roanoke, Virginia, an eighth grade class went through all of ninth grade algebra in half a year using simple teaching machines and programs. Their grades were as good as those of the ninth grade and, a year later, their retention was better. You would think that if the American educational establishment really wanted students to learn algebra well they would have said, "Well, this is *great*! We'll do it this way." But that experience has been largely forgotten.

We need to utilize our understanding of the conditions under which organisms learn well. The main thing is to break material into small parts and give the student assistance so that he or she is almost always right. This is, in itself, highly motivating. You don't need to give them *reasons* for paying attention; they just do. When I visited that school in Roanoke, nobody looked up when I walked into the room. They were all working with the machines. Alan Calvin, the man who designed the program, said to me, "Keep your eye on the students," and he jumped up and came down on the floor with a great bang. Not a single student looked up; they were studying, working really hard.

Huddle: How could these principles be used in improving our national security attitudes and policies?

Skinner: I am in no position to counsel the State Department on what it should be doing in areas of foreign policy. But I could at least offer them a concept of human behavior against which to check what they do and what they propose to do and to observe the consequences. For example, what effect do they want their action to have on the behavior of the other party? My hope is that the studies of my colleagues will lead to a clearer recognition of what human behavior really is, and that this will trickle down to the people who deal with human beings and make them more effective. At present, we are using completely out-of-date and unscientific concepts of human behavior, so we're in trouble. It's quite understandable that we're in trouble.

Huddle: How do you think we can stop and reverse the arms race with the Soviet Union?

Skinner: I am in no position to comment on the specifics. I don't know the facts and anything I would say to someone who did know the facts would sound quite silly, I'm sure. I believe, however, there is something to be said for a program proposed by Charles Osgood. He suggested that you pull back a little and then wait and see if the enemy pulls back. If he does, then you pull back a little farther, and so on. You can test out this kind of thing quite easily. Obviously, the only problem is that the Soviet Union is scared to death and we're scared to death; under such conditions, we don't act very wisely. Instead, we all build up our defenses and increase our military budgets. I really don't want to make pronouncements on this, because I don't know the facts. All I can say is that I don't like what I understand to be the current theory of human behavior which underlies political, economic, social and educational action. That theory doesn't work.

It has often been charged that the methodologies implied by my research are manipulative, but I don't think that is a real issue. You don't push a button and get anybody to behave in one prescribed fashion. You arrange *consequences* of behavior: It is very effective, but then, you don't want educational or social systems to be *in*effective. The trouble is that if you make a system very effective, people will fear it and of course they should. We fear complete power, and quite justly. But if we want teachers to teach well, if we want families to rear children well, if we want a husband and wife to get along with each other, we must turn to behavioral practices that are more effective than the current ones.

Huddle: What do you consider the primary national and global security problems? How can they be handled?

Skinner: The number one problem in the world is overbreeding. How do you go about changing that? If we can believe what we read, China offers an interesting example. They have set up some very strict sanctions. A one-child family is fine; two children are acceptable, and you get your wages cut if you have three children. So, instead of giving them more money for an extra child, they give them less. That provides an economic incentive to control the number of children in the family. They will then pay more attention to contraception, abortion, and so on. That's one way to go about it.

Exhaustion of resources is another key threat. One proposed remedy was to add a fifty-cent tax on each gallon of gasoline. If gasoline were two dollars a gallon, we'd have more carpools, smaller cars, and so on. The money would come back to motorists in better goods. The consequence of higher prices would be contingent upon the behavior one wanted to support. There are many other practices that would have similar effect.

During a war you can appeal to the future and the security of the country. For example, during World War II signs were posted which said, "Is this trip necessary?" That would be a good thing to do now. Thousands of people working in Boston drive fifteen or twenty miles a day from Lexington or Concord. When I walk to work in the morning, around eight-thirty, I play a little game. There is a crossing with a big flow of incoming traffic, and as I wait I count the cars with only one person in them until I get to a car with two or more and then I start counting from zero again. Usually, I get eight or nine cars in a row with only one person in each. The other day, I got twenty-three in a row; a couple of days ago, I broke that record and got thirty-three. Each car is probably traveling fifteen or twenty miles—a terrible waste of gas.

Huddle: What is your positive vision of the future? Of how to manage our nation?

Skinner: Ideally a government should be run by these people who best understand human behavior. They would be able to create conditions in which people work productively, get along with each other, learn things readily and so on. Who should those people be? They shouldn't be people who gain personal advantage; the criteria for selecting them should be *whether the whole culture gains or not.* In the long run, a set of governmental practices can be considered good if the government survives by solving its problems.

Howard Kurtz

Howard Kurtz is the director and co-founder, with his deceased wife Harriet, of War Control Planners, Inc., a not-for-profit corporation. His organization distributes reports and publishes articles promoting research and development of global war-prevention systems, all-nation security and development systems, and global "compassionate power" systems. He lives in Washington, D.C. This interview took place in the summer of 1981.

My wife Harriet and I worked together for more than thirty years trying to understand the roots of war and how to achieve a lasting peace. Back in 1946 I was working in an upper management position with American Overseas Airlines, when the Civil Aeronautics Board granted us the certificate for the New York to Moscow route. I was made responsible for the long-range planning of the operation and was sent back to school for two years of graduate study at Columbia University's Russian Institute. As it turned out the actual operation didn't start for another twenty years, but if it had, Harriet and I and our babies would have all moved to Moscow.

　　Then in 1947 I got a call from my boss, telling me to drop out of school temporarily and leave early the next morning for Washington, D.C., where my passport and visa had been arranged secretly. I learned I was to leave the next day for Moscow. We had chartered three planes to carry the American delegation and the press from Washington to Moscow for the foreign ministers conference. I had to go ten days in advance to set up navigation, diplomatic, and other arrangements for the first U.S. civil airplanes to go behind the Iron Curtain. About nine weeks later we brought the planes in again to take everyone back to the U.S., but I stayed another five days with some newspaper correspondents to watch the 1947 May Day parade. During that parade I saw Soviet-made jet fighters, in quantity, flying over Moscow. As a lieutenant colonel just out of the air force, this had real meaning to me. I returned to Columbia, telling Harriet that I had just seen World War III already beginning to form, and that not only our two babies but many, many young people from all over the world would be sucked up into the next firestorm because the atomic bomb had changed the picture of war so completely.

This got us started on our study of the endless cycles of war and peace which have plagued humanity since the beginning of recorded history. The biggest disillusion came when we realized that none of the scholars seemed to have the slightest idea of what lay behind this endless repetition of war. As we got deeper into the subject, Harriet recognized that behind walls of secrecy, cloaked in the respectable rhetoric of "national security," small groups of men in the White House and in the Kremlin were in hostile confrontation, brandishing power capable of destroying humankind. She saw that it was a power of really mythological proportions, power which most religions claimed that God alone could command. She concluded that the tiny power elites of neither the Kremlin nor the White House were informed enough or noble enough in their goals to command appropriately such God-sized powers. This drove her through six years of study at Union Theological Seminary in New York. She went half-time, commuting seventy miles a day, taking care of a couple of babies and a house, and somehow managing to make many of her own clothes as well. Her search took her into all the world's religions, looking for what sorts of purposes or goals were noble enough for this God-sized power which was now in our human hands. In 1964 she was ordained in a unique ceremony in which Catholic, Jewish, Ethical Culture, Unitarian, and many different Protestant clergy participated. She was ordained in the belief that people of all faiths, and those professing no faith, were created in the image of God and therefore possessed creative powers which would enable us to create new history rather than remain chained to dead history of past wars and suffering.

In the meantime from 1932 to 1954 I worked in key airline

management positions in American Airlines, American Overseas Airlines, and Pan American World Airways. From 1954 to 1965 I was a senior associate with Handy Associates, a management consulting firm. In 1965, however, I lost my job with them because two of their clients, who were defense contractors, put pressure on the firm to let me go. So since 1966 I have devoted full time and energy to War Control Planners, working together with Harriet until her death from cancer in 1977.

Early on Harriet and I made an important decision. We agreed that we wouldn't go forward with another step in our conceptualization process until, coming from our very different perspectives and backgrounds, we could both agree on that step. Sometimes the gulf between us seemed unbridgeable, but there was so much love between us that we really tried to understand what each other was saying. Perhaps one reason we were able to work together so completely was that even though I am about as far outside of institutional religion as you can get, my work as a pilot and airlines manager had taught me the Golden Rule in action: no pilot can find safety and progress for his passengers and himself except under the universal disciplines of air traffic control. So Harriet and I both realized that in the present age of ultimate danger, anything less than the Golden Rule among nations is unsafe: Do unto others as you would have them do unto you.

Way back in 1969 the editor of *Esquire* read hundreds of pages of our published articles and condensed everything into one paragraph: "Since right now international arms agreements are improbable because no country trusts any other country, the purchase plan would first provide something trustworthy and then ask the military powers to begin trusting it."

What Harriet and I have been proposing is a transition process to help us break out of this terrible cycle of war–peace–war–peace. Before you can ask the present military people to trust this transition process you have to say, "Continue with your defense. Meanwhile let's start a fantastic experiment to design and build, over ten or twenty years, an international system capable of providing military protection to patriotic people of all countries. Only *after* this system has been built and shown to work, only then will we ask nations to begin to support it." People we've talked with at top levels of the United Nations, even in the disarmament section, agree with this. It's a great deception to play on the public's yearning for disarmament. There's not going to be anything like disarmament until after a very long period of developing and testing world systems which prove that it will be safe for nations to begin cutting back on their arms. It's not safe today and it won't be safe until someone does this other creative thing. Now *who* is going to be able to do this? Decisions like this are made by chief executives; only someone like a president of the United States can fight a war with one hand and start something vast and experimental like this with the other.

To draw a parallel from history, when the airlines first found that their piston-engine airplanes were becoming obsolete they didn't immediately get rid of them and say, "What are we going to do now?" For another ten or fifteen years they continued to operate piston-engine planes, and even bought, maintained, and sold new ones while they had another group of people develop and test jet transports until they were ready. You can't simply leap from here to there; you need a transition period.

At present I am aware of almost nobody working on developing this sort of massive project, with possibly one exception. In May 1978 the president of France, addressing the General Assembly of the United Nations, proposed that there be set up a United Nations earth-sensing satellite system of a military character to monitor peacekeeping and arms-control agreements among the nations. This was a conceptual breakthrough. The Americans at the General Assembly opposed it right away and abstained from voting. The General Assembly passed a resolution instructing the secretary-general to create a committee of experts to explore the idea's feasibility. He did so several months later, selecting a committee of experts from twelve different nations, excluding the United States and the USSR. They made a year-long feasibility study and their preliminary report says that it's feasible but that there are a great many problems. Which is all obvious. The United States, meantime, is way behind in this sort of conceptualizing. We have one group of people, with white hats, called NASA, working on space exploration, and another set of people, with black hats, working on military space programs for war purposes. Nowhere in the whole American mythology or government is there anybody working on military satellites for the purpose of peacekeeping.

There are so many groups of fine, dedicated people concerned about the issue of world peace. For thirty years Harriet

and I followed the work of the World Federalists, the world
hunger people, the environmentalists, and so on. We saw they
were all wonderfully dedicated to sustaining life, and yet year
after year we saw the world situation getting worse, not better.
Even with these fine people and conferences and all these books,
there's something gone wrong. And so our search was for a
missing strategic factor somewhere.

Looking at history, we found a parallel in the problem of
smallpox, which has killed more human beings than all the wars
of history combined. In recent times a decision was made to do
two different things: first, to continue to fight each new case of
smallpox the best we can, and second, to set up a completely
independent group of people to analyze the whole phenomenon of
smallpox. This group would ask the question "Is there some one
factor which might be touched and controlled to bring smallpox
to an end?" That factor turned out to be a particular virus. Until it
was controlled the disease continued to plague humanity. Today,
thanks to this realization, there isn't a single case of smallpox in
the world. That this has been achieved is a total miracle, as big as
any written in the Bible.

Think what we might accomplish if we tried this same sort
of approach to solve the phenomenon of war–peace–war–peace!
There's a beautiful two-volume classic called *The Study of War*
written by Dr. Quincy Wright, a leading scholar in this field. In
chapter after chapter he enumerates all the different causes of war
all back through history. When Harriet and I got into this search,
we felt discouraged: if there are that many different causes of war,
it's hopeless. Nothing is ever going to change. But as we got
deeper and deeper into our theoretical analysis of the phenomenon, we found one very tangible factor, and until it is brought
under control, nothing else can matter. When you name that factor, it seems so obvious as to be unbelievable: enemy military
power.

The process goes something like this. After each war there
are generally two major powers which emerge that are within
range of each other. They each have an entity like our National
Security Council whose job it is to look around and say, "What
may be the source of our next trouble?" Then they focus attention
on each other, and the whole buildup process starts again. It is a
purely gut-level response to fear of the enemy. Each side does the

"reasonable" thing—it builds up its defenses to protect itself. This is morally supported by the leaders and everybody, who all say, "Oh, yes, that makes us feel safer." The problem is that each side's actions have intensified the anxiety of the people on the other side. And they view the "enemy" with alarm: "Look what that guy has done; we must do something." So they do the instinctive thing, which is to increase their *own* defense weapons. And all their moral and political leaders and the public itself says, "Ah, good, I support you. That makes me feel better inside." But once again that intensifies the anxiety on the other side. This action–reaction behavior goes back and forth slowly, without particular form or timing over ten, twenty, forty, sometimes one hundred years, with each side doing the justifiable, moral thing, each building its own propaganda on the same imagery. The buildup doesn't happen overnight in such a way that you can see the pattern. In fact most people have forgotten the last set of major moves by the time the next escalation comes along. But both sides soon begin to play on all of the religious, economic, and other forces that can be used to mold or manipulate public opinion to show that "Look out! Mobilize! If they come over here, they're going to threaten your religion, your economic system, and your very life." And so on. Both sides do this, all on a "morally justifiable basis."

So the one factor we could isolate was military capability, whether it's a spear or a gun or a guy on horseback or the cavalry or an airplane or an atomic bomb. Today, however, we have an entirely new situation: the range of potential fighting has expanded until the whole world is involved in it, and if this war–peace–war epidemic breaks out into a new cycle of war, we can effectively destroy civilization as we know it. We have such a little bit of time left, but nobody in the White House or in the Pentagon seems the least bit interested in the subject. They are like firemen in the firehouse polishing their engines and getting ready to go out and fight the next fire. They're apparently not interested in tackling the critical and urgent problem of how you build a fireproof house. That requires an entirely different kind of mentality than either Henry Kissinger or Brzezinski has. And yet all the capabilities are here to mobilize American creativity to help the world develop the system we need to build a war-proof world. The problem is that the guys who control what flows into the mind of a president are all from the same financial institutions that are profiting from the current way of doing things. But the reality is that if we continue in this same direction, we are going to kill ourselves. Yet nobody in power dares say that, because the public will lose faith in the system. The whole pyramid of political power in a nation is very much like a religious institution in that it is built on faith. For example, if I give you a hundred-dollar bill, it seems very real to you; but the reality is that the paper on which that bill is printed is worth about 1.8 cents. All the rest of it is faith. Everything we do in the government here in Washington faces about that same ratio of reality to faith. Building on this system of faith, you get into dogma: "Believe this because I tell you it's true, not because you discover it to be true." And just about everything comes right down again to being controlled at the top by a little elite group around a Vatican, a Kremlin, or a White House. They determine what we're going to do and then they hire the public relations people to sell it to the public.

I was first introduced to studying unconscious anxieties of people back in the 1930s when I was in charge of all the stewardesses and food service on American Airlines. When people are trapped in a closed system over which they have no control, they feel a strong sense of anxiety at a subconscious level. If something happens to the plane, this unconscious anxiety wells up and influences the behavior of every passenger on that airplane, no matter what church he goes to or what political views he has. These gut-level anxiety reactions are common to all human beings when they're trapped and feel endangered. And it's only on that gut-level that you can begin to explain what is going on.

Let's go a bit into the geographic story of war. Some two hundred years ago as the thirteen colonies banded together, they perceived threats in the form of Frenchmen coming down through Montreal, Spaniards through Florida, others through Mexico, and Indians in many areas. Each of these groups presented a threat to this "tribe" called the United States. In this situation of threat there is one predictable pattern all through history: defensive expansion. When the tribe is threatened, it expands. The United States expanded, gradually killing off the French and the Spaniards, expanding to get more of a sense of security. We did the same thing to the Indians even though they got to a point where they were not really a threat—just a potential threat; so we just walked in and mowed them down until finally we dominated this entire continent. We didn't have to totally dominate Canada or Mexico because they were so weak and were no longer perceived as a threat. We then entered a period of our history where this unconscious anxiety could relax and the conscious mind could begin to have more control over our behavior. We could see rationally that we were protected by great oceans and by the Arctic Circle, and that we had no enemies. This was the unconscious object of all the U.S.: to expand defensively with our military until we got a feeling of security.

Now let's look at Russia. Right after World War II, as soon as they could, Russia did the natural thing from its standpoint of trying to protect itself. It started expanding its influence and gaining control over neighboring countries. This went on until the United States stopped them with our one unique advantage: we had nuclear bombs—and missiles to deliver them just about anyplace in the world. At that point, around 1947 or so, we said, "Stop, or we'll zap you. We will contain you and you will not expand any longer." One thing you learn in studying the phenomenon of anxiety in an airplane is that the mere fact that you say "You're locked in and can't get out" doesn't cause the anxiety to go away. In fact it causes the anxiety to become even more intense. And in the last generation the United States has really done nothing to eliminate the sense of threat felt by the Soviet people.

Pearl Harbor showed us what happens to a nation when it is threatened. The American people reacted to Pearl Harbor by turning themselves over, as one person, to an authoritarian leader, Roosevelt, saying, "Take us, lead us; we will do anything you say. Take our boys and send them into the trenches. Whatever is necessary. We will suffer, we will do without gasoline and rubber." Threat or attack is a unifying thing. Every move that the United States has made in the last generation—increasing the number of our bombers and missiles stationed around them, increasing our threats—has intensified the threat perceived by the Soviet people, which has caused them to turn themselves even more firmly over to their authoritarian leaders: "Take us, we will suffer and sacrifice and die—whatever you need to do to defend our motherland." There's nothing weak about Soviet *patriotism,* and we have given it impetus at every stage.

During the Cuban missile crisis, while the Russians were putting missiles in Cuba, we pulled this containment number once more. We humiliated them in front of the whole world by making them turn around and go back—which we were able to do because we still had this threat of superior atomic weapons. At that time they said publicly—almost everything they do is public knowledge and can be found in speeches or books, in Marxism and Leninism— "You will never again do this to us." And they went back and, in addition to their basic military strategy, they took on a supplemental strategy: to build enough missiles and nuclear bombs to cancel out the American advantage in that area. They have done this fairly effectively. The arms race itself, the missile race and the hydrogen bomb race, has reached the point where if either side launches a war the other will respond so quickly that, literally, world civilization will be ruptured. It is to the Soviet advantage to continually focus American attention on the nuclear armaments race because that's the only weapon the United States has had that is holding back what the Soviet leaders believe destiny has in mind for Russian power. We have had only one thing to stop them: our nuclear capability. Their one job was to counter that and to focus our attention wholly on nuclear war, which they have done quite successfully. Most of our peace groups have been sucked into this thing and into just talking about the horrors of nuclear war since it is so awful that we must do anything to do away with nuclear war. And the Soviets for a whole generation have been saying, "Let's negotiate about cutting down on missiles and cutting down on nuclear bombs; let's have disarmament talks." They will not talk at all about disarming their basic strategic forces, conventional ground forces, to use in taking over more Afghanistans and places like that. They will not discuss them at all. The way our American leaders think is very short term, holding their elections and changing their policies every few years, whereas the Soviet leaders are working on hundred-year strategies. There's no real rush; they can go as slowly as they need to, seeking to dominate the Eurasian continent and then the world. Wherever there is trouble they move in there because they truly believe that all these people really resent being owned or controlled by the United States and that sooner or later they'll try to break away.

A purely defensive response by the United States is not going to solve the fundamental problem. Instead we must begin to mobilize the creativity and resources of America, in all the different areas, to begin providing the research, development, and experimental operation of future global operational systems which will be able to guard the national security of all one hundred fifty-seven countries and release their energies for the production of food, clothing, housing, and other things their people need to ensure their real security.

This system of global security would function in the same way that air traffic control guards the safety and the progress of all airplanes. About fifty years ago the airlines came to the realization that something needed to be done about the situation of a large number of airplanes flying blind in the clouds, because without a system of orderly control they are all in great danger of colliding with each other. There is no future for an industry which cannot guarantee the safety of the passengers—which at that point they couldn't. Thus there was no future for the entire airlines industry until somebody came up with the concept that is now called "air traffic control," a superior discipline combined with the enforcement of laws completely committed to the safety and progress of every airplane in that cloud, large and small. The golden rule of "Do unto others as you would have them do unto you" is the only rule that works among pilots in an air traffic control system—for unless I'm totally committed to your safety and your passengers' safety, I will never find safety for myself.

And so it is among nations. To set up this sort of global security system is the challenge for the next generation to pioneer. And for the first time in history there are global technologies and global systems available for us to begin this experimental process of testing, finding and eliminating the weaknesses, and building a system which can be properly tested by the nations of the world. There will be no peace until something is developed which convinces the people of the world that it is safe to disarm; at present it's not the least bit safe, and they're not going to do it.

What we're talking about is a third option: instead of either the U.S. or the USSR dominating all these global satellite systems and other systems, there must be an international control. Instead of either of us gaining control over all the resources of Africa or Latin America and other areas, which the people there oppose, there has to be a system created which enables people in every single nation, large and small, to provide their own food, clothing, housing, and health for themselves and their children and grandchildren.

One of the problems we must solve is that of communicating these ideas to the public. About ten years ago the editor of one of the major national magazines told Harriet and me that he could envision a picture on the front of his magazine which would sell lots of copies, a vivid picture of war with dead bodies scattered all over the place. He said, "The problem is that I cannot think of a picture that I could put on the cover of a news magazine which would sell the thing and tell the story you're talking about. How can you create a visually gripping picture of a device through which people are managing to keep from killing themselves? You're talking about the Golden Rule among nations militarily, and throughout history no journalist has been able to communicate vividly the story of the Golden Rule."

Sometimes it is quite discouraging to see things getting so bad in the world and to feel so frustrated at being unable to reach the one person, the president, who would be able to make the kind of decision to launch the kind of program which we need to break this cycle of war–peace–war–peace. But I suppose the thing that keeps me going is the driving conviction that we can and must do this thing. And along the way a number of important people have urged us to continue. One of these was Robert Muller [see pp. 251–55], who ten or twelve years ago told Harriet and me, "You must continue the conceptual work you are involved in. Thirty years ago when I went to work for the United Nations, I didn't believe it would ever function properly; but I wanted it to, and so I gave my life to serve it, even though I didn't really believe it could happen. Today I know from my position here that human skills and knowledge in every profession have expanded enormously, across national boundaries and around the world. Today for the first time in history human beings have the capability to build an operational organization to protect all nations. *The problem is that nobody is ordering it to be done.* But for the first time in history we do have the capability, so you cannot cease your work no matter how broke you become, how deep you go into debt. Because for the first time in history humankind has these powers and we are waiting for somebody to provide the necessary leadership."

Buckminster Fuller

At eighty-five years of age Buckminster Fuller was considered by many to be one of the creative geniuses of our times. Inventor of the geodesic dome, Fuller developed a powerful scientifically based view of the underlying principles of the universe and the geometry of thinking. His recent book, Critical Path, *is a penetrating analysis of the historical trends and powerful forces of politics, economics, and ideas which have led us to our current situation, as well as a blueprint for going on to the next stage of human evolution. Dr. Fuller was well known for the World Games, an annual series of simulations for solving world problems. This interview took place in the spring of 1981.*

Humanity is moving ever deeper into a crisis which has no precedent. It is a crisis brought about by evolution being intent on completely integrating differently colored, differently cultured, and intercommunicating humanity, and by evolution being intent on making integrated humanity able to live sustainedly at a higher standard of living for all than has ever been experienced by any. Probably ninety-nine percent of humanity does not know that we have the option to make it; *we do.* It can only be accomplished, however, through a *Design Science Revolution.*

Those in supreme power, politically and economically, aren't yet convinced that our Planet Earth has anywhere nearly enough life support for all humanity. They assume it has to be *either you or me,* that there is not enough for both. Those with financial advantage reason that selfishness is necessary and fortify themselves even further. That's why the annual military expenditures of the USSR, representing socialism, and the U.S., representing private enterprise, have averaged over two hundred billion dollars. This makes a total, so far, of six trillion, four hundred billion dollars spent to develop the ability to kill the most people at the greatest distance in the shortest amount of time.

Neither the great political or financial powers of the world nor the population in general realize that the engineering-chemical-electronic revolution now makes it possible to produce many more technical devices with ever less material. We can now take care of everybody at a higher standard of living than anybody has ever known. It does not have to be "you or me," so selfishness is unnecessary and war is obsolete. This has never been done before. Only twelve years ago technology reached the point where this could be done. Since then it has made it ever so much easier to do. With the highest aerodynamic engineering facilities in the world redirected from weapons-delivery production, all humanity now has the option of becoming enduringly successful. The capability has come through the continual dealing with the invisible world of electronics, of alloys. But you *have* to know what you are doing.

Weighing only fifty-five pounds, with a wing span of a hundred ninety-six feet, the human-powered Gossamer Albatross was able to fly across the English Channel because the structure of the materials with which it was built had enormous tensile strength, sixty times stronger per unit of weight than the strongest structural material available to Leonardo da Vinci. This enabled us to finally realize the design of his human-powered flying machine. To give another example, a quarter-ton communications satellite is now outperforming the message carrying capacity and transmission fidelity of one hundred seventy-five thousand tons of transatlantic copper cables. Human-powered pedal airplanes and communications satellites are only two of the hundreds of thousands of examples of technologies which can now accomplish much greater performance with much less material. You *have* to understand this. This is *not* a visible revolution and it is not political. You're dealing with the invisible world of technology.

Politics is absolutely hopeless. That's why everything has gone wrong. You have ninety-nine percent of the people thinking "politics," and hollering and yelling. And that won't get you anywhere. Hollering and yelling won't get you across the English Channel. It won't reach from continent to continent; you need electronics for that, and you have to know what you're doing. Evolution has been at work doing all these things so it is now possible. Nobody has consciously been doing it. The universe is a lot bigger than you and me. We didn't invent it. If you take all the machinery in the world and dump it in the ocean, within months more than half of all humanity will die and within another six months they'd almost all be gone; if you took all the politicians in the world, put them in a rocket, and sent them to the moon, everyone would get along fine.

There is more recognition now that things are changing, but not because there is a political move to do it. It is simply a result of the information being there. Our survival won't depend on political or economic systems. It's going to depend on the courage of the individual to speak the truth, and to speak it lovingly and not destructively. It's saying what you really know and feel is the truth—not just the truth per se, but all the truth, the integrated truth, in all the directions. Our greatest vulnerability lies in the amount of misinformation and misconditioning of humanity. I've found the education systems are full of it. You have to examine each word and ask yourself, "Is that the right word for that?"— the integrity and the courage of the individual to speak his own truth and not to go along with the crowd, yet not making others seem ignorant. After a while, if enough human beings are doing it, then everybody will start going in the right direction.

Most of this change is going on invisibly, technologically. Take all of the people working with computers; we don't really know all that's going on. By the time something gets into the newspaper it's often ten years old. There's something *enormous* going on. It means housecleaning all around the world, getting rid of the misinformation that we're all exposed to. It's a daring attitude that you can't let up. You have to do it twenty-four hours a day. For example, almost all of academic science is today operating on mathematical systems the universe is not using. Academic science doesn't know what it's talking about. At times when I've been invited to speak to important scientific bodies I've asked any scientist in that audience who does not see the sun going down in the evening to please raise his or her hand: no one did. I said, "For five hundred years we've known that the sun is not going to go down. There's no such thing as 'down.' The sun's not doing anything—the earth obscures the sun." But what are we doing about this kind of error? Nothing.

We're not just dealing in willingness. *Humanity has to qualify to survive.* You have to have some confidence. We're all born naked, with no external equipment and no experience. Therefore we're terribly ignorant. We're hungry and thirsty, driven to find food by trial and error. So *we're designed to live by trial and error.* Don't worry about making mistakes. Study your mistakes; admit them, study them, and be terribly excited about them too. If this isn't true, what *is* true?

As for weapons, there's no sense in weapons. But we have had to learn by making mistakes. If I thought "There's not enough to go around," then I have to say, "How come God put me here?" and "Maybe I have to do away with you because there's not enough to go around." My responsibility is to me. I could under those circumstances rationalize my response selfishly. I could say, "My family is a little more devout than other families; my family is better than yours." That's the kind of rationalization we've been doing. I find that through a proper understanding of the basic principles of the universe there is *ample* to go around. I know this is so, not intuitively but by actual knowledge of the figures involved. So we come back to the question of the weapons: weapons are invalid if there is enough life support to go around. Since there is ample to go around, I don't talk about weapons because they are obsolete tools.

Now as far as using atomic energy, I say, "Nature has already given us all we need—which is the sun." Big government, big business, and big religion don't see any way to put a meter between the people and the sun, so they don't do anything serious about developing solar energy. These organizations are predicated on people not having enough to go around and they have to have big money to survive. All ideas coming from these organizations are based on the idea of humanity's being a failure and that everyone should be in pain and suffering. Their business is "Come down and get a turkey dinner from us and we'll get you into heaven." There *is* enough to go around, but the church is not interested in that because it would put them out of business. The Roman Catholic church, for example, is terribly rich. They have an enormous amount of real estate all around the world. Big businesses too are at the top of the heap. They'd all have to go out of business if humanity is a success. There's a built-in resistance to letting humanity be a success. Each one claims that *their* system is the best one for coping with inadequacy. We have to make them *all* obsolete. We need to find within technology that there is something we can do which is capable of taking care of *everybody*, and to demonstrate that this is so. That's what geodesic domes are about and that's what my whole life has been about.

Eldon Byrd

Eldon Byrd is a research scientist with the Naval Surface Weapons Research Center. He lives in suburban Maryland. This interview was conducted in the summer of 1982.

Since the only experience I have is my own, I really can just tell you the things that make *me* insecure. Then going from the personal to the global level, I can speculate that insecurity probably comes from several sources. One is lack of knowledge: if I don't know something about situations that affect me, I feel insecure about them. So perhaps the first thing we need is a better information-transfer system so that we all have a better idea of what's going on. I don't mean information of the sort we get now, because the way it is currently presented we are not encouraged to evaluate anything. We are given information to form *opinions;* we need information and training so that we can *evaluate* things. You turn on the news at night and you hear ads by political candidates; they tell you what's good about their guy and what's bad about the other guy and you form an opinion. You don't really know if the guy is telling the truth or not. There's an emphasis on commercialization; one candidate is portrayed as good or bad; the same is done with countries. You have to pick sides. If we had facts presented, that would help.

Another thing that makes me feel insecure is when I think somebody might hurt me. I suspect countries are no different. I thing the Soviet Union has been reacting for a long time, and has been pretty paranoid about what they think we might be up to; and we are reacting the same toward them. So the idea of a threat, real or imagined, causes insecurity. People and countries walk around shaking sticks or rattling chains, pretending to be strong, whereas in reality they're afraid someone might attack them: "Don't mess with me because I'm so strong."

One thing we can do is to take some very sensitive issues and get people to laugh about them. Once people can laugh, they don't take things so seriously. "All in the Family" did this with the situation of blacks in America; here was Archie Bunker, a guy portrayed as a bigot and a funny slob. So if we can get people to laugh about their really deep insecurity that we really *might* destroy each other and that the world as we know it really *might* end pretty soon, perhaps this would raise their consciousness so they see how absolutely crazy—really insane—the current situation is. Then perhaps they will be empowered to do something about it.

We need to start looking for a common cause to support, for example, the sort of thing Jim Hickman and Michael Murphy are doing, running an exchange program with a few key people in the U.S. and the USSR. This goes back to my point on information. If you don't want someone to be paranoid about you, then you have to let them know who you are and what you're doing. If you can convince him you're not a threat, he will treat you differently. This is clearly difficult, because if you truly believe another country will do you harm, you don't want to believe that it might *not* happen; you're afraid of being conned.

In the eye of the beholder, real or imagined threats are all the same because people don't *know* if it's real or not. If there is no real threat, then they have to make one up to fit their worldview. People seem to act on the basis of asking "Who poses a threat to me?" whether it's a country or an individual. Survival instinct may have something to do with it; anyway, somewhere along the line this is what we're taught. We need somehow to get people to come from dealing with each other from a position of mutual respect, rather than "who's a friend and who's an enemy." Possibly we can do the sort of thing we did with racial relations, introducing these concepts in schools gradually. Eventually kids got used to opening a textbook and seeing pictures of black kids and white kids playing together happily, and it became an accepted and natural thing through the educational process. In dealing with the arms race, the problem is that there are all sorts of contradictory information; sorting this out creates a time lag, and we may not have time because our current situation is so precarious. We need to find ways to provide students *and* citizens with accurate information, teach them how to evaluate it, and get them interested in cooperative rather than competitive ventures. Distrust is spawned by competition; cooperation seems to breed trust. Our current economic and social systems run, and I must say, rather poorly, on competition. If the government wants to buy something, for example, they have to get competitive bids. They end up with a corporation's promise to turn out an item at the lowest possible cost, but they may get a poor-quality product. Competition seems good because it drives prices down, but cooperative ventures need not cause prices to rise if the spirit is to cooperate and not to gouge your customer. The fundamental attitude we each bring to our interactions is really the key. Right now the idea of cooperation, which isn't really new, seems to be a change from the current way. People have to be ready to accept change. Right now we mainly need to remind people that there is another way of doing things.

We used to think there were only two ways of changing things: through evolution, which is long and slow, and through revolution, which may simply replace what you've got with something else that doesn't work. What I'm talking about here is a third way: transformation. Anything we look at and can see isn't working very well is a prime candidate for being transformed, given a whole new form. The root of transforming a society comes with transforming the individuals. In observing my own process of transforming myself, I got to a point where I simply became aware that nothing else worked for me. At some point I realized that making little piecemeal alterations wasn't getting me anywhere; a whole new order seemed necessary, a new context or framework for looking at everything. In the case of national or global security, we currently have the context that it is a "you or me" world: in order for me to survive, the hell with you. This holds true both on an individual and on a national basis. Technologically we are at a point where it is no longer necessary to have that attitude. One thing being discovered is that *both* parties can win when they have the attitude of helping each other rather than "What can *I* do to survive, even if it's at my neighbor's expense?"

Until recently the strategy game was "Look at the big stick I've got, and don't mess with me or I'll whomp you." The other guy would look at that and say, "I need to get a bigger stick, otherwise he won't be afraid of me and might hit me." If you keep playing this game, it comes to a point where you can't find a bigger stick, so you go out and find something different from a stick—like a knife. And things become increasingly unstable and dangerous because now the other side is motivated to do the same thing. If people and countries can start being honest with each other, we wouldn't have to come from a position of "Gee, I wonder what he's up to? I'd better get a knife. . . ."

How do you get people to be honest with each other? One thing that might help is to mount some sort of program to educate people to the fact that we're all human beings and that if we don't start cooperating with each other we really might actually do ourselves in. We also need to educate ourselves about our potential and about our positive alternatives. In some ways we've gotten very rational about the bomb: we "know" that it kills large numbers of people, and for most people it stops there. As long as the people of the world feel insecure and have the technology to do something drastic, we are all in danger. We need to figure out how to generate within people the conviction that we're all in the same boat and we can't point a finger at a single group of people or some country and say, "Your end of the boat is sinking!" We need to encourage the kind of thinking that observes when and how institutions and methods aren't working, and then knows how to do something about it. I don't think it's possible simply to patch things up; I think a whole new way will have to emerge. Almost every major country is essentially bankrupt; technically we're going to have to scrap the current world economy and start over again from some common base, perhaps with resources a little more evenly distributed, before it will work.

Another source of insecurity is poverty, which is very widespread. At the same time people with more possessions feel insecure about losing what they possess. But eventually, if things keep going the way they are, they will have no choice. Faced with the high probability they'll lose it all through revolution or war, they might be willing to give up part of their wealth voluntarily. Otherwise our current trend is toward anarchy, the collapsing of major institutions and perhaps of the entire world economy. It may be a trite example, but if enough people don't pay taxes there won't be enough jails to put them in, or money to support them in jail. It doesn't take long for any country to collapse if enough people stop paying taxes. There are different ways of not paying taxes: one is refusing to pay because you've lost faith in the government; another is not having the money because you don't have any work. If enough people are out of work because there's no demand for what they do—and sometimes there's no demand because other people can't afford to pay them—the country's economic base would be eroded quite quickly. Just look at our housing and automobile industries. If these two major industrial sectors collapse, it could conceivably trigger the collapse of our entire national economy. That's *certainly* a way to make a country insecure: to have people lose faith in the government and the economy because it no longer provides them with jobs.

A transformed society would be one that works; right now very little works. How do you get people, an entire nation, the entire world, to recognize that there is another, more effective way of handling their problems? If I can convince you and one other person, and you both go out and convince two more people apiece, and they do the same the next day in thirty days the whole world is convinced. If you look at the numbers it really would work. The problem is that you can't get to everybody: not everyone *can* understand; not everyone *wants* to understand because they have a short-term vested interest in *not* having it work for everybody. In the long run they too would benefit, but they don't think in those terms. What we really need is a massive program to look at this whole transition process.

Right now the arms race has become a vicious circle, with both sides probably terrified of trying to break the circle: "If I make the first move toward defusing this escalation, I'll appear weaker and that'll make me vulnerable." Both sides feel the same way; that's the problem. If we can get enough people thinking it's a good idea to break this pattern it can happen, but it requires enough people on both sides. We need a great deal more dialogue with people in the Soviet Union. It may not be possible for the ruling generation in either country to change things right now, but perhaps through people-to-people contact we can begin to transform things. One thing I've noticed with my own children is that usually they will accept people when they've had a chance to play with them on an equal basis. They get a sense that "This person may look or talk different from me, but it is a person just like me." If we can somehow get American and Soviet children involved, perhaps through international gatherings and exchanges, then perhaps kids on both sides would develop the attitude "Hey, those kids on the other side of the fence are just like me. Why should we grow up hating each other and wanting to hurt each other and taking things away from each other when there are much more interesting and fun things that we can do *together!*" Maybe we could kick this off by setting up something like "Pen Pals for Peace." The nuclear arms race is literally insane, and kids understand this right away. I'm not sure how long it will be before the rest of the people realize that it's a waste of time, resources, and human energy.

Scientists have much to contribute to the solution, but research follows money and scientists often prostitute themselves. Also, for them any unsolved problem is a challenge and often they don't think too much about the implications of what they're doing. Someone in a political position says, "We need something that will do such-and-such. If only I had this, I would be more powerful and our country would be stronger." As long as our governments are coming from a fearful "you or me" position the money will be poured into weapons research. And that will simply generate more fear and suspicion. Right now it looks as if we're on the threshold of a whole new scientific breakthrough which has enormous implications for humanity, both in terms of new weapons as well as of life-enhancing technologies. There is speculation that it might be possible to use certain precise electromagnetic signals, especially in the extra-low-frequency (ELF) range in which our brain functions, to influence very selectively specific processes in the brain and in the various organs of the body. It has already been demonstrated that a very weak electromagnetic field applied to the body can retard insulin-producing cells in the pancreas, alter heart rate in laboratory animals, or alter the firing rate of neurons in the brain, thus upsetting the organs' or the brain's function. We're just in the early stages of research in the U.S.; how far along other scientists are, I don't know. Dr. José Delgado, who is considered to know more about this than anyone in the West, has been spending some time visiting labs in the Soviet Union and apparently they're way ahead of him. And this is coming from a guy who can control the motor behavior and emotional states of monkeys just by using electromagnetic fields, and no wires or electrodes implanted in the brain!

This whole area of research needs to be regulated by international agreement. We must come up with positive, peaceful ways to use this technology to move us toward positive shared goals. Since every living process is basically an electrical process, and since all chemical processes taken down to their basic forms are electrical in nature, the implications of this research are staggering. Moreover this does not require devices that cost billions of dollars; these are cheap. Even more urgently, we really must figure out how we can get along better.

We are truly on the threshold of a whole new science in which we have much to learn from our Soviet colleagues. Western science has primarily evolved in a linear manner, whereby you go into a laboratory and set up experiments, keeping all the variables except one from moving. You let that one "wiggle" and study what happens. Then you nail that one down and let another variable change, and so on until you have looked at all of them. Then you superimpose all the results to get your answer to the problem. That is a linear process. Most living processes, however, are nonlinear. An example of how our methodology doesn't work very well is seen when you try the following experiment. Give an animal a small amount of a tranquilizer, not quite enough to impair his ability to perform a learned task. Then take the same animal after the tranquilizer has worn off and irradiate it with very weak microwave signals, again not enough to impair the animal's ability to perform a learned task or to show up in analyses of the blood chemistry. In neither case is there an observable effect. But now take an animal dosed with a subnoticeable amount of the tranquilizer and irradiate it with a subnoticeable dose of electromagnetic radiation and you will see that the combination will produce *profound* effects on the animal. That is a nonlinear, synergistic process; you put something in and get something completely different. Our standard Western scientific approach doesn't generally do research in that way; in contrast, Soviet scientists look precisely for that sort of thing. They do their experiments under conditions that very closely mimic nature or the actual situations they want to learn about. That's why they have come up with much lower standards of microwave radiation considered to be allowable doses for human beings. This seriously challenges our methodological approach.

This new electromagnetic technology also offers some enormous potential benefits. There's an indication, for example, that we can actually alter the morphology of a growing fetus by changing the genetic coding on the DNA molecules with externally applied weak electromagnetic fields. This might mean, for example, that we could eradicate conditions like Down's syndrome. Scientists have also been able to alter the immune response in animals; so far the experiments have mostly been done to suppress it, but enhancement is the other side of the coin. This whole technology makes drugless treatment much more possible. You could conceivably build very lightweight, inexpensive devices that generate a very specific field that could react with the cells in the pancreas that produce insulin. Very simple and effective hearing aid devices are also possible. For an epileptic, when the spike and dome wave occurs, which happens before a seizure, a little ten-dollar chip in your pocket could be programmed to recognize that signal and automatically turn on a weak electromagnetic field and entrain your brain waves temporarily and avert the seizure. This would happen automatically, and you wouldn't even know you were about to have a seizure. Another possibility is a mood-altering device; if you started feeling depressed, you could stimulate certain centers of your brain, causing chemical changes which would alter your mood. This could all be done without drugs, using the body's natural ability to regulate such things. I also assume you could go through training like that of biofeedback so that eventually you could get rid of the device and just do it yourself. Although this is speculation, this all looks very promising and is not pie-in-the-sky. In my opinion this whole area of technology is about where nuclear technology was in the 1930s.

At the same time this technology could be used to create *negative* chemical reactions and electrical interactions that would cause disease, respiratory or heart failure, and so on. It also looks possible to focus these kinds of fields at a distance, over quite great distances in fact. The only way to counter the effect, so far as we know, may be to generate locally a field that isn't harmful, which will interact with the incoming signal and alter the input. Meditation and physical exercise could be useful. There may also be some combinations of vitamins which make people react less to certain kinds of radiation.

It's really clear that we need to improve relations with the Soviet Union to the point where we can both share what we're learning for the benefit of everybody. One thing that keeps countries fighting each other is an imbalance of power. If someone has the edge, the other side can get very paranoid about the possibility of getting pounded. Until recently the Soviet Union was probably more paranoid about us than we were about them and we had things like Khrushchev pounding his shoe on the table, making threats, and telling big lies. Now we're paranoid about them too, and keep telling our people, "We have to be careful of the Russians; they're building up and they might attack us." This made our government want to keep ahead of them in the arms race. Today, from what I understand, we may be behind in terms of numbers of warheads, but our technology is probably somewhat better; there's enough of a balance or raw parity so that no one has been willing to hit the button. Also, there's the recognition that if either of us hits the button, then both of us will lose. Now the Soviets have been building fallout shelters, which is a way of cutting their losses, while we've done very little in the way of civil defense. On the one hand that makes them even more paranoid. They see this and say, "Gosh, they're not even scared enough of us to have a civil defense program; therefore they must feel pretty secure that they could win!" If we *did* build civil defense shelters that might be interpreted as a signal that we are taking the possibility of nuclear war more seriously; in fact *their* fallout shelters make some people here paranoid. It gets very complex when there is so little trust because anything either of us does could be interpreted in many different ways.

Basically, anything destabilizing has severe implications for global security. Now these new technologies seem to have the possibility of causing such a destabilization if, for example, they are based on the Tesla technology. [Nikola] Tesla was a rather strange scientist who made all sorts of wild-sounding claims back around the turn of the century, and at some point people stopped taking him very seriously; yet some of the devices he talked about could make very effective weapons, for example, taking off from the particle-beam weapon concept and developing something much more potent. He talked about a set of waves that were not electromagnetic in nature, what we call "Tesla waves" today; he claimed you could put a lot of energy into these waves and then take it out again at a distant point. Some of the recent soleton research now suggests that we can indeed transmit a lot of energy over long distances in such a way that it doesn't dissipate.

You may recall that in SALT II the Soviets also proposed that we make a treaty that neither side would develop any other kinds of weapons of mass destruction. We wondered why they said that. Maybe they wanted to see if we had any other technologies we were developing—or maybe *they* do. It may be that they are making a shift from nuclear to a whole new kind of weapon. This is conceivable, but this is not to say that they have actually succeeded in doing this. Now as long as the people who are in control continue to be, it is not unreasonable to assume that technology will be used to develop more effective weapons. The Soviets I met recently at a scientific exchange were clearly interested in health. They were somewhat equivalent to scientists in our Environmental Protection Agency, and they were the ones who set the strict microwave standards. They seemed genuinely interested in doing research that would be beneficial to mankind. Meeting them was a really interesting experience for me because I had never met any Soviets before. There was an initial surprise: "Gee, they look just like me!" And when I got over that, it was "Hey, they look kind of paranoid, as if they think we're going to get up on this side of the table and go over and beat them up or something." They seemed to be very sad, their faces, and how they talked. They were very witty though, and things got lighter as we talked. They had brought over some good Russian vodka, and even though we didn't sing any drinking songs we did a lot of toasting in socializing periods. They had a great sense of humor, but there was a sense of heaviness. I talked most with one man; we felt a really strong connection. As I was leaving he told me through the interpreter that the next time we met he hoped relations between our governments wouldn't be so up and down. As I pondered that on the way home, it dawned on me that at that level everybody was the same: we were all interested in sharing what we'd been doing as scientists, and were interested in learning more about each other's countries and ways of doing things.

I have a paradoxical set of feelings about the future. I have a very negative vision about the way things *look* as if they're headed; on the other hand I can also see that it doesn't have to be that way. Each of us must work toward shaping the future in a more positive direction. The problem is that some people have the idea that a positive vision is one where all people are fed, clothed, sheltered, and have decent opportunities to develop themselves;

yet there are people who want their country to be Number One in the world, they want to own all the oilfields and so on. So people are working toward very different visions. At the same time technology has advanced to the point where we really are on the threshold of being able to provide universal abundance to a degree undreamed of in the past. That would make far greater security for everyone. So the question is "How can we get everyone to start catching on to that universal vision?"

It is almost inconceivable to me that anyone with any degree of sanity would think war is a good thing. Of course it serves to rev up the economy and create jobs and provide military people with the opportunity to get promoted and so on, but there are better ways to organize all of that. I rather like the idea of having exchanges between the children of the leaders of both countries; that way no one would push the button. But unfortunately it seems that the most obvious and reasonable solutions to big problems are not very well thought of because it seems that the big problems should have big solutions. We need to remember how Alexander the Great solved the problem of undoing the Gordian knot: he cut it.

I'd also suggest declassifying of virtually all research going on in anything. The only information that really needs to be classified is that which protects another person, like names of CIA agents. The public really needs to be better informed. Also, why build a war machine except for defense? It's pretty hard to convince your enemy that your intentions are peaceful if you're building offensive systems, and that's all we've ever done. We don't even have a defensive ABM system; they do. We rely on our capability to destroy the Soviet Union in order to deter war; that simply drives them to go build something similar. I'd also promote lots of cooperative efforts, like joint peaceful exploration of outer space and the development of the new technologies I've mentioned. We can develop stronger trade relations and cultural exchanges. We need to come to see each other as people, to appreciate how small the world really is and how similar we people are in very fundamental ways: if you stick a pin in someone, it hurts; we all hurt the same.

Yuri Antipov

At the time of this interview Yuri Antipov, a Soviet citizen, had been working for about five years with the Soviet delegation to the United Nations. Since then he has returned to the USSR. He is married and has one daughter.

I was born in Siberia. My family is very well educated and well-to-do by Soviet standards. My father was a professor at the university and my mother was a chemical engineer at a large factory. So even though I have a somewhat different background from, say, the average Soviet citizen, I don't think my views are very different on important subjects. The rest was very ordinary—I went to school and then to the university. I studied mathematics initially, but I was discouraged. I saw many people so much more gifted than I am, and felt I was taking up a place which another person deserved more than me, someone who would be more gifted. I was somewhat lost; my grades were above average, but it wasn't my path of life. Then I was drafted into the army. That is a duty of every Soviet citizen who wants to serve, male and female. I spent a little over three years in the army, where I was first trained in computer science and served in different parts of the Soviet Union. My work involved servicing intercontinental missiles; many people now serve in this branch so it is not so special.

I was in the service in the early 1960s, after the Cuban missile crisis. That was when we started building up our military capability. After World War II we felt the United States was directly threatening us with the cold war and [Secretary of State John Foster] Dulles's policy of containment of the Soviet Union.

With all the military bases and nuclear weapons surrounding the Soviet Union, we didn't know if the United States was going to drop bombs on us. After all, it was the United States which used atomic bombs on Hiroshima and Nagasaki; and it was the United States which produced atomic and hydrogen bombs, strategic bombers, ICBMs, nuclear-powered submarines with long-range ballistic missiles, and all the rest. So in a sense it became a race. We were forced to build up our nuclear weapons arsenal because we felt threatened all the time. This had a great impact on our population. I was too young to realize most of that. I do remember, at the time of the Stockholm Peace Appeal around 1952, that somebody from our community came to our home and asked my father to sign a petition to ban nuclear weapons. And they did. Later I discovered that about a hundred million people signed that petition throughout the world. That greatly impressed me.

Nevertheless despite all the negotiations we *still* have not reached an agreement to ban nuclear weapons—just to ban underground tests. Our official position was, and still is, that we are ready to ban and to destroy all nuclear weapons provided that the U.S., France, China, and other nuclear powers do the same. I think the thing holding it up is that the U.S. scientific community wants to continue its nuclear explosions to guarantee the reliability of stocks of weapons: when the weapons get older they are less predictable. Also, the U.S. says that the targets have changed, requiring technological innovation and testing of new weapons designs. Third, the U.S. says the Soviet Union would retain all the scientists who work on nuclear weapons, so that they could be set to work again very quickly if the Soviet Union decided it needed to resume its nuclear research. Whereas they say they could not do it so quickly in the U.S. because scientists would go to other fields and lose their expertise. But I think the main problem is that people in the U.S. government and military-industrial complex have a vested interest in producing new types of weapons for the arms race. It means big profits to them.

From what I know, the chances of nuclear war are very slim because the people who would give the command to use those weapons know the destruction they can cause. If war ever started it would be due to misperception, misunderstanding, or an error. I do not believe there can be a limited nuclear war as is stipulated in your government's Presidential Directive 59, because in reality you cannot stop the exchange of nuclear warheads; each side would calculate how much damage it could inflict on the other and what the response would be; and the other side would weigh it. Now that's pretty stupid, right? Pretty irrational. And I believe that people in America and Russia and around the world recognize what terrible destruction there would be. We are all afraid of nuclear war because we understand what it would mean.

People in the Soviet Union are particularly sensitive to what a nuclear war would mean, more so than the public in the United States. You must remember our history: twenty million people were killed in World War II. That memory is in our blood; it is a part of everyday life. In every family someone died. In my case my mother's brother and my father's two brothers were killed. In the United States many people are out of touch with what war means. I don't mean everyone, because Americans were in wars— although not on her own soil. The perception of people in Europe and the Soviet Union is vastly different from that of Americans. The last major war the U.S. was involved in was World War II. Do you know how many Americans lost their lives in that war? It was three hundred eighty thousand. That is quite different from losing someone in every family. This is a very stupid example, but I wish Americans could imagine an atomic bomb the size of the one dropped on Hiroshima, dropped at Forty-second Street in New York City during the working hours. Imagine how much destruction that would cause. And that is only a fourteen-*kilo*ton nuclear weapon; the ones both our countries now have measure in the *mega*tons. That is a stupid example, but you see what I mean? By the way, I pick this example because there are some studies, based on official U.N. estimations, of just what that size bomb would do if dropped on that area. This information should not only be available, which it is, but also widely publicized. So I believe that we have to go to the people and try to get them to understand what nuclear war really means.

In the Soviet Union we believe that our social system is much superior to that of the United States; we really believe so. Based on the theory of Marxism–Leninism, which is a philosophical concept of human society, nature, and science, we believe that in due time, with increased productivity, the Soviet Union would provide every Soviet citizen with a quality of life that is better than any country in the world. If there were really peaceful coexistence we believe we could increase productivity faster than other countries. Then people in the working class in the capitalist countries, like the United States, would see that their social system is very unfair to them. They would compare it with that of the Soviet Union and would establish what we call a "socialist society." That is what we believe.

The people of the Soviet Union are of one hundred twenty-four different nationalities; more than a hundred fifty different languages are spoken. But I would say that all they want is peace. In the Soviet Union the military-related industries are not built into our system; I mean, we don't really need them for our economic system to prosper. Instead of building mighty armed forces, we could use the same resources in a more productive way; that is, to increase the standard of living for every Soviet person. Our concept of society is different; we believe that we live in a community in the first place, then in a larger community, and then in a country. So we believe that everybody has to develop one's capability for one's benefit and for the benefit of the society—not only for our personal benefit. One axiom is "Those who do not work do not eat." Another is "To each according to his contribution." What we want, then, is to have peace in which to develop all our capabilities for the benefit of the whole society.

In the future, under communism, it would be "From each according to his ability and to each according to his need." But right now we cannot provide every citizen's needs because goods and services are somewhat limited. It isn't fair, but for right now the axiom is not "accccording to one's need" but "according to one's contribution to the society." Society itself determines what is the contribution. In a factory, for example, those who produce more get more benefits; those who produce less get less. It is very complicated how this actually takes place in the society, but essentially it is a reward system.

In my opinion the momentum for the arms race is dictated by the influence of the United States, or at least by our *perception* of what is going on in the United States, particularly in military-related spheres. Also, the Soviet Union has certain national security requirements because so many countries are on our borders. We are persuaded that we must keep our armed forces at a certain level of preparedness. I do not believe that we can get rid of nuclear weapons until we create a network of national security guarantees which take into account the legitimate interests of all not only of the superpowers. It is very difficult to say what this network could be at the outset. I have done some thinking about this, but probably my answers would be somewhat premature. For one thing we must strengthen the role that the United Nations plays in world affairs. We must also develop a system, probably through the United Nations or on a regional basis, which would create more incentives for cooperation and better understanding and fewer incentives for fear and misunderstanding.

We live on a very tiny planet and we have *so* many problems. From the point of view of humanity, can you imagine that every year more than five million people die of malnutrition? Just simple hunger. The vast majority of countries live in such poverty that the notion of human dignity doesn't mean anything. And this is largely our fault because we don't provide them with assistance. We *could* do so, and we should. But how can we if we're building up our armed forces and consuming large amounts of materials to build weapons? Look at what is happening in the United States. It's really incredible for the Reagan government to slash thirty-four billion dollars from programs designed to solve the problems of people who need help and to put that money into the military. To get what? Except from the point of view of the extreme right wing, that is a real waste.

Probably I am not entirely correct, but to a great degree the United States depends on Third World countries more than it used to. Say, two-thirds of the volume of U.S. trade goes to the Third World countries; so you sell them goods and services in order to get a favorable balance of payments. Second, the United States depends to a great extent on raw materials from Third World countries. You have to make sure you continue to get those materials even if there is social change in those countries. What is El Salvador today? It is fourteen families controlling ninety-five percent of all developed land. I mean, *fourteen families!* And the junta supports those families. They say they tried to conduct land reform; what kind of land reform is that? They expropriated only eighteen percent of the land, and yet the government kills people there and the United States would support that government. Support them in order that they may do what? To ensure that their investments are safe. For the multinationals, countries like El Salvador play a very important role for their investments and profits. After all, in

American society, which functions on the notion of making a profit, you can't do anything if you think that you will not get a profit. Right? It's true that historically there have been people like [Robert] Owen, a socialist who built a textile mill in Massachusetts. He wanted to abolish profit and distribute the income equally among all people in the community, but he went bankrupt. There have been other experiments in the United States and in other capitalist countries; they all went bankrupt. Why? Because the law of your society is such that making a profit is the main motive.

The problem is how a person can get income. In a socialist society like the Soviet Union the means of production are nationalized; in the U.S. they are private property. So you get profit by exploiting labor. The less you pay labor, the more profit you make; the better technology you use, the more profit. But the main source of profit comes from exploiting labor. In the Soviet Union society is developed according to a plan. We try to design an economic plan which will satisfy the most important needs of people and of national security. Again, it is the duty of the government to provide all people with housing, with free medical service, free education, and a job. This is all provided according to our constitution, which is the fundamental law of the Soviet Union. To establish this plan we have special organs on the local and on the state level. Each factory knows what it is capable of producing, how to increase productivity, how much capital they need, and what kind of expansion they desire. They go to the authorities at the local level and give them all their information.

But whether we are in a socialist society or a capitalist society, we are all human beings—in the first place, because we all suffer. On the personal level I do not believe in God. I feel I am a strong enough person so that I don't need to rely on anything "supernatural." I know that I came to this life, to this world, and someday I will be gone. It's not that I am not afraid of death—that is natural. But I don't believe in an afterlife. I know that death will be the end of my suffering and of my enjoyment, the end of my existence as a human being. And certainly this idea frightens me that somewhere there will be an end. I mean, it is an end to me, but of course mankind will continue. I will be, so to speak, replaced by another human being. As I can see it now, my duty is to give other human beings my understanding and to encourage the best part of every human being that I am in touch with, to develop those best parts to the benefit of those human beings and of the society in which they live. I don't see that this has anything to do with religion; it is a basic human outlook that's very common. After all, we cannot exist very well if we fight and are afraid of each other. The continuation of mankind here in this world is our main duty. Or so I see it.

When I think about what religion is, the first thing I think of is architecture, of many kinds of churches. Also music and paintings and human voices. They sound somewhat interesting in such places, in that they affect you. It's . . . very personal. It affects me that I do not share their beliefs, that I am not a part of them. I have nothing against them. If somebody feels it necessary to believe in God, why should I stop him? However, I feel that I should encourage this person to rely more on himself. Throughout history some of the most agonizing atrocities against humanity have been done in the name of God; this is still going on among Christians, Muslims, and Buddhists.

I have read Jesus' Sermon on the Mount and other things like that. They reflect basic moral behavior without which no human society can exist, whether a socialist, capitalist, primitive, or a highly developed future Communist society.

Throughout the years I have come to a few very simple and common ideas. One is that we should each have respect for the dignity and integrity of other human beings. Another is that we are all equal in the sense that we are all suffering. Probably the basic characteristic of a human being is the ability to suffer, or more broadly, the ability to share things. Despite the fact that some are more gifted than others, we are all equal in this way. Over the centuries those who are more gifted have perhaps been the most humanistic in their outlook, in that they've had more respect for every human being. I believe there are more good people than bad people around and that you can rely on people in bad times. I believe we shouldn't be afraid of people. And our life's meaning, if it has any, is to work for the benefit of the society. This is true for *all* human beings, no matter what their race or their abilities or whatever.

I believe that human beings have come into existence as an accident of nature, though I do not exclude the possibility of living beings on other planets elsewhere in the universe. But I *do* believe life was an accident. I don't believe there is anything supernatural about it. Or is there? I truly believe that life on *this* planet is an accident . . . in particular on *this* planet it is an accident. I believe so. [*Agitated*] It has no meaning. Well, what kind of meaning does it have? With all this evolution we know that life started here on this planet. And we're pretty sure, according to plenty of credible scientists, that one day it will stop existing. That's it. Right? Anyway, we will go to another subject.

You know, I think one of the key things is the concept of guilt. That is where alienation started. In practical terms this means that people who would press the buttons to fire nuclear weapons would not feel in touch with the destruction. They are alienated. They don't see that it is *they* who are killing people. It is not one person killing another one directly in cold blood. That is what alienation means right now. It has nothing to do with your conscience, with your sense of guilt or of duty. *That* is what frightens me. It is one thing to kill another person; you would feel guilt. I mean, at least a *normal* human being would feel guilt, or at least *odd*. Except a mentally disturbed person.

We live in subcultures, and here I am talking about both the United States and the Soviet Union. We live in subcultures: there are those who have power and those who don't. There are those who issue orders and those who fulfill orders. That is a subculture: if you have power, you feel differently. You know what the late Senator Dirksen said to John Foster Dulles? He said that if you want to build up the military might of the United States, then you've got to scare people to death. That's what they do. That is a simple, prosaic thing that has nothing to do with human conscience. Or there is one thing—for that is approved consciously, not unconsciously—*it must have some benefit to somebody, otherwise it wouldn't happen.* In the Soviet Union, well, it might be of some benefit to some people to increase military might—perhaps those in the military who rise through the ranks by fulfilling their duty in these things. But there are *many* in the United States who benefit. For God's sake, when the rumor started to circulate that the Pentagon was going to have a huge increase in outlays, do you know what happened on the New York Stock Exchange on Wall Street? All the transactions in stocks related to companies involved in the military-industrial complex—companies like United Technologies, McDonnell-Douglas, and others—*went up eighteen points per day!* Do you know that they sell stocks for building the MX and people buy those stocks? There are people who invested in those stocks even though it has no real meaning, because the MX has not yet been built. But to build the MX people have invested money, on paper at least. They will get a profit—and a good one.

I guess we can hope that the people in power now realize that if they persist in trying to keep things from changing and if they resort to nuclear war, then they too will be destroyed. That is one deterrent.

One thing greatly upsets me in the United States. When I was a student, many people in this country were against the Vietnam War. There were huge demonstrations. I mean, it was *so* impressive on our TV. We were so greatly influenced by that spectacle. Because we know that it is not that easy to go and say to people in power, "You are wrong. You have to stop that." Right? Even though the government didn't stop immediately, those people were successful. But where are all those leaders now? Where are all those ideas now—which were beautiful and justifiable on the social level? One man who was a member of the Weather Underground is now a successful broker on Wall Street. Another one is going to run for the Senate. I mean, either they disappeared completely from public life or they adapted themselves, making careers and money. *For what?* I mean, I don't need five suits; I probably need only one. And I really don't know whether I even need *that*. It is a custom which is imposed on me by society, and I do accept that custom; but why does it make a difference whether I wear this tie or that tie, one is two bucks and one is twenty? For some people it does make a difference. I could go to unlimited discussion on this. . . . But just tell me, where are all those people now? Where are all those beautiful ideas? What has happened? How has the society changed them? *You have to identify those forces. How have you been manipulated?*

From what I know, and I guess I know something, a limited nuclear war between the United States and the Soviet Union is not possible because it would be impossible to control. And I can't rule out the possibility that nuclear weapons could be used in certain Third World countries. Probably it would not be started by my country, but I know that some people here in the U.S. speak very loudly about that possibility. I am really very much afraid of that talk. I really am. I think those are corrupt intellectuals with no sense of social responsibility, or maybe with a sense of social responsibility but with a distorted, upside-down way of looking at the world. Sometimes I think that if we can't abolish nuclear weapons altogether—and we can't, realistically speaking, because we are too far from each other right now, though we shouldn't be—I wonder, why can't we, the Soviet Union, go and unilaterally stop nuclear testing? After all, we have systems similar to those of the United States, like the Polaris submarine, Trident I. After all, Trident I has twenty-four submarine-launched ballistic missiles, each equipped with ten nuclear warheads, with each warhead being around one megaton. So it could destroy two hundred forty big cities. That is enough of a deterrent. I really think so.

On the other hand I know that technology is rapidly developing. People are now talking about antiballistic missiles in space and around silos. There is a real possibility of a breakthrough in the years to come of building an ICBM system capable of intercepting missiles. That would close a window of vulnerability. On the other hand with the new levels of accuracy achieved it is possible that the ICBMs could be destroyed in the silos and in other places. Sometimes I do such calculations. And sometimes I think, if the Soviet Union alone would explode nuclear weapons just on her own territory, the fallout would be so bad that the whole of human life on this planet would be destroyed.

At the same time I realize that in the best interest of the Soviet Union such unilateral disarmament might be a wrong step. I will tell you why. I have heard it said many times that if you build a beautiful garden, you have to put a fence around it to keep pigs from destroying it. It's very simple and many people believe it. We have to first get the pigs out and then we can destroy the fence. And then we can build a whole beautiful garden everywhere, have one beautiful garden in the whole world.

Now as to who are the pigs, that is very difficult to say. I don't want to be unfair. I might say to someone, "You are a pig," and they might say, "No, I am not; I don't have a vested interest in the arms race. I would be happy if it were stopped." So I don't want to point the finger. Even members of the military-industrial complex can be good people in their families. I think that the "pig" is a natural force that divides our countries. We believe that the United States wants to preserve the bad governments on this planet and to preserve corrupt social systems in many countries. The whole of Latin America is a case in point, except perhaps

Mexico. There is also competition for world resources. All this leads to fear of each other, fear of each other's enormous nuclear potential. We know that we can't stop you and you know that you can't stop us. Fears come from misperception of the most fundamental intentions of the other country. There's a substantial lack of information in the U.S. about the Soviet Union; we have more information about the U.S., but still it is limited.

The situation in U.S. politics is becoming really serious. For example, [Senator] Jesse Helms from North Carolina. He was reelected two years ago not because he is smart or the most qualified candidate, but because he spent four to five million dollars of his own money to promote himself. He bought time on television and sold himself, just like a product. That is what your politics are becoming. What discouraged me most of all during the last election was the fact that about fifty-six percent of all the eligible voters didn't bother to vote. That is *very* discouraging, because some say that they didn't vote because they didn't have a candidate whose position they could support. I think that's nonsense. In New York, for example, there were twelve candidates from the extreme left, from the Citizens party to the Liberal party to the Libertarian party. All varieties of choices and programs. And yet they didn't vote. I am afraid this is a pattern which is going to get worse in the future. That people feel so alienated that they don't feel that they can change things in this country. And that is wrong. That is an attitude you have to change. I am very concerned that if people are alienated from the voting process, then the worst candidates will get through because groups like the Moral Majority are so well organized and financed. At this time I do not see any force which will change this.

You know, politics is very difficult in any one country. Can you imagine how difficult it is to conduct politics *between* our two countries? Just imagine Brezhnev and Reagan together at one table. They have different lifetime experiences. Probably very different knowledge. Imagine their conversation. It would be—and I don't mean this as an insult—but it would be like a conversation between two deaf men, talking words to each other but not understanding each other. That's what it would be. The best one could hope for is that they would really try to talk to each other and not try to undermine each other.

I guess the one hope is that today, with more travel and

better communications, we are all becoming more global in our outlook. But it has yet to achieve an outlet in a creative way to bring us together. There are certainly many places where we are working together and can increase our mutual efforts. For example, medicine, solar energy, outer space exploration, math, fundamental physics. There are so many positive things I have gotten here in the U.S. After all, it all depends on the attitude of a person, don't you think? One might go and look for garbage and that is what he will find. Whatever you are looking for you will find. I went for the bright side and I found very good and very intelligent people here in the United States. What has surprised me most is that even such bright, intelligent, and well-educated people have allowed themselves to be so manipulated and so extremely alienated. They are committed to their families and jobs, and that's it. There is no outside work for most of them. They are simply afraid. They are afraid of something unknown, some unknown force which they think could break them into pieces. Whether it is in your society or mine, one of the most important things human beings want is stability. That is one reason why the relationship between our two countries is so important to people here and in my country—because it affects the basic stability.

I also discovered a great sense of humor in the United States. I really love it. I guess that is the most important characteristic of human beings of every nation. The sense of humor here is very sharp and very optimistic—if you define optimist as a "well-informed pessimist"! I also found many people to be very energetic, always trying to find or invent something new. One thing which surprised me was that so many people want to stand out from other people, to be a star or something. I find that so different from my way of looking at things. I don't want to be somebody, a star; it's not important to me. I'd like to be part of a group, have a sense of belonging and of being equal to others. Maybe your mass media somehow creates that—we have something of the star syndrome in the Soviet Union too, but I think it is less so.

There are really, I think, no basic differences between the U.S. and the Soviet people. The main problem is the fear that we have of each other—you are afraid of what we could do to you and we are afraid of what you could do to us. That's the main problem.

Bob Aldridge

After sixteen years of working for Lockheed in systems development for the Polaris, Poseidon, and Trident ballistic missile systems, Bob Aldridge resigned for reasons of conscience. Today he writes and lectures widely on the need to change current defense policies. He is the author of The Counterforce Syndrome. *He lives with his wife and the youngest of their ten children in San Jose, California. This interview was conducted in the winter of 1980.*

I was born and raised south of Santa Cruz, California. During World War II, I served in the Philippines, after which I attended California Polytechnic College; Janet and I were married after my first year. After my second year, which was during the pre–Korean War recession, no aeronautics jobs were to be had, so I worked six years in state forestry. When Lockheed moved their missile plant to the Bay Area, I was hired into the engineering department. At the same time I finished up a degree in aeronautical engineering at San Jose University.

During my sixteen years with Lockheed I worked on a submarine-launched ballistic missile, the navy's leg of the United States's strategic nuclear triad. I worked on all three generations: the Polaris, the Poseidon, and the beginning of the Trident program.

When I started work on the Poseidon about 1965 I helped develop what's known as the "reentry body," the special package for the hydrogen warhead that brings it back down through the atmosphere without burning up from air friction. This was the beginning of the MIRV program, the Multiple Independently

Targeted Reentry Vehicles, where many warheads are put on one missile in order to destroy many targets. The Poseidon missile can carry as many as fourteen hydrogen warheads.

By the beginning of the Trident program I was the lead engineer, or design group leader, with several design engineers working under me. I was given the concept design studies for developing a maneuvering reentry vehicle for Trident. In reviewing reports, I could see increased interest on the part of the military for greater accuracy in the weapons—accuracy of the type needed to hit those targets which would deter the opponent from striking first. In other words, we seemed to be preparing ourselves to be able to strike first in order to destroy underground missile silos, command posts, and other "hard" targets where you need pinpoint precision.

It was at this point that I realized the United States was moving toward more aggressive weapons systems, and I was coming to appreciate more fully the devastation that would result from the type of weapons I was working on. Janet and I talked it over, began making new plans, and eventually we separated from that type of work.

At Lockheed I didn't find many people concerned about these things. While you're working on it you don't really think about or discuss such things too much. One of the games you play with yourself to justify what you're doing is that you don't think about the bad parts of it; you just think about the good parts and rationalize why you should be doing this. Or "If I don't do it, somebody else will." Or you tell yourself that you don't have all the information. Things like that. Also, before you actually quit job security seems like a big deal. But after it happens and you have tangible events to work with it doesn't seem so big.

In the eight years since I left Lockheed I've been doing research, writing, speaking, and consulting to other groups. I'm trying to use my engineering background to pull together all this widely scattered technical information in a way that the average person can understand it. I've been examining various technologies which would supplement our very accurate missiles in forming an aggressive policy; I have found that *all* of these technologies are in development. Many of these programs are presented as "defensive" programs, but in actuality they do give the United States what I would have to call a "disarming first-strike capability." We'll start putting these weapons in the field probably about the middle of the 1980s. I really believe we are making our nation less secure by developing this sort of first-strike capability.

There seem to be five aspects of this capability. First, if our country wanted to launch a first strike against an opponent, one thing they would probably like to do is to destroy the early-warning communication satellites. That would prevent the opponent from knowing what's happening and slow him up from firing off his missiles. This would give us time to destroy them. In looking at space warfare I see many things are going on. For example, we've developed small interceptor missiles that are not explosive but have very great precision; they usually have infrared devices that enable them to home in on an orbiting satellite and destroy it by impact energy.

We hear a lot about the Soviets' being ahead of us in anti-satellite warfare. Over the past twelve years they've had about seventeen tests, out of which only about two or three could be considered at all successful. Nevertheless our government is using this as an excuse to go ahead with antisatellite warfare.

Farther down the line are things like killer lasers and particle beams. These programs are actually being developed, although as far as I know none of them has been developed in space yet.

So the first aspect of a first-strike capability would be the *development of space warfare*. The second aspect would be the *greatly increased accuracy of the missiles,* which I've mentioned.

Under the so-called deterrence policy you aim your missiles at the enemy's large cities and manufacturing areas. This is supposed to deter the enemy from striking us first. It's a very gruesome type of policy, but even so, it's based on assuming a *second* strike on our part. As we develop more accurate missiles, however, we acquire the capability of destroying missiles in silos, command posts, communication depots, bomber fields, submarine pens, nuclear storage bunkers, and all types of land targets. Even if it's not our *intention* to use these precision missiles for a first strike, it still gives us the *capability*. Since the Russians look at capability rather than intention, you can see the danger in this sort of shift. Ironically, improving your weapons capability may even force the opponent to strike first in times of crisis, thinking that he'd be better off to use his missiles rather than wait until they were destroyed. So this shift is very destabilizing. Of course the

Soviets have always lagged behind the United States, but they've always sought to catch up. If they get a similar capability or some other counterforce, then both countries will be geared up for a first strike. In a time of crisis it will be very touchy because each country will want to be the one to get the first volley off. That's very dangerous. What has increased the precision is a new navigation system composed of constellation and navigation satellites. Missiles would have a receiver aboard and be able to correct any position errors while actually in flight. The maneuvering reentry vehicles could sense the target and correct the flight course to hit within about a hundred feet of the target. That's *very* close.

The third aspect of the emerging first-strike capability is *antisubmarine warfare*. Right now we are making all kinds of improvements in weapons for destroying submarines—rockets that drop torpedoes and depth charges, depth charges that can be dropped from aircraft, and so on. The main challenge is to find enemy submarines, to keep track of them, and to be ready to destroy them at a moment's notice. That's all based on underwater sensing. Within ten miles of our house, at Moffett Naval Air Station, is the antisubmarine headquarters for the Pacific Ocean region. Their underwater acoustic laboratory coordinates the development of underwater sensors to pinpoint enemy submarines. They have an Iliac IV, one of the world's most powerful computers, that processes all sorts of data from host and surveillance satellites, weather reports, and various types of oceanographic information. With that data the Iliac IV can actually compute background noises in the ocean, cancel them out, and bring out the sounds of submarines. Then those submarines can be matched with what they call the "sonic signatures," which are sort of like the "fingerprints" of different classes of submarines. These are stored in the computer and can be used to identify the submarine as friend or foe, and even determine what class or type of submarine they are. By about 1982 I estimate that the United States should be able to track every submarine in the ocean under all conditions. They can do it now under ideal conditions, but we don't always have ideal conditions.

So if we can keep an oceanwide surveillance of submarines and pin them down within a hundred-mile radius, then we can use local antisubmarine warfare—like these planes that fly out of Moffett Field and off aircraft carriers. They can take turns staying on the submarines' tails along with the hunter-killer attack submarines.

The fourth aspect of a first-strike scenario would be a *ballistic missile defense and a bomber defense*. This would enable us to destroy, before they hit our targets, any enemy missiles that survived the first strike or that were launched in retaliation. Those things are in development too. As a matter of fact almost the same things being used for satellite warfare will be used for ballistic missile defense, for example, small homing interceptor technologies, hit vehicles, killer lasers, and particle beam devices.

The killer laser is somewhat analogous to a lightning bolt; it can deposit a tremendous amount of energy on a very small area, physically damaging the opposing side's weapon. In some cases even a near miss with the particle beam will destroy the weapon's electronics so that it will not function. Shot from a satellite, you can destroy an enemy missile shortly after launch, before it starts spewing out all the little individual warheads—"get all your eggs in one basket," so to speak.

Other interceptors being designed are very similar to the old ABM system we used to have, only the technology is more modern. These would destroy incoming missiles with radiation. If they hit up in the upper atmosphere where there's not much energy absorption from air molecules, they wouldn't have to hit very close because the radiation would travel almost indefinitely; whereas if they hit in the air, the radiation would be absorbed and diminish over distance. Neutrons and gamma rays, particularly neutrons, would be the most destructive. The incoming warhead would be bombarded with neutrons to destroy it.

I have my doubts about the effectiveness of terminal defense, because you only have a few seconds to respond. When a reentry body is coming in at mach twenty, twenty times the speed of sound, it only takes ten or twenty seconds from the time it hits the atmosphere to reach its target. In that time you'd have to take a couple of breaths, distinguish the missile from things like booster tank fragments and all the other stuff up in orbit, fire at it, and blow it up. Frankly I have very real doubts about whether that's feasible.

The fifth and final aspect of the United States' move into developing a strong first-strike capability is the thing that ties everything together: *C-3, or "command, control, communication."*

These are early-warning computers and a massive computer network which collect all your data and put them into usable form
for making decisions. It includes all the communication satellites,
communication devices, and to a limited extent the underground
system they are putting in Michigan and in Wisconsin. This information is used to coordinate all the other technologies I've mentioned to enable almost instantaneous decisions to be made. All of
these systems are now in development. Some of them, like the
navigation satellites, are gradually being put into work now.
About five or six are already in orbit; eventually there'll be eighteen or possibly twenty-four.

There are many ways of comparing Russian and American
military capabilities. In most technologies the United States is at
least five years ahead; in some areas they're even farther ahead. In
key technologies for first-strike capability the United States has a
very significant lead. This is very obvious from things you read in
the papers about how anxious the Soviets are to get U.S. computer technology.

The way Soviet capabilities are presented to the American
people is deceiving. We hear so much about the number of missiles and missile-launching submarines they have, and the mega-
tonnage. These are areas they are ahead in, and they were allowed
this lead back in the SALT I treaty because we had superior capabilities in other areas and were working to deploy the MIRV
system I was working on. MIRV allowed the United States to put
many more warheads in use without increasing the number of
actual missiles or missile-launching submarines. Right now, for
example, the Soviets have thirteen hundred ninety-eight intercontinental ballistic missiles; we have a thousand fifty-four, minus
maybe a couple of Titan IIs that blew up. The Soviet Union has
about sixty-four nuclear-powered ballistic-missile submarines; the
United States had forty-one, but I think it's decommissioned a
couple of Polaris submarines so it may be down to thirty-nine
now. But while the Soviet Union has about five thousand strategic warheads, the United States has almost ten thousand, because we put more warheads on each missile. So you can see the
difference. The game of "catchup" continues, however, and the
Soviet Union is following our example and starting to put the
MIRVs on their missiles, at least on land-based ones. Also, some
of the submarine-based missiles are being deployed with three

MIRVs on them, not fourteen like the Poseidon. But while they're catching up there, the U.S. is advancing in other technologies, such as sensing technologies, counter measures, and the "Stealth" fighters. I don't know too much about the "Stealth" aircraft. In some way it absorbs radiation from radar rather than reflecting it back so the enemy can't get a radar reading.

Basically, five or six things tell how capable missiles are of destroying targets such as missile silos. Probably the two most important are the *yield,* or explosive power of the warhead and the *accuracy.* Of these two, accuracy is much more important. Now the Soviets usually have bigger bombs, but the United States has more bombs which are smaller and more accurate. Our smaller bombs, being more accurate, can do more damage to Soviet missile silos than their less accurate, bigger bombs can do to our missile silos. To figure it all out you get into a lot of formulas, which I have done in some of the documents I've written.

Another important consideration is *reliability.* Our weapons are much more reliable; in other words, the probability is higher that U.S. weapons are going to work properly after being launched than it is for Soviet weapons. As far as I can determine from available information, the newest Soviet missiles are something like about seventy-five percent reliable; in other words, three out of four of them would work properly. That's the rate of reliability for their best systems; it drops down to sixty-five or seventy percent for some of the older ones. The worst probability for any of our systems is about eighty percent.

Another important factor is *availability,* which means the number of weapons available to fire at any one time. The U.S. has fifty-five percent of its submarine ballistic missiles ready to fire at any one time; the Soviet Union has about twelve to fifteen percent. All the rest of their fleet are in port. They only have about fifteen percent of their submarines out at sea at any time; the U.S. has fifty-five percent. We have almost a hundred percent of our Minuteman missiles ready to fire at any one time. The Soviet Union only has about thirty percent of their intercontinental ballistic missiles ready. If you take thirty percent of their fourteen hundred and almost a hundred percent of our one thousand, then you can see that at any one time we have many more missiles ready to fire. You can do that same comparison with submarine-launched missiles.

So when you hear that the Soviets have more missiles and

more submarines, that's giving you only a very small portion of the picture. That can be very misleading because it gets people to believe that the Soviets are ahead of us. I believe the main source of the misrepresentation is the military–industrial complex, which makes profits from developing these weapons systems. It is very similar to a lot of the advertising you see on television: it doesn't give all the facts, and emphasizes certain facts but omits others. In this military–industrial complex I see industry as the strong arm pushing for more and better weapons. As far as I can tell, the military is more the action arm that's needed to provide the contracts, to guarantee the support of overseas dictatorships to provide cheap labor, land, and resources for the big corporations.

Powerful ties link the military and industry. For example, the flow of personnel goes both ways all the time. Going from the military to industry, you have all these retired senior officers—navy captains, army and air force colonels, and above. After retiring they take jobs in key executive positions in various industries. For instance, when I was first starting at Lockheed we were developing the Polaris missile to be launched from underwater. There was a certain Admiral Rayburn, the so-called father of the Polaris, who was the one in Washington in charge of developing the Polaris missile and submarine system. When he retired he went back to Sacramento as an executive to Aerojet General Corporation, which at that time was making all the motors for the Polaris. That's just one tiny example.

I don't remember the numbers, but they're high. One research group figured that about twenty-five percent of these retired senior officers were in conflict-of-interest situations. In other words, after retirement they took jobs that dealt with the same branch of the service they retired from, which is considered a conflict of interest. I think this should be investigated carefully.

The flow the other way probably brings even more business to the corporations; business people are being put in decision-making positions in the Department of Defense. For instance, under Carter, Dr. Perry was the undersecretary of defense for research and engineering, probably the Number Two position in the Department of Defense. He's from ESL, right out here in Sunnyvale, which is a subsidiary of TRW, one of the big satellite companies and electronics companies that handles a lot of government contracts.

Another example is David Packard, one of the founders and

president or chairman of the board of the Hewlett-Packard Corporation. He was a deputy defense secretary about the time Lockheed got its bailout. He also was instrumental in what they call the "famous golden handshake," when Lockheed filed a claim for many millions of dollars overrun. Although I'm not sure of the exact figures they're in about this proportion: David Packard assured Lockheed of thirty-six million dollars, although a later study showed only about a seven- to twelve-million-dollar overrun. But since Packard, who was deputy secretary of defense, had promised Lockheed the thirty-six million the government had to pay that, even though it was obviously a gross overestimation.

This is called "white-collar welfare." I think the main reason nothing is done about it is because of a couple of fears in the minds of the American people. One is fear of Russia and the other is fear for the economy, the fear that we need the weapons contracts to provide jobs to keep the economy going. I've touched on the fear of Russia. Fear of a deteriorating economy is an enormous factor. When the B-1 bomber was cancelled, the last arguments for saving it were not that it was needed for national defense but rather that it was going to cause so many people to be out of work. As soon as you cancel a contract you have to worry about unemployment. As far back as the early 1960s legislation was introduced to initiate economic conversion studies; such legislation always gets lobbied out or dies in committee or something like that. As far as I know, none of them has ever reached the floor for a vote. And nothing is ever done to retrain people for other types of employment.

The military-industrial lobby is this country's strongest lobby. When budget season comes around the military starts making presentations to Congress. They bring in high-ranking admirals and generals from all over the world to testify that we need all these weapons, that our equipment is in terrible shape and needs to be brought up-to-date. Industry is the same. I understand that corporations have two hundred offices within walking distance of the Capitol building. I think their power goes far deeper than their sheer numbers; it's pretty clear that corporate campaign donations have helped put many politicians in office. I think this influence extends beyond the legislative branch too.

It's my opinion that political conditions right now represent a backlash, because much of the resistance to weapons is starting to become effective. I don't think the B-1 bomber is dead, but it has been slowed down a lot. The neutron bomb can't be manufactured outright. The MX is in big trouble; they can't find a basing mode that anybody will accept. Since the U.S. started negotiations with the Soviets on eliminating long-range theater weapons, the Pershing II and the ground-launched cruise missiles for Europe are also in big trouble.

Many of the problems are not directly related to resistance movements. For example, Trident submarines are twenty-six months behind schedule now and it looks like they might slip again. This combines with the political atmosphere of many countries wanting nuclear-free zones, so business needed somebody like Ronald Reagan to get in there to overwhelm everybody. What they're going to do is to step things up and do everything that's possible to do right now. From the perspective of business interests, things don't look good. If you look at magazines like *Aviation Week* or *Space Technology,* they had editorials awhile back that had nothing to do with the need for NATO defense or security; they were strictly bemoaning the fact that talks with the Soviets were undermining negotiations to convince NATO that they needed missiles in Europe. They blatantly focused on how damaging these talks are for business in the aerospace industry.

We who are concerned about the arms race ought to recognize that when we start becoming successful there's going to be a backlash from business because they're strong and won't give up these profits easily. We shouldn't be intimidated by all this strong talk and should continue pushing for some sincere negotiations.

The main danger of the current shift from a defensive posture to a more aggressive first-strike capability is that it causes instability. I hope that nobody in the United States really intends to *use* the first-strike capability. I think it's more that it's to keep the arms-production business going; to do so you have to keep improving your product. With military products the ultimate end is to be able to destroy the enemy without any response from them. This is destabilizing in times of international crisis and also in arms-control negotiations because there's no evidence of a sincere interest in reducing arms. So we get attempts at treaties like SALT II which don't do anything. If both countries are prepared to strike first, each starts thinking that he might lose his weapons if he doesn't launch them first. That makes the chance of nuclear war much more likely.

Looking at this logically then, if you become more desta-blized you're certainly becoming less secure. And let's face it: there is no defense against nuclear weapons. I don't think even the first-strike capability would work right. It's very complicated, very sophisticated. The more complicated something is, the more likely something is going to go wrong. I know from my engi-neering experience that you have to test and test and test to work the bugs out of things: first-strike capability can't be tested; you can only test it once.

The Soviet Union probably has less defense than we do. In the U.S. the propaganda is that the USSR has more defense be-cause they have an ABM system. In reality, however, they have sixty-four old, 1950-vintage interceptors ringing Moscow (there have been rumors that they have taken some of those out) that probably wouldn't even be able to touch our modern missiles as they're coming in. They do have a greater defense against bom-bers, quite a sophisticated radar network, and interceptor aircraft and surface-to-air missiles. This will maybe make the effectiveness of the cruise missile very tenuous for a while, but it flies very low to the ground and is very accurate. That's supposed to be the main thing we're working on right now. But then of course the Soviets would soon develop capabilities to intercept that.

We need realistic steps toward disarmament. We need to bring other countries into the negotiations. The real, positive step we can take toward disarmament is sincere negotiations and some real treaties. Even before we get that far, however, the United States could take certain unilateral steps without endangering na-tional security and probably enhancing it. First, we should stop developing these first-strike technologies, particularly the MX, Trident, and cruise missiles. And second, we should make a pledge of no-first-use of nuclear weapons. I think that these steps would set the stage for moving toward some sincere negotiations.

A third step we could take, one that is very close to comple-tion, is to adopt the Comprehensive Test Ban Treaty, which would ban all testing of nuclear weapons. I don't know if it could ever get ratified during the Reagan administration, but it would be a good treaty because without testing nuclear weapons you can't develop new ones.

I do not advocate unilateral disarmament. To make disarmament work you have to prepare the country for something besides a military defense—a nonmilitary, nonviolent defense strategy. People aren't trained in that right now. Disarmament will have to be a gradual transition, and these unilateral steps of stopping first-strike weapons would remove the immediate threat and instability. This would give us time to negotiate a Comprehensive Test Ban Treaty (CTB) which can be verified with a little improvement on seismic detectors. Along with radiation monitors, satellite surveillance, and other technical means of verification, we should be able to monitor things very capably.

Ever since CTB negotiations started there's been a strong lobby against it by the military, the Department of Energy, and the corporations. One of their biggest arguments is that if we don't occasionally test our weapons we won't know the capability of our stockpile. But that also works for the Soviets. In fact when it gets to the point that neither country is very confident their stockpile will work, then we're going to become more stable yet, and we'll be more apt to want to get rid of that stockpile.

After getting a CTB Treaty we could negotiate other bilateral or multilateral treaties. Both countries could ban flight-testing of all missiles, which would also be very easy to monitor. Without flight-testing you can't develop new weapons, maneuvering reentry vehicles, missiles, or new types of super-accurate navigation systems. We could also start removing the ICBMs and bomber forces, reducing weapons on both sides little by little. I think that's the way to go. I don't think we can see the role right now because there's too many "ifs" in the way, but as we go along the way will open and we will gain confidence and more trust in each other. Hopefully we can also get away from the fear tactics.

Verification capability is of course terribly important in all of this. When SALT II was presented before the Senate, all the experts testified that we could verify everything in the treaty. Some of the things seemed to me very difficult to verify. For example, how do you know how many reentry bodies are under a nose shroud? Or how many cruise missiles are in a submarine? Or how far a cruise missile will go? Mostly verification can determine numbers, but even those numbers are sometimes hard. It's hard to verify quality. I think the best way is not to verify precise capability, like how far a cruise missile will fly, but rather to verify whether they're building cruise missiles or not. Both the Comprehensive Test Ban Treaty for nuclear weapons and a treaty to ban flight-testing of missiles could be verified fairly easily.

As corporations got out of the weapons production business they could start making decent transportation and housing that doesn't fall down in fifty years. Eventually, though, I think it'll require more than just converting corporations from making weapons to building something else with another big government budget because you don't automatically get rid of the basic problems from which the arms race springs—like greed. Corporate greed is an institutionalization of individual and collective greed. Many of our society's problems spring from some basic roots, and the arms race is just one manifestation of those basic problems. Our jail system is another. We are not solving our social problems effectively; we're not giving due consideration to the people who need help. In other words, we're oppressing some people so that other people can make a lot of money. Naturally this will create a backlash. I think a lot of people in jail don't realize consciously that they're stuck in there because they got caught for striking out against some sense of social injustice. There is far too great a gap between rich and poor in this and many countries; the rich are getting richer and oppressing the poor still more in order to get still richer. The poor feel they have nothing to lose, so they create a backlash of crime and violence. The arms race is another aspect of this whole big picture.

I don't see any way of tackling these fundamental issues except through a mass movement. Each person must become aware of these issues and try to make his or her own lifestyle less consumptive. When you don't buy a lot of fancy gadgets and use so many resources, there's more for the other people; you're not exploiting the land and labor resources of Third World countries.

A lot of things changed my viewpoint. It didn't happen overnight but over a period of years. One catalyst was exposure to people working for things like the National Peace Academy Campaign.★ Or my own children, when they were going to col-

---

★For information, write: National Peace Academy Campaign, 110 Maryland Avenue NE, Washington, DC 20002.

lege, discussed some of the demonstrations during the Vietnam War. Initially I was all for the United States' standpoint. I thought we were the good country that was saving the world, but as various stories came out and began to unfold the true nature of things—soldiers' testimonies, and the *Pentagon Papers* and so on—I was forced to reexamine a lot of things I had taken for granted. Like civil disobedience and the burning of draft files. I began to see the symbolism: the connection between burning draft files and burning people in Vietnam with napalm. I started questioning everything.

I've been through World War II. I never liked war. I had a real hatred and even a fear of war. When I saw the Trident missile system was going to be a more aggressive type of weapon, I finally realized there's a point beyond which you cannot go, a place where you just have to draw the line. Looking back, it really wasn't that big a deal to get out of the business of making missiles, but it seemed pretty big when I was on the inside looking out.

Once in a while I talk to other people who are still on the inside looking out. There's not much you can say. Each one of us has to work through this self-delusion, this fear that prevents us from making changes. I had one advantage: I'd done other work besides engineering so I knew what other types of work were like. For a person who gets out of college, goes into engineering, and knows nothing about any other type of work, this kind of change might seem very scary.

Around here I work with Pacific Life Community in non-violent symbolic actions, hoping to break through the intellectual approach which creates so many defenses against seeing what is really going on, and to help people connect more with their feelings. We use many different symbols to communicate—blood, ashes, all of these. We have developed what we call the "Trident monsters," a large parade-type thing made of two columns of rope strung on bamboo poles with four hundred and eight black flags hanging on them. Two columns stretching out for the length of two football fields—that's the actual length of a Trident submarine. Each black flag represents one of the warheads. When you see these things stretched out for blocks and blocks on a street, and when you realize that each one of those flags is a hydrogen bomb, and when it hits you that it's all on just one submarine, you begin to understand how massive it is. But if you say "four hundred and eight warheads," that's just another number.

I've been warning people we only have a few more years to stop these weapons, after which it will be practically impossible to stop them. Each day, with each new weapon, the chances become greater that we will trigger a nuclear war, even if it's accidental. My real prayer is that we can stop developing the next round of nuclear weapons and start looking for new ways of creating security for everyone. It's a race with time.

Seymour Melman

Dr. Melman is a professor of industrial engineering at Columbia Univer-
sity. Among his many books on the political economy of the military are
Pentagon Capitalism: Our Depleted Society *and* The Permanent
War Economy. *His most recent book is* Profits Without Production
(1983). In 1981 Dr. Melman received the prestigious Rolex Prize. This
interview was conducted in the fall of 1980.

I was born in New York City in 1917; I have one younger
brother. My father was a pharmacist and my mother was a housewife. We were lower middle class. Nobody went on welfare; they
just scraped by. I grew up during the Great Depression and we
were living in the East Bronx, on the famous Charlotte Street
where Jimmy Carter went during his campaign. It looks like a
ruin now, but I was brought up right on that corner where he
stopped to give a speech. After graduating from the public high
school I went to City College for undergraduate study in economics and to Columbia for my Ph.D. I didn't bother to get a
master's degree; "straight on," I said. I have been teaching at
Columbia since 1948, in the Department of Industrial Engineering. I play flute and harmonica.

I've always studied economics and production because that's
the linkage between technology and economics. I started out ana-
lyzing how economic factors affect technology, which factors affect productivity, how factories get designed, and so on. I got
interested in this because I thought that if you understood productivity you could understand a lot about the development of a
society. And I was right. The early books I wrote on productivity

during the 1950s were to prove important as background for sus-
pecting that the military economy probably has strong counterproductive effects. It didn't take long before I realized the
tremendous impact of the military on the economy and on production. That was around 1960 or 1961. Increasingly I realized
that we must turn this whole thing around if we are going to save
our country from the terribly damaging effects of a permanent
war economy. So I continued to study it, making more and more
connections—jobs, the economy, the military, and so on. I just
hope we can change things around before it's too late, but that's
going to require that a lot of people wake up.

Our traditional business process has long yielded instabilities
of a familiar sort. These come from considerable inequalities in
the distribution of income, price manipulation in the marketplace,
a readiness of firms to make money by producing less, and a
corresponding readiness to close productive enterprises and move
them elsewhere (including out of the United States) in order to
maximize profits. A company's typical priority has been to make
money—never mind the details of how, as long as it is sensibly
within the law. But making money per se will not necessarily
satisfy the basic survival requirements of a community. In order
to live, a community must produce what it needs; it is unreasonable to expect that others will sustain it on any long-term basis.

It is critical to note what has happened to productive compe-
tence in manufacturing, that is, in the output per person. Lately
American industry has been doing pretty poorly. For about a
century the output per person in manufacturing—called productivity—had an average annual increase of about three percent.
This was largely due to the progressive mechanization and sys-
temization of work. Business found it attractive to purchase new
machinery because industries producing that machinery worked
hard to keep the cost of their products down. As a result the
prices of the machinery rose progressively less than the cost of
labor. During the last decade productivity has slipped to only a
two percent increase per year or less.

Let's look at this drop in productivity more closely, taking
an example. An enterprise may have paid twenty percent more
per hour in wages, but it then redesigned its product or its manner
of production so as to require fewer hours of labor per unit. So
the price of its product increased *less* than twenty percent, or not

at all. Productivity growth made it profitable for businesses such as the machinery makers to offset all sorts of cost increases, so that progressively wage rates rose faster than prices of machine tools. This was very striking in the period from 1939 to 1947: wage rates, i.e., average hourly earnings of industrial workers, rose about ninety-five percent while prices of machine tools rose only thirty-nine percent. This was characteristic of a long period of development in U.S. history. In fact visitors from Great Britain saw evidence of just that sort of process going on in the United States all through the nineteenth century. Then in the 1960s that process of cost minimizing, not only by machinery users but also by machinery makers, changed dramatically as major machine tool companies became producers for the Pentagon.

The Pentagon doesn't function to minimize costs; it is a customer that can pay whatever it wishes in order to get a given production capability. Inside the Department of Defense higher prices can be used to justify a bigger cash flow, which means a bigger budget—which benefits everybody in the Pentagon. Their argument has been that more money flowing to the whole country is good for the national income. But what we actually have is *more money flowing for fewer goods.* The process is destructive of economic values and contributes to inflation.

Furthermore the Pentagon has wanted to increase its military capability. When they have wanted a plane or gun to do certain things, they have always been ready to pay any price for it. For example, right now a new forty-ton tank is being designed. Over about three years its unit price has gone up from about half a million dollars to two million dollars. How did that happen? They wanted a very specific product, a tank that's very heavy yet also able to move very fast over broken ground and able to keep a tank turret absolutely level so as to fire with great precision. In other words, that requires an extraordinary combination of power and mechanical capability, needing all sorts of new technology.

They did *not* put a price limit on the tank; what they wanted was the *performance,* which in fact they are not quite getting. But that very effort to satisfy those requirements has run the price up by a factor of more than five.

Doing business in this way has affected the entire system. Some of the machinery producers are now doing the same thing. They have stopped minimizing costs in their own operations, and the result is now there for all to see. What happened to the machine tool industry in the United States during the 1970s was that machine tool prices went up eighty-five percent while the average hourly earnings of industrial workers increased only seventy-two percent. In other words, the price of machinery went up faster than labor's wages. One effect of that was to make the purchase of new machinery less attractive to users. Another result was that the users do not get a productivity boost from the use of new machinery.

Japan has had the opposite experience. From 1971 to 1978 Japanese machine prices went up fifty-one percent, but average hourly earnings went up one hundred seventy-seven percent. With wages going up three times as fast as the price of machinery, machinery users found a big advantage in buying new, more productive, more specialized machinery and using less labor time. That's why in the last decade Japanese productivity has gone up ten percent per year, compared to the United States' two percent per year. Japan has been repeating the classic U.S. pattern of increasing mechanization and thereby productivity.

As productivity failed to rise inside the U.S., managements could no longer use that growth to offset their cost increases. They then developed "cost pass-along," which means adding cost increases to price. As that accelerated, the rate of price increase became inflation. They passed it along to the consumer and that became price inflation. As U.S. price inflation proceeded, foreign producers of the same classes of goods saw they could undersell us, so they proceeded to export their products to the United States. In 1980 twenty-seven percent of the autos sold here were imports, twenty-five percent of the machine tools, fifty percent of the shoes, eighty-five percent of the black-and-white TV sets, and so on.

As these goods were now being imported, American factories that used to make them here were shut down, rendering the workers unemployed. And that's how we've gotten unemployment together with inflation.

To get us out of this jam we must reverse the flow of capital and technical brains out of the military and into civilian work. We need a planned conversion from a military to a civilian economy, plant by plant and base by base. Civilian factories which have been shut down need to be converted into viable enterprises once again. To do that will require very detailed local planning all over the country. Alternative-use planning will have to be done in every factory. In the recent past it was recommended that this be done by alternative-use planning committees comprised of fifty percent management and fifty percent employees. The aim would be to design economically viable enterprises that could produce competently for the domestic market, as well as provide opportunities for productive livelihood. Industries and government in America have forgotten the goal of providing productive (which simply means "making useful things") livelihood in favor of making profits.

New prestige, importance, and understanding must be given to productive livelihood. Simultaneously our government has to be used to put large blocks of capital into new productive undertakings. For example, at the present time sixty-nine percent of the American machine tools are over ten years old, whereas in Japan it's only thirty-nine percent. Upgrading the U.S. machines would take an outlay of about thirty-four billion dollars. Rather than buying this stuff outright, one strategy our government might pursue is to give a major tax incentive for purchasing new machine tools, making them cheaper and more attractive for companies to buy. It is interesting that this figure of thirty-four billion dollars compares with the lower cost estimates for building the MX missile system. So we have an interesting trade-off: *either we can rehabilitate the metal-working machinery of U.S. industry or we can build the MX; we cannot do both.*

There are four reasons we aren't making the necessary shifts in our spending priorities. First is the confused and widespread belief that making money is all that counts. Second is the judgment that since military spending increases the amount of money in circulation, it is a good thing. Third is the false assumption that military spending is a key factor in employment, which it is not. In fact, as I explained earlier, military spending is indirectly a key factor in generating *unemployment*. Fourth, there is obviously a major sector of a ruling class in our society that is hell-bent for a power play against the Soviets, supported by a large cadre of intellectuals who are ready to justify their move.

We will not be able to turn the situation around until large numbers of people come to see the connection between the war economy and these consequences and get good and fed up with them. It is a matter of enormous importance to explain these linkages clearly. Certainly anyone who has just been laid off would understand perfectly. Because these analyses are all about their lives, the closer to production people are, the more easily they understand them. If they are working in a steel mill they could organize production teams everywhere in the plant and think about how to run the place competently. They could use that knowledge in collective bargaining with management. If management decides to fade out, they can figure out other ways to run the plant. If management wants to drop the plant or close it or clear out of the country or go make money on the stock market instead of making steel, then the union should start taking practical steps toward possibly taking it over. There aren't many models yet for how to do that, but there are near models based on ESOP, the Employment Stock Ownership Plan—schemes that have been worked out whereby people working in companies being shut down by management can buy them up and run them. There is a federal law to that effect, and the Economic Development Administration in Washington runs the program. Incidentally, EDA is being shut down by Reagan and Company.

The machinists union (IAM) is setting up a school to run for ten days this spring (1981). The purpose is to get their people to understand enterprise planning and other functions they've left to management until now. If it works, this approach will be an example to other unions. Management really can't be relied on any more to organize work. While multinational corporations are sending money abroad for short-term profit, our state managers are promoting military nonsense. In essence our managers have been wrecking the United States as a production system, and the only alternative that seems to make sense is that the people whose lives are rooted in production work have to find a way to organize things so they function properly.

Recently I was asked whether I put the onus for various international difficulties on the USSR. Actually *both* the United States *and* the Soviet Union have been pushing military buildups into the overkill range, and it is unilaterally irrational on *both* sides. Also, *neither* government has anyone formally thinking about reversing the arms race or planning conversion from military to civilian economy. The ruling classes of *both* countries are responsible for this; therefore my judgment is to condemn them *both*.

Intellectuals in both countries, including the media, have the task of explaining the war economy. Working people have the need to plan for productive livelihood because both the private and the state managers are less competent to do so. In the U.S. all sorts of groups should use every means available to them to explain, to clarify, to lay out the connections, to show why the Reagan national security program, which accelerates all the trends in the direction of deterioration, is the worst kind of bad news for this country. There is no one villain; the main villains are all who formulate and knowingly participate in carrying out the current program.

The reversal of the arms race is the last available military strategy for improving the security of America. Military and international relations people are needed to give good advice on how to carry out a mutually agreed upon (U.S.–USSR) roll-back in armed forces. That is largely a military-political problem, and military-political considerations and advice are needed. Unfortunately, mainstream military people are not thinking along these lines, omitting such planning as part of military contingencies. We laid out our basic formula on Economic Conversion in legislation put before the last Congress. There is basically no shortage of useful work that needs to be done in our country. For example, it would be nice for the United States to be able to make a railroad or a bus—a *good* bus.

Ordinary people follow the buck and the ruble; the managers follow power and privilege. Translating this, what can happen in American society and in Soviet society to force those with power and privilege to stop perpetuating the military economy? Two things are going on now: first, Reagan and Company are frightening our people; it's terrible to see the devastating emotional effect on ordinary people because they really don't understand what's going on. Second, the economy is being smashed. Most of our population has never known economic depression, and certainly not a pattern of technical/economic industrial decay and they aren't prepared for it. In the United States the Reagan administration has been pushing war in El Salvador and it's about to push something that will cave in on their heads: civil defense. Reagan is currently asking four billion dollars for civil defense. Can you imagine what lunacy that is? Just picture this: bulletins over TV and radio to "leave in an orderly fashion; even-numbered license plates on the first day and odd-numbered ones on the second. . . ." Do you know how many rifles and guns are distributed in our country? Imagine someone pulling up and the guard saying, "Nope, your license plate's an odd number; wait until tomorrow." If you just look ahead a few steps, it starts being Cloud Cuckooland.

Young people today have no prospect of being economically better off than their parents. They can't buy houses or save money because inflation melts their money. This is a "bad scene." Reagan and Company are promising all sorts of things they can't deliver, so I expect strange things to happen. Before long the AFL-CIO will turn against the military. We've got to make reversing the arms race *the* main issue of the next presidential race. At the same time we've got to consider the Russians too. We're setting up a U.S.–Soviet economic conversion symposium. The truth is that the political-economic issues involved here are at the core of concern in reforming both of our societies. In both our societies centralism is the main method for controlling the war economy. This is covered in detail in my book *Pentagon Capitalism*. In it I pointed out that Soviet society was organized on the theory of concentrating political, economic, and military decision-making power in the same hands: the Politburo. In the United States we have now evolved to the same point: political, military, and economic decision-making power now largely rests in the hands of the Pentagon and its directorate in the White House, while the Pentagon operates the biggest industrial central administrative office in the United States and probably in the world.

Dick Gregory

Dick Gregory, a nationally famous comedian, has since the 1960s become equally well known as a peace activist. He was interviewed in front of the White House in the fall of 1980, where he was picketing on behalf of the campaign to end world hunger.

It's difficult to say how I got to be doing what I'm doing now; it's like your hair growing. I went from a ten- or fifteen-thousand-dollar-a-night show business comedian thing to protesting all sorts of things I see wrong. And if someone would've said "Here's what I want you to do," I would have rejected it. I guess I got to where I am now because my mother, my brothers and sisters, and my wife never put demands of glamor on me, although I wanted them. So if I'd married a woman who wanted glamor and enjoyed show business, things would've turned out different. Maybe it was also the cowboy movies. I wanted to be that cowboy. And when the civil rights movement hit it gave me a chance to be a cowboy; it gave me a chance to be right and to have a showdown with the bad guys. Every time I hit that front line I felt the way I felt when I used to sit and look at cowboy movies.

Anyway, I kinda grew and got more wrapped up in the whole peace movement, and I came to believe that nonviolence can be more than just a tactic or ideology. I also got into vegetarianism, and found that as you change your diet and your body then you change your head.

One problem with the peace movement is that the people in it do not have peace within them. When they get that things will change. You see, peace is not the absence of war, it's the presence of peace. Now that means peace deep down in the pit of your body, recognizing the God-force, the unity of all creatures and all human beings. That means sympathizing with hungry people and people who want peace, but also recognizing that it's a violation of God to hate the food manipulators or the war mongers. It took a *long* time for me to come to *that* understanding. As I raised my level of consciousness I came to expect more and more of myself than I did as an ordinary comedian hanging out. So I decided not to work in places that served alcohol, because alcohol is not a symbol of peace—it's a symbol of war. In fact one of the reasons we tolerate all the things we tolerate is that most of the people are either high, on their way to get high, or just finished getting it.

The problem with America and most of the world is greed. Greed feeds back into itself. We will become secure when we reach the end of that rope and find that greed is not the answer. We're a very greedy, frightened, and cowardly nation. You and I can walk down the street with some Iranians. Who'll get jumped on? *They* will. If we walk down the streets with some *Russians, they* won't get jumped on. We don't jump on no one what jumps back on you. I recently listened to a judge say, "Well, uh, what we ought to do, uh, is get them Iranians out of here, uh, ought'a export 'em . . ." Never said that about the Mafia, and most of the Mafia isn't citizens here. *Ain't gonna mess with nobody that has power.*

Greed, pride—all that is a violation of God. In order to change it you have to deal with self. You have to go into yourself and turn your light on. If ten thousand of us are sitting in the basement in the dark and you come in and turn the light on, we *all* have the light. If you just let that light shine there's no way I can't recognize it. So when we turn our lights on, people who felt comfortable in the dark, 'cause they been there for a long time, some of them gotta shield their eyes, and that's all they're doing when they resent you—they're really just shielding their eyes because they been in the dark so long. Once you start understanding how important that light is, don't go puttin' it under a basket. Let it shine. That's what's gonna turn things around.

One thing you gotta understand: there ain't never been a "world war." Take World War II: it was mainly fought between white folks, and not all of them participated. Moreover most of the world is not white. So you just have a few percent of the world involved, which ain't a world war! It works like this: they have a war and then they have a PR game and *project* that it's a world war. The dudes that make war are just makin' it as big as they can; like a little child who comes in, "Ooooh, mommy, I was out there'n there was a *big* bully. . . ." They do it to feel important. Sure, 'cause the bigger my war is, when I come home and tell my children, the more power I get. *That's* their game.

If you plant the seed of war in our subconscious "mind garden" then you're gonna harvest war. You plant the seed of nuclear bombs and one day you got to harvest that. We gotta go through that garden an' pluck it out! And we got to say, "Ain't gonna be no world war, an' you not gonna drop no nuclear bombs."

Let's go and review war for a minute. I'm your husband and you're my wife; we have a son. Because of the perverted sex patterns we have in this country there comes a time that my son challenges me for your love. My son don't know nothin' about this. It's in *my* head. That's why fathers keep puttin' sons out, but they have compassion for a girl that did the same thing because the girl's not challengin' me for mother's love. That sort of thing spills over into society; as an older dude I see the young dude challenge me for young women, and because my perversion makes me freak out over young women, now I gotta find a way to put him out'a the house. That's called war. But in order to play war I gotta play games; I gotta make you patriotic. Patriotism is from a Latin word, *patria,* meaning "father." And "army camp" is from a Latin word meaning "castrate." Okay? So the deck's already been stacked. The rest of it's just manipulation. It ain't got nothin' to do with nothin'. That's why war is puttin' young men on both sides in the front lines to kill one another, while we old men stay back home with the ladies. That's why you got to go to the Pentagon one day and say, "If old men gonna *make* war, then let old men *fight* war." Once you start seein' how it works, it's incredible. It's totally insane how they whoop a game on us, how they project. When you get right down to it, it's a racial thing— men of one race afraid of losin' their women to men of another race, which means losin' the children, which is their immortality. You see how it works?

When you watch the Game and see it and start figuring what

it's about, things start to fit together. And the only way you can figure it out, or figure out what to do, is to sit quietly and watch.

We make things difficult for ourselves because we try to structure our God around a capitalistic system, and God was here before capitalism and will be here after it's gone. If you understand universal law, it says, "If you give, it's gonna come back." Once we understand how that universal law works then we're better off in figuring out what to do in society. But it starts with yourself.

So where do we go from here? We go inside and start finding the truth. We start breaking up all the incredible negativities that destroy our true power. Once we do that, then we can find out where we're going. Take greed. When you recognize that seed in you, then you just tell yourself "I'm not gonna be greedy, I'm not gonna be greedy . . ." and then "I'm gonna give one of my dresses away to someone that needs it; I'm gonna share my food; I'm gonna share my love; when I pray for *my* children in school I'm gonna pray for *all* children." You don't wait for someone else; the God-force says "*You* are responsible." You have to do it for *you*.

We gotta look with fresh eyes at everything we're doing in our culture. In order to keep the war game goin' I gotta make you aggressive and violent. The most violent period on television is not them cowboy movies or them detective shoot-'em-ups; it's every Saturday morning when they show them *cartoons* for our children. That's why Bugs Bunny uses dynamite. And if you get around little children after they been lookin' at those cartoons, you'll see they get very violent. Look at our nursery rhymes too: "Jack and Jill went up the hill. . . ." Before it's over both of them gonna fall. "Humpty Dumpty sat on a wall. . . ." Before it's over he gonna break himself into a billion pieces. "Little Miss Muffett sat on a tuffet. . . ." The spider *scared* her. . . . Why do all our nursery rhymes end in violence? See how the seed of war is planted? It goes so far back!

I've been protesting what I've been seeing for a long time, and I'm getting tired of talking about these things over and over. I'm not quite sure what exactly to do now; I'm just formulating it now. I'm thinking about maybe not talking for twelve years to protest all the things we're doing wrong in our society—world hunger, war, violence, all that. I want to plant something in people's minds. I have a six-year-old son; he'd be eighteen when I started up talking again. Maybe folks would listen; I want to be among the first to call, "Break down your nuclear equipment; get rid of it." So that's the seed I'm planting: "Get rid of it; tear it up. Tear up those nuclear plants. If you've used up all your legitimate energy, then go to bed when the sun goes down!" I want to make a statement for elderly people, for mentally insane people, for people in jail, for handicapped people, for women, for children . . . a statement against racism and sexism. I figure that in our society, when you decide to give up making millions of dollars with your mouth then maybe everyone'll want to hear your last words; and twelve years later when you come back, they'd pay you millions to hear your *first* words!

When you think about me, I want you to think about no war, about peace, about the right way to treat elderly people, about how to treat drunks or drug addicts, about how to treat handicapped people. And I want you to start working; shine your light, and touch others. That's my dream. But even if nobody else ever listened I'd still be a better person after twelve years of silence. When I think about all the cussin' I've done in my life, I'd have been better off if I'd stopped talkin' long ago . . . or if I'd been born without knowin' how!

Thing's are going to work out; I really think so. You see, people are out there and they are lookin'. That's where I've got my insight from, talkin' with people. Traveling across the country, looking at this country change. Hearing the news as it's manipulated in the large cities; but it flows free in the little bitty towns. You start seeing it; you start feeling it. In fact when I walked from New York to the White House it was on the back roads. Something very interesting happened; not one time did I see a Carter, an Anderson, or a Reagan sign, even in this peak campaign period. How close have you ever been to an election where every car that passes by hasn't got a campaign sign on it? I tell you something—that's really weird. Something's fixin' to happen. People are getting really disgusted. They're catching on. When they *really* catch on and start changing things, I hope and pray that we can get some *real* security. It's up to us, and we can do it with God's help.

Ina May Gaskin

Ina May Gaskin is a member of The Farm, a spiritual community of about 1500 people located near Summertown, Tennessee. She is actively involved in the Farm's midwifery program and in educating the medical profession and the broader public about the role and art of midwifery; this is discussed in her book Spiritual Midwifery. *This interview took place in December 1980.*

I was born in 1940 in Marshalltown, a town of about twenty-five thousand in central Iowa. My father was raised a farmer, but his parents lost their farm during the depression. I went up through junior college in Marshalltown. Although my grades were good, I didn't get a scholarship I think because I was a girl, so I worked my way through the State University.

One of my earliest memories was the great celebration in town when the Second World War ended. Nobody had known how far the war was going to reach . . . was it going to come into the middle of the country? It's hard to believe, but even in central Iowa we had blackouts. At the time we kids were not aware of what ended the war, of the atomic bomb. I read John Hersey's book *Hiroshima* when I was about fourteen and I was horrified.

When I was about twenty-two I went to California on a vacation and briefly joined the peace movement, walking with a group of people up the coast from San Diego to Vallejo, a naval base north of San Francisco. I wanted to see if this kind of method could do anything. It was a very quixotic thing; only about twenty people walked the several hundred miles, joined at times by others. When we entered towns which depended for their livelihood on the military industries, I could see how threatened those people felt and how we were touching off more hate and fear in them. Although I was glad to have participated, that was my last peace march.

After college I joined the Peace Corps. Kennedy was shot while I was in training, just before we were to go overseas. I spent the next two years in Malaysia, where I saw how much he had touched people abroad. Although Americans had a bad reputation at the time, he was well loved by many people. A lot of that was because of the Peace Corps; Kennedy was pretty idealistic, which was rare in the early 1960s.

I found the Peace Corps experience very valuable. We Americans really must get out and see how others live and think. When we can see our country as other people see us and see how most Americans live overseas, we can understand why many people abroad don't like us much. It was very educational for me, although I can't say that I did anyone much good by teaching English to hungry kids.

By this time I was getting quite depressed; it was 1964 and the Vietnam War was escalating. I felt pretty alone and unable to do anything to change what I saw as the basic situation: more and more military buildup, using the vast riches of America to squash some very poor people whose main problem wasn't ideological but survival. So few Americans know what it is to live in poverty. We have this Horatio Alger idea that anyone who really tries not only can survive but can even become rich and probably president. American optimism is very nice if it's got some generosity to it; it's not so nice when it assumes that anyone who is not doing as well is somehow at fault. It may not be their fault at all; if the system they live under is unjust and oppressive, they may be working very, very hard and it still won't be enough.

When I felt the first wave put out by the hippies and heard of their real cultural renaissance, I realized that there were *thousands* of people like me flocking to San Francisco. The first signals were very pure and idealistic, and they went all the way around the world. Several of my Malaysian students started to grow their hair and look for guitars; the Beatles were a large part of that. I saw their first movie, *A Hard Day's Night,* in Singapore, and it made me want to go home and check it out. I didn't feel so old and useless (at twenty-five).

I met Stephen Gaskin in San Francisco. He started the Monday Night Classes which I went to for a couple of years. We were already together at the time the Caravan started traveling around the country. That is when I became a midwife. Several of the ladies traveling with us were pregnant, and the first one gave birth while we were in a parking lot at Northwestern University in Evanston; fortunately everything came out all right. It was the first birth of *anything* that I had ever seen: I learned a lot from that lady, from just how easily she did it. After that I began studying. I read only medical and obstetric books for the next few years.

When we settled on our land in Tennessee, we started keeping our delivery statistics and comparing them with those of hospitals. We realized we had rediscovered something very good—that women can take care of each other.

I am convinced that natural childbirth and midwifery have wide implications for national and global security. Today's overreliance on technology and the passing of the decision-making process in childbirth from women to men have made for a really strange situation. In our mothers' generation a whole lot of our mothers were totally knocked out when they gave birth to us; they were told by men how they [the men] would deliver us, and from then on they were told by the men how to raise us and what to feed us. When women lose the power of decision, especially about this really basic stuff, a lot of them have a hard time for the rest of their lives. At the same time many of the men of that same generation have gotten kind of crazy. Instead of being protective they sometimes do things that run counter to survival.

The protective instinct of the mammalian mother for her young is very strong, yet our generation is accustomed to thinking of mothers as weaker than fathers: if mother doesn't feel well, she goes to the doctor and he gives her a pill. I don't mean that all of our mothers fit this pattern, of course, but that generation was the most drugged—from childbirth on through menopause, and perhaps even still: the "Valium generation." And these women were confused, too, when it came to sending their sons off to war: the Korean War, the Vietnam War.

Childbirth is an empowering event for women who go through it with the support of their loved ones and people they trust, and with the idea that it is a strong experience requiring bravery but one they are equal to. On the other hand if a mother is convinced that it is beyond her strength and she is put under anesthesia, childbirth can be a lot like rape.

For a time we lost some good vision in the women. I think a lot of it had to do with the disappearance of the midwife in America. We never had schools of midwifery endowed by the philanthropist millionaires, as they did medical universities, so midwifery was not regarded as a respectable profession in the U.S. The invention in England of forceps also reduced the power of midwives. It only took a few very well-placed women whose children's lives were saved by this magical device for the word to get around that the male midwives had it more together than the women—even though there were also a lot of birth injuries caused by misuse of the forceps. Then in the late nineteenth century America started to have a glut of doctors as more people sent their sons to study medicine in England, Scotland, and Germany. They then came back here to practice and teach. We began to get some very well-endowed, all-male medical schools. Before long the doctors were strong enough to squelch midwifery through propaganda, social pressure, and withholding funds. Some are still doing that.

We lost something very great when that happened because there is a limit to what a doctor can do. For example, he won't be very good at advising teenage girls about their sex lives, because most girls are too embarrassed to talk to a man about that subject. He can't often advise well on how to breast-feed because he has never done it. He can't give as much hands-on care to a woman because of the possible alienation of affection and the anger of her husband or his own wife. So he's not able to find out how much comfort this gives the woman. Because the doctor has never been in labor he may not know that a mere *look* can stop that process. I've seen this happen.

Many women in our mothers' generation went to a narrower vision. Maybe it was partly because the world situation was too much to look at. Or disempowered by their childbirth experience, they were made to distrust their instincts and to think their opinions didn't matter much and that they needed to be dependent on men. This led them to displace their sense of what provides security. Wanting security for their children, they turned to *material* security. It became important to have a big house, wall-to-wall carpeting, a college education, and so on. But they didn't extend their minds to consider carefully whether the war that was going on was really necessary.

When you look at the polls today you see that a lot of the people thinking about alternatives to war are women. Far more women than men thought that Reagan was a hawk. There is a new spirit among women now, more self-respect. We see the world is all interconnected and interdependent; what goes on in the Middle East or Central America might have a very strong impact on our families. Women are also getting more interested in addressing these issues collectively with other women.

One great contribution of the late 1960s was the concept of sisterhood. Increasing technology, urbanization, and suburbanization have split women apart from each other and made them distrust each other; women lost the natural ceremonies, like childbirth, that formerly bound them together. As I was growing up little girls were taught to be competitive with each other, not cooperative. If you look at successful tribal societies you see a very high level of cooperation among women. This is significant when you realize that they've figured out how to survive harmoniously for many generations. You don't find the "Miss America syndrome" where you pick out the young woman among the millions available and say that she's the best looking. A lot of tribes have ceremonies where you see all the women together in a dance, and they're *all* beautiful. And they all *know* they are beautiful. The competitive mode makes women distrust each other. Cooperation is pretty clearly a survival trait. When you cooperate you place your attention on the things that really matter. Are the kids making it? Is the water clean? Is there enough food? Are kids learning what they need to pass on to the next generation? Are the men using their strength and aggressiveness to protect the women and children? These are real central questions.

It seems to me, those of us born in the 1940s and 1950s were not brought up in ways conducive to survival. We need only look at the events of the last few years to see that the world is not on a very good track and that we're going to have to be some smart cookies to get ourselves out of this mess.

Sisterhood is something we cannot do without. We have to use our intelligence in a collective manner to solve problems. I have a gut feeling that the women of Russia and the women of the U.S. would find a lot in common. Our men are quite similar. A lot of men in high positions drink too much, and the aggressiveness of the Russian military and of the U.S. military looks more alike than it does different. It's part of the same problem.

Women's communications skills are really needed in these next few decades. Women tend to be good communicators and peacemakers; certainly any mother who spends any time living with kids learns to be a peacemaker. Yet we do not put many women into high positions where they can use these skills.

Change is coming about on all fronts. More women have to get involved, to inform themselves. We have to find out what is going on beyond the spoon-fed version of the news we get on the television. Watch the tube, but find out what's going on in other places too. If you don't, you might miss something that might mean your life, your children's lives, our continued existence. Try to understand other women. Look for global solutions to global problems. Learn another language and reach out to people in other cultures.

I would change morning TV entirely. Television has terrific possibilities, but I'm appalled by what is shown to the people, mostly women, who watch it at home during the day. I'd like to see a channel that teaches skills we need. For example, a really skillful mother taking care of her children in front of the camera. This is how skills are taught in any village society; you just watch how the best ones do it and you learn. They could show a woman breast-feeding her baby, giving a little explanation. Or a lady sorting out a fight among children and bringing about a peaceful resolution.

When Thomas Jefferson and other Founding Fathers studied the Iroquois Six Nations as they were designing the American Constitution, they left out some of the most important elements of their form of government—for example, the part played by the women. The men sat as chiefs, but it was the women who chose the chiefs. In their clans there were clan mothers, women who were highly respected and who spoke for the other women. And they picked the chiefs. They had been watching them from the time they were young girls until they were grandmothers. They knew these men, their total history—how long they sucked their thumbs, if they were greedy at the table, if they were bullies as kids. They could spot those with natural leadership tendencies pretty early: who were the ones with compassion, who were the ones they could trust, and who were too impetuous to be given a lot of responsibility over other people. What an intelligent way to choose! The safety factor in there—because we know that power can corrupt—was that if a chief became unacceptable to the women they could pull him down. And the other men would back up the women. Another important clause was that the women decided what wars were fought. Now doesn't that seem intelligent?

We women must all understand that we can't see ourselves as only being powerful in the way that we see men are powerful. This is not necessarily where our power resides. If we only go into competition with each other and with men we won't find the answers. We also need to understand the power mothers have to change society. If enough women became aware of what is going on in society we could solve an awful lot of problems. We could wipe out most sexism in a generation. Men have pretty much taken the rap for sexism; many people have forgotten (although a lot of men remember) that it was women who mostly raised the men. How can women raise men so that other women's daughters can live with them in a fair and compassionate way? We need to examine our attitudes and practices, changing them so we don't keep perpetuating the problems. It can be done and this would contribute to having a more peaceful society.

I'd like to go back to the role childbirth plays in knitting a society together. When it's not controlled by an elitist group and when women have their way about it, in some way their men become involved. When men participate in natural childbirth they come to respect the courage, strength, and endurance of the women. A lot of our men on the Farm have told me that they believe that if every man in our society saw their child born that there would be no such thing as war. It does something to you that's very good. You consider the children and the future more. In all of their actions the people of the Six Nations were supposed to consider the consequences of their actions as far as the seventh generation of people. This creates a different attitude about what you teach your kids. If you unleash your anger on your kids, you see that you're cutting a track there that will affect your grandchildren, and they're going to pass it on to your great-grandchildren, and so on. This way of thinking gives you a different attitude about everything. For example, when we sell the Third World pesticides that we have outlawed in the United States, how will it come back to us? We'll have it in our coffee and in our cereal. What we put out *will* come back to us.

James W. Prescott

Dr. Prescott is currently working on a book which develops the themes included in this interview. Recent personal and professional events that are only briefly mentioned in this interview have led to the loss of his seventeen-year federal career in science administration, a home and a marriage of twenty years. This interview was conducted in the spring of 1982.

I was born in Eureka, Illinois, in 1934. My parents divorced when I was four, at which time my three brothers and I were placed in a Catholic orphanage. The post-depression years made it impossible for my mother to support us and we spent nine years in the Guardian Angel Orphanage. We all recognized the necessity of the orphanage and did not interpret it as "maternal abandonment," but it definitely helped shape my thinking about emotional security and the importance of the mother-child relationship. When my mother remarried, we all rejoined her. Unfortunately the marriage did not work out and I can still remember the four of us protecting her from our stepfather who became violent and abusive after a head injury received in an auto accident. She died in 1973 from injuries received in an auto accident when she was hit by a twenty-one-year-old woman who was drunk at the time.

After finishing high school in Illinois, I went to Marquette University in Milwaukee, graduating in 1954 with a major in psychology and minors in philosophy, theology, and mathematics. My Jesuit education was instrumental in helping me reevaluate my personal belief system, but it took me about ten years to dismantle a quarter century of education, training and Catholic belief, a process I began as an undergraduate. Such efforts are, of course, incomplete since certain emotional residues from early childhood remain with us throughout life.

After completing my master's degree in clinical and child psychology, I spent two years with the army's Human Resources Research Office in California. From there I went to McGill University in Montreal, receiving a doctorate in experimental-clinical psychology. I moved to Washington, D.C., in 1961 and after a couple of other positions, I went to work in 1966 for the National Institutes of Health's National Institute of Child Health and Human Development (NICHD), where I established and developed the Developmental Behavioral Biology Program. This program was responsible for initiating, promoting, and administering grant and contract research programs, particularly on the effects of early experience upon brain development and behavior.

Ultimately, the effects of sensory deprivation upon brain development and behavior became a major focus of my program. I was particularly interested in understanding the sensory processes and brain mechanisms responsible for the variety of abnormal emotional-social behaviors which result when infants are reared away from their mother—so-called "maternal-social" deprivation. Numerous important studies were done by the Harlows, psychologists at the University of Wisconsin Primate Center. Dr. Harry Harlow conducted a breeding program of rhesus macque monkeys. He separated the infants from their mothers and reared them in cages by themselves but in a colony room where they could see, hear, and smell other animals but could not touch or be touched by them. Dr. Harlow thought this would be a more "efficient" breeding system. What happened, however, was that these infant monkeys developed profound depression, autistic behaviors, stereotypic rocking behaviors, chronic toe and penis sucking, and hypersensitivity to touch. They had an overreaction to all sensory stimuli but touch was a particularly traumatic experience for them. Later, as juveniles and adults they manifested extremely violent behavior toward themselves (such as self-mutilation) and toward other animals. The juveniles would viciously attack infant and adult monkeys—behaviors which non-isolation reared monkeys simply do not engage in. Furthermore, the Harlows discovered that when these monkeys became adults, they had a variety of abnormal sexual behaviors and were useless as breeders. Dr. Harlow developed two means to correct this situation. One was the development of a "rape-rack" where the isolation-reared female monkey was restrained in a sexually receptive position so that the male monkey could mount and impregnate here. The other way was the use of a very patient male who finally was able to mount and impregnate some of the isolation-reared females. But when these "motherless" monkeys gave birth they either totally neglected their offspring or would viciously attack them by throwing them against the wall or crushing their heads against the floor. Human intervention was necessary to save the infants' lives. The findings from these experimental animal studies of maternal social deprivation has established the best animal model for the study and understanding of human child abuse.

Dr. John Bowlby, the famous English psychiatrist who brought to the world's attention the importance of the maternal-infant relationship in his report, *Maternal Care and Mental Health* (1951), presented to the World Health Organization, visited Harlow's laboratory and pointed out to Harlow that his abnormal monkeys had characteristics similar to those seen in children reared in institutions. This observation led Dr. Harlow to look for the critical elements in the maternal–infant relationship which resulted in such profoundly abnormal behaviors in infants reared in isolation.

In a 1964 paper, Dr. Harlow revealed what was, in my opinion, a major conceptual error when he stated, "The most extreme deprivation condition we have studied is total social isolation (not *sensory* isolation, only *social* isolation)." A similar statement was made by Rene Spitz, the famous psychoanalyst who reported on the profound depression and death of infants who are hospitalized and not given maternal affection. Spitz wrote, "In recent years a great deal of illuminating and interesting work has been done with animals and humans on the effects of sensory deprivation. . . . It should be realized that sensory deprivation and emotional deprivation are not interchangeable concepts."

My research convinces me that both of these authorities were in error in directing scientific inquiry away from the sensory neurobiological processes. My understanding of developmental neuropsychology makes it very clear to me that sensory processes *had* to be involved. After all, our sensory systems are the means by which the organism and its brain communicates with the outside world. The question was not *whether* the sensory systems were involved, but rather, were *all* the sensory systems equally important or were some more important than others. This question led me to a critical review of the literature on isolation-reared mammals, not just of primates. This review made it clear to me that deprivation of *touch* was the critical sensory modality; deprivation of vision and hearing does not result in pathological behavior if touch and body contact are received by the infant.

My conclusion was modified in a significant manner by the extremely important study of Dr. William Mason and Dr. Gershon Berkson who raised infant monkeys in cages by themselves in a colony room where social communication could take place through vision, hearing, and smell—but not through touch or body contact. The critical difference in this study was that some of the infant monkeys were reared on a "swinging" mother surrogate while others were reared on a "stationary" mother surrogate. The difference in the results were profound. The monkeys reared on the swinging surrogate did not develop classic isolation-reared behaviors, while those reared on the stationary surrogate did.

Drs. Mason and Berkson, who were behavioral primatologists, interpreted their findings to emphasize the importance of dynamic social interaction. They did not recognize the significance of the neurobiological processes involved in their study nor their associated brain mechanisms. From my perspective as a neuropsychologist, it was clear that the *vestibular* sensory system (which mediates movement stimulation in three-dimensional space) is *crucial* in determining the presence of pathological behaviors. Within the brain, neural impulses travel from the vestibular receptors to the cerebellum and the brain stem. It is the cerebellum which mediates the complexity of emotional-social and behavioral abnormalities, particularly the stereotypical rocking behaviors. Subsequently, I demonstrated the existence of structural and functional abnormalities in the cerebellum and limbic structures of the brains of maternally-socially deprived monkeys. I also did extensive theoretical research to demonstrate the necessity of neurological connections between the brain's cerebellum and limbic structures, two parts of the brain principally involved in emotional behaviors.

I next initiated four neurobiological studies to determine whether the brains of these abnormal monkeys were also abnormal.[1] And indeed, the findings from these studies established both functional and structural brain abnormalities.

In addition to laboratory research, I conducted a set of cross-cultural studies. Although developmental and clinical studies supported the linkage between child abuse and subsequent adult violence, I felt we should be able to validate this in much larger human populations. Fortunately, anthropologist Robert B. Textor had recently summarized in a massive set of tables the statistically significant relationships among coded behaviors of 400 cultures in the Ethnographic Atlas that had been collected over the years by cultural anthropologists. In that volume, I selected *all* the primitive cultures in which there was information on a) child-rearing practices, b) sexual behavior, and c) violence. Forty-nine such primitive cultures had this information available.[2]

In summary, after making corrections for coding errors in the original data, thirty-nine out of forty-nine cultures with high and low levels of violence were accurately predicted just from the variable of infant physical affection. The remaining ten cultures whose violence was incorrectly predicted by the infant physical affection variable was correctly predicted by taking into account whether premarital sex was permitted or punished. In brief, four cultures were characterized by high infant physical affection and high adult violence when it should have been low. All of these cultures punished premarital coitus. My interpretation is that the advantage of early infant physical affection can be negated later in life by deprivation of physical affection through repressive sexuality. The other six cultures had low infant physical affection and low adult violence. These six cultures all permitted premarital coitus. Here, my interpretation is that disadvantages of early deprivation of physical affection can be compensated for by rich physical affection through expressive sexuality.

In overview, the physical violence high and low in forty-nine primitive cultures distributed throughout the world could be accurately predicted with the two measures of physical affection in two stages of development: parent/infant relationships and adolescent sexual expressiveness.[3]

To sum up, the essence of what we have learned is this: *physical affectional pleasure is the major regulatory control system over violence.* If the neural pleasure systems of the brain are stimulated or activated they will automatically inhibit, reciprocally, the activity of neural systems that mediate violence. Dr. José Delgado demonstrated this relationship when he stimulated the brain pleasure centers of a charging bull and brought an immediate end to the bull's rage and charge. This reciprocal relationship between pleasure and violence was even more dramatically shown by Dr. Robert G. Heath who stimulated the septum (with an electrode) of a woman who suffered from uncontrollable rage. All forms of therapy had been unsuccessful. Electrical stimulation of this limbic pleasure structure brought an immediate halt to her rage, followed by the experience of pleasure and ultimately of orgasm.

When physical affection is absent during the formative periods of brain development (and this period goes beyond adolescence), the dendritic structures of the neural pleasure circuits do not develop properly and are malformed. Thus, sensory deprivation causes the brain's pleasure circuits to be crippled in their ability to control and regulate the violence circuits.

Another aspect of this theory which needs mentioning but which cannot be extensively discussed is that for affectional and sexual pleasure to be effective in controlling, regulating, and preventing violent behaviors, this pleasure must be integrated into higher brain centers.[4] It is for this reason that physical affection during infancy and childhood is so important because it lays the neurobiological foundation for pleasurable sensory experiences to be integrated into higher brain centers and consciousness.

As various environmental factors shape the development of the *individual* brain and its associated behaviors, individuals who group together with others for collective action come to express a sort of "cultural brain." Thus, if the culture creates violent individuals, that violence is reflected in the larger group, appearing as collective violence or warfare or in other ways with which we are all too familiar—for example, chronic alcohol and drug abuse, which research shows is also a consequence of physical affectional deprivation. Given the prevalence of barbarity, torture, and sadism in the history of Western civilization (for example, the Catholic Spanish Inquisition and the Christian Nazis) and given what we now know about sources of violence in the individual, it may not be an exaggeration to suggest that *the cultures of Western civilization are essentially brain-damaged cultures.* I don't wish to imply that we alone hold that dubious distinction, but that fact combined with the highly developed weapons technologies we and the Soviets now possess makes this a matter of very serious concern to all of us.

Clearly we need to develop some short-term and intermediate-term programs and institutions to deal more effectively with specific international tensions as they come up, but in the long run I am convinced by my research that *we will only find solutions to our violent tendencies by carrying out a fundamental reorganization of our culture, in a way which permits a more wholesome development of our brains along the lines I've suggested.* We can learn a good deal about potential elements of a new culture by studying those cultures which have developed quite a different "cultural brain"—one which places them on the path of peace, harmony, equality, affection, and nurturance, and the acceptance of the intrinsic values of sexual affectional relationships in youth and adults alike. This would be an important topic of discussion among U.S. and Soviet scientists and sociologists—and we both could learn a good deal from studying cultures which function better than our own.

This proposal will, no doubt, step on an enormous number of "cultural toes" because the issue of sexual pleasure is so powerfully loaded for many people. I suggest that nothing less than our survival may depend on our reexamining our fundamental attitude toward our child-rearing practices and our sexuality.

Basic to these considerations is the answer to these two questions: first, what is the primary function of human sexuality? and second, why is the human female, unlike other primate females, able to engage in sexual behavior at any time, without regard to ovarian cyclic control? The answers to these two questions are highly interrelated and provide insights into a totally new view of human sexuality and, in particular, of that of the human female.

The human female is unique among all mammalian females[5] in her ability to be sexually receptive and active at any time she chooses to be, and in the functional significance of her orgasmic state. Since the human female can copulate with any male and as many males as she prefers and whenever she chooses, it is clear that *reproduction is not the primary function of human female sexuality.* Copulation is done only a few times in the sexual life of most couples for the purpose of reproduction. What, then, is the explanation for all nonreproductive sexual behavior? The answer is obvious: *pleasure!* What function, then, does pleasure serve in the evolutionary scheme of things?

Part of the answer has already been suggested previously by many observers of the human sexual scene—to develop affectional bonds and to promote pair bonding. Implicit in the argument is an assumption of *monogamous* sexual relationships which, interestingly, is not supported by the higher order infrahuman primates (great apes), nor by human history itself.

I maintain that pleasure is the primary process for affectional bonding beginning with the parent-infant relationship and extending into the sexual relationship. However, the primary function of pleasure in establishing and maintaining affectional bonds must be understood in its ultimate evolutionary significance for humans.

The first stage of affectional bonding for the human primate is the maternal-infant bond. The second stage of affectional bonding is the sexual pair bond which is a transition bond for the third stage of communal affectional bonding.

Sarah Blaffer Hrdy has pointed out that multi-male mating by certain infrahuman primates (the Barbary macaques studied by primatologist David Taub who reported their copulation at mid-cycle about once every seventeen minutes and with each male in the troop at least once) has certain advantages. For example, males that have mated with the female will care for and protect her and her infants, while stranger males may well prove a threat to the infant's life. Infanticide is rare among troops characterized by multi-male-mating females, but it is not infrequent in troops of harem-dwelling primates where the Alpha male maintains exclusive mating control over all females. In these species, when the Alpha male is overthrown by a younger and more powerful male, it is not uncommon for the new Alpha male to kill nursing infants sired by the previous Alpha male. Although Hrdy didn't comment on this, I would predict that fighting and aggression are less within multi-male-mating-female troops than in harem troops.

These infrahuman primate behaviors suggest that also for the human primate there may be a powerful role to be played by physical affection and sexual pleasure mutually shared in a communal living group. Also, it needs to be noted that the inability to experience sexual pleasure is one of the best predictors of those who abuse children.

Thus human female sexuality assumes a significant new dimension in communal living groups where she is the mediator of peaceful and harmonious relationships realized through multiple affectional bonding shared throughout the group.

But the unique role of human female sexuality does not end here because there is another evolutionary stage of her sexuality— that of her *spiritual sexuality*. Unlike other female primates, the human female is capable of experiencing multiple orgasms; profoundly altered states of consciousness that are characterized by altered states of consciousness—such as sensations of "flowing," "drifting," "floating"—sensations that can be characterized as "interuterine" or "oceanic." These are all vestibular cerebellar sensations. Accompanying these somatic sensations are *perceptual* changes that include losing perceptions of body boundaries, a sense of union or uniting with one's lover as if their "bodies were one," and a "sense of unity with the cosmos or universe." Finally,there is a mystical or transcendental state of consciousness which can involve "out-of-body experiences" and a profound sense of joy, contentment and unity.[6]

Although there isn't time here to go into crosscultural data on primitive human cultures which support this position, I can say from my cross-cultural studies that it is almost without exception the exclusive matrilineal cultures that are characterized by high physical affection and nurturance of infants and children, acceptance of premarital and extramarital sexuality, and either the lack of a high god in their cultures, or if present, a high god who is not involved in affairs of human morality. These are very peaceful and harmonious cultures, a mirror image of those multiple-male-mating primate communities described by Hrdy.

Conversely, almost invariably, exclusively patrilineal cultures are not affectionate toward infants and children, they punish premarital and extramarital sex and abortions, and they have a high god in their culture who is involved in affairs of human morality and who is very violent—a mirror of their patrilineal cultures.

These ideas clearly have enormous implications for individual, community, national, and global security. Indeed, I would suggest that survival may depend on our taking a clear and unbiased look at the evidence and on making appropriate cultural changes. I am not saying it will be *easy* for our societies to change because there are so many irrational forces to deal with—

however, I *am* saying that it may be *necessary for our survival.*
This is the theme of the book I am currently writing.

Notes

1. These were 1) the brain implant studies conducted by Dr.
Robert G. Heath, 2) the neurosurgical studies of Drs. A. J. and
Doreen Berman and me, 3) the neuroanatomical studies of Dr.
Austin Riesen's research group on somatosensory cortex, and 4) the
neuroanatomical studies of Dr. William Greenough's research group
on the cerebellar cortex.

At Tulane University Medical Center in the late 1960s, Dr.
Robert Heath implanted electrodes in the cerebellar nuclei and
limbic structures of isolation-reared monkeys who were patho-
logically violent. He found abnormal "spiking" (high voltage
electrical discharges) activity in the cerebellum, septum, and other
limbic structures. This was the first evidence that "maternal-social
deprivation" of these Harlow animals had abnormal brain function.
Subsequently Dr. Heath identified extensive cerebellar-limbic
interconnections.

Dr. Heath also used an implanted cerebellar pacemaker to
stimulate with mild electrical current the paleocerebellar cortex
(vermis) of human patients who had uncontrollable violent behavior
where all other forms of therapy were unsuccessful. Dr. Heath
demonstrated that this mild electrical stimulation of the paleo-
cerebellum resulted in a *profound* reversal of the hostile, distrustful
and violent behaviors of these patients. Consistent with the
neurosurgical studies, electrical stimulation of the neocerebellum
(lateral cerebellar hemisphere) was not found to be effective in
changing the emotional-social behaviors of these patients.

Meanwhile, in the late 1960s, Dr. Saltzberg (an associate of Dr.
Heath) had developed under an NICHD contract, a complex signal
analysis methodology to detect the occurrence of abnormal sub-
cortical "spiking" (high voltage discharges) from ordinary scalp
EEG recordings in the isolation-reared monkeys. It was my conviction that we would find such abnormal sub-cortical "spiking" in
violent criminals, particularly, violent sex offenders, who invariably
have a childhood history of deprivation of physical affection, abuse,
and neglect that is compounded with impaired or nonexistent
affectionate/caring sexual relationships during youth and adulthood.

If proven successful, we would have a neuropsychological
diagnostic test of "dangerous" where, today, there is no such test
available in the disciplines of either psychiatry or psychology. Such
a test that could identify the *dangerous* violent offender (impaired
brain function) would result in the placement of such individuals in
a secure, rehabilitative environment that would translate into the
savings of human lives, particularly children and women who are
the usual victims of physical and sexual violence. We would have a
test not only of "dangerousness" but also of therapeutic effectiveness: i.e., does therapy eliminate the sub-cortical spiking?

Unfortunately, it was my attempt to develop such a collaborative federal interagency research study with Dr. Robert Powitzky, Administrator of Psychological Services, Federal Bureau of Prisons, Department of Justice, that led Dr. Norman Kretchmer, then Director of NICHD, to block such interfederal agency collaborative research efforts. Subsequently, Dr. Kretchmer abolished entirely the NICHD's responsibility to support basic research on the causes and consequences of violence against infants and children, including the assessment of brain damage/disfunction in infants and children who have been abused and neglected. Today (1983) these critical research studies have yet to be conducted. If successful, such studies would benefit everyone—the violent offender, the public, and the judicial-parole system.

2. Information on child-rearing practices was developed and coded by cultural anthropologists Barry, Bacon, and Child and were measures of infant physical affection defined by how much physical touching and carrying of the infant on the body of the mother or caretaker (vestibular-cerebellar stimulation). It was this *movement stimulation* of the infant provided by the carrying of the infant on the mother's body throughout the day that was the critical variable. The measure of sexual affection was provided by cultural anthropologists Ford and Beach; and John T. Westbrook who characterized cultures that permitted or punished permarital coitus. The measure of violence was provided by cultural anthropologist Philip E. Slater and was a measure of "killing, torture, and mutilation" of enemies captured in warfare. It is the most violent of coded behaviors in the Ethnographic Atlas.

3. I know of no other theory or data that can predict violence high and low in so many primitive cultures around the world with 100 percent accuracy. It is emphasized that this is not a simple correlational study but an experiment of nature with a triple-blind control based upon data collected by anthropologists who were unaware of each other's codings (triple-blind measures).

4. When sexual pleasure is rooted at the "reflexive" level like a spinal reflex, then this pleasure is superficial and transitory—it is "apparent pleasure" which reflects the reduction of physiological tension but does not constitute a true state of positive integrated pleasure. It is disassociative pleasure and it is at this level that sexual exploitation and violence occur.

5. Despite the fact that certain infrahuman primates (e.g., chimpanzees and orangutans) have the ability to copulate on any day of the cycle, anthropologist Sarah Blaffer Hrdy has noted that in captivity "orangutans may copulate on any day of the month; in the wild they are somewhat more cyclical." It is well established that captivity and cage-rearing can and does produce various emotional, social, and sexual disturbances in primates, as replicated in single-cage housing. Therefore, extrapolations about primate sexual behavior from laboratory or captive-reared primates is very hazardous when attempting to make inferences about normal or typical sexual functioning of the primate. It is suggested that the

non-monogamous and multiple mating of males by certain infrahuman primates represent an important evolutionary transition for
the understanding of the ultimate significance of human female
sexuality.

6. These altered states of consciousness are infrequently experienced by the human male and it is for these reasons that I have
suggested a four-stage process of orgasmic states that is based upon
the degrees that pleasure is integrated into higher brain centers that
makes possible "spiritual sexuality." These stages are 1) reflexive
(male), 2) associative (male, female), 3) integrative (female, male),
and 4) transcendental (female).

The first two stages are nonspiritual, stage three is spiritual but
not mystical, while stage four is both spiritual and mystical. As part
of this formulation, I have predicted that the interneuronal
connectivity between the forebrain-limbic system and the cerebellum is more greatly developed in the human female brain than in
the human male brain which makes possible her spiritual-sexual
state. It must be noted that deprivation of physical affection and
pleasure is more injurious to the human female with respect to her
total functioning as a "persona" than it is to the male and can
preclude the development of spiritual sexual states because of the
lack of neural integration networks necessary for such states of
consciousness. This is also reflected in the greater frequency of
"anorgasmia" in the sensorily deprived female than in the sensorily
deprived male.

Robert Muller

Having worked with the United Nations from its beginning, Muller has had a ringside seat in watching this international consultative body develop. For twenty-five years he had the unique job of keeping up with developments in all the U.N. programs and agencies and reporting on these directly to the secretary-general. At the time we conducted this interview in the summer of 1980, Muller was the secretary of the Economic and Social Council; today he is an assistant secretary-general. He has published his autobiography, Most of All They Taught Me Happiness, *and* New Genesis, Shaping a Global Spirituality.

The present condition of humanity was best described by the philosopher Gottfried Leibnitz a few hundred years ago when he said that humans would be so occupied with making scientific discoveries in every sector for several centuries that they would not look at the totality. But, he said, someday the proliferation and complexity of our knowledge would become so bewildering that it would be necessary to develop a global, universal, and synthetic view. This is exactly the time and juncture at which we have arrived. It shows in our new preoccupations with what is called "interdisciplinary," "global thinking," "interdependence," and so on. It is all the same phenomenon.

One of the most useful things humanity could do at this point is to make an honest inventory of what we know. I have suggested to foundations that they ought to bring together the chief editors of the world's main encyclopedias to agree on a common table of contents of human knowledge. But it can also be a dangerous idea. Why? Well, when the Frenchman Diderot invented the first encyclopedia, the archbishop of Paris ran to the king of France to have the book burned because it would totally change the existing value system of the Catholic church. If we developed a common index of human knowledge today it would similarly cause a change in our value systems. We would discover that in the whole framework of knowledge the contest between Israel and the Muslims would barely be listed because it is such a small problem in the totality of our preoccupation as a human species. The meeting might have to last several days before the editors would even mention it! This is exactly the point: some people don't want to develop such a framework of knowledge because they want *their* problem to be the most important problem on earth and go to great lengths to promote that notion.

So that is what I believe to be most necessary for global security: an ordering of our knowledge at this point in our evolution, a good, honest classification of all we know from the infinitely large to the infinitely small—the cosmos, our planet, humanity, our dreams, our wishes, and so on. We haven't done it yet, but we will have to do it in one way or another.

After observing the world scene since World War II, two years ago I began at long last to write and to speak. I grew up in Alsace-Lorraine where I was "wired" in a certain way by my two-country culture, France and Germany. Each gave me quite different messages, which made me suspicious about the absolute value of what each was teaching. Because of this I was very happy to come to work with the United Nations and to get wired in by world knowledge. I suppose I am a somewhat unique individual on this planet. I have knowledge in many, many fields, from astrophysics to atomic science, from world population to individual human rights, because all these problems come to the United Nations. Finally, I was "submerged by complexity," and in the last few years I tried to see things in their right place. Today I can see the whole evolution of our little planet and of life and of humanity in space and in time. And what is happening now makes great sense to me. I should say that I have no merit in achieving this understanding, because it has been imposed on me by the facts. Of course having seen people kill each other for certain values helped me remain very open-minded while I looked to understand evolution and for ways we could all live better.

The changes we need are happening almost all the time because things are accelerating so fast. Things which seem completely impossible today might become possible not in two thousand years but in twenty or thirty years. This is why I have become an optimist. I would like to put up a sign "Never give up hope" at the entrance of the United Nations, because it is here that the shape of the planet's future is being molded. People here are really trying. Of course often they do not succeed, because it is still the cave age of global living. Like little children, we burn our fingers. There are accidents. For years we thought everything was unlimited and suddenly we discover that it is not. Until 1951 we didn't know the size and growth rate of the world population. We wanted to keep so many children from dying, but we forgot to tell the mothers not to have six or seven children. As a result, today in the developing countries fifty percent of the population is under twenty-five years of age. There are major mistakes, incredible mistakes, made by a species that has entered suddenly into its global, planetary age. Yet once a warning is given, as it was the case with population, things change. Now fertility rates are going down. It is no longer estimated that in the year 2000 the world population will be seven billion; now it is estimated that it will be 6.2 billion. And by the time we are actually there, the figure will certainly be lower.

The human species is very mature in scientific and technological fields. We are able to look millions of light-years into the universe and into the inside of the atom. We have expanded our knowledge fantastically. Yet we must now make far greater progress in improving the way we live together, in using our knowledge for living happier lives for all. In this spiritual dimension of life I would say that we are still living in the cave age. Most people who want to do good give much greater consideration to their group than to the world and to the good they are doing. This is what the parable of the Good Samaritan teaches. As a matter of fact one of the great contributions the United Nations is making to enhance global security is the way we promote international cooperation. We make people forget they are Russians, Americans, Chinese, Hindus, Catholics, or Muslims. As we work together to solve critical problems we are all human beings looking at the substance of each problem: hunger, poverty, illiteracy, four hundred fifty million handicapped, the blind, people with smallpox, people who die in accidents, our deteriorating environment, the threat of nuclear war. Progressively Russians, Americans, and Chinese begin to forget their isolated nationality and unite to seek solutions to these problems. If we can continue this evolution for a number of years more, then we will have made it. We will discover there is only one real problem: a stream of people renewing themselves all the time, trying to find their fulfillment and happiness on this little planet in the universe. All the languages of the world say the same thing; all the religions of the world say the same thing; and all nations are trying to do the same thing. When you talk to people in corporations and other institutions they will be able to prove that they too are working for the good of people. What is required, however, is a fundamental revolution in our approach: we must think of the good of the human species as a whole. We are a planet and a dominant species. We must find our place within the total reality, which means within the universe from the infinite beginning to the infinite end. If you see yourself in the framework of total time you find again the relevance of Christ's teachings and of Buddha's concept of karma: each action at any moment has an effect on the entire universal society over the total time of our species. To tell this to a species today that doesn't think more than twenty years ahead, that means a long time until you get there! But we have to keep saying it because we are at a critical juncture of human evolution. Survival depends on such bold new efforts.

World problems and interdependencies are so big and complex that few people dare to absorb them. Nevertheless the universe has always been complex. We have simple instruments, like the eye and brain which hold in one word but which see and process billions of bits of information. Similarly we have simple one-word concepts, like faith, hope, joy, and love which are *incredible* notions that permit us to live whole and integrated lives within all the complexity and mystery of the universe. Even the scientist, when he takes his eyes away from the microscope, moves beyond his dissections and can exclaim, "It is a fantastic world!" A woman consists of miles of blood vessels and trillions of cells, but she is infinitely more than that; she is a person you can feel love for. Creation exists in its entirety, and in the end science has to be sublimated by religious and cultural concepts which appear in all ages—concepts with simple names like "faith" which suggest a miracle, a mystery. Creation is both a mystery and a miracle.

The United Nations is not yet at this philosophical stage. You have to seek particular individuals who have reached this understanding. Two outstanding ones were Dag Hammarskjöld and U Thant. They knew that their understanding of the outside world was very dependent on their inner disposition.

Today I do whatever I can to promote these ideas. I give lectures to the U.N. staff, and many young people come to see me. I also make about a hundred eighty speeches a year. The goal of my writing and speaking is to give people confidence. The head of an international institution in Geneva told me he had all his staff members read my book on happiness. He said, "I want my people to understand that they cannot cave in to complexities. I want them to have a positive attitude and faith in their work, like you." This is what you can do as one individual; each one of us can make a difference in the outcome.

I do not know of any universal method to obtain clarity and good communication. The main way I cope with it is to be wide open to all perceptions, people, ideas, and to whatever touches me from near and far. I try not to draw any conclusions or to think during the day. I just open my "computer" to receive information. At night I let my computer digest it. Then I usually wake up at four or five o'clock in the morning and listen to myself. It seems that during the night my brain rearranges everything, and my alarm clock is those new ideas. I go to the living room and write down what comes out. I don't think about what I'm writing; perceptions flow out naturally. Then I look at the product, noting what seems important and adapting it over the years.

You get insights in the strangest ways. A child might make a remark that opens you to a completely new perception. Another great source is speaking to audiences and getting their responses. More recently I realized that I also get the same feedback and learning process from writing. I never imagined I would learn so much from the many responses I have received from the readers of my little book on happiness.

When I retire from the United Nations I intend to spend the rest of my life digesting the totality of what I have learned and to draw the lessons and conclusions of what it meant to have had a life like mine, to write it down so that others can continue to work on that basis and make their own contribution to the further transcendence of the human species in the tremendous universe.

Tony Buzan

Author of several books on the brain and on learning theory, Tony Buzan is the founder and director of the Learning Methods Group, a London-based institute which gives seminars on learning methods and self-knowledge in Europe, Africa, the Far East, and the United States.

I was born in England in 1942 and went to school in a small fishing village. There I had my first major experience which set me on my present course. In school our classrooms were divided into the A, B, C, and D streams. Although we were told it didn't make any difference which stream you were in, the children all knew that A was the bright kids and that D was the dumb kids. Within the individual streams you were also ranked by your most recent test score. The bottom child in the class sat in the front right-hand seat and the top child was in the back right-hand seat, and a snake of children wound back to that prize spot. At that time I was always in the A stream and my best friend was always in the D stream. I was always in the back row, between number three and number seven. I was never number one or number two; the only two who got those were Mummery and Apse.

One day the teacher was asking us such questions as "What's the difference between a spider and an insect?" "What's the difference between a moth and a butterfly?" "Name three fish you can find in an English stream." Now nature study was my entire life at the time. After school each day my "dumb" friend and I used to do nothing but go out into the fields and study nature.

Two weeks later the teacher came back and said, "Somebody in the class has got a perfect mark on a paper." Everybody, including me, whipped around to see if it was goddamned Mummery or goddamned Apse who was first again. And the teacher said, "Buzan." Which shook me to the roots because I had *never* been perfect before. And also I knew I hadn't gotten a perfect mark on a test. I *knew* that. So we all got shuffled around and there I was, for the first time, in the back right-hand seat, seeing for the first time the right profiles of Mummery and Apse. That was a major sense of security—at first! But as I was sitting there, I realized there *must* have been as mistake . . . that maybe Mummery had blotted his name. Mummery could, by a stretch of the imagination and an inkblot, become a "Buzan." So I thought my stay at the top would be shortlived. Moments after, the teacher handed out the exam papers and I saw it was the paper on which I had written those ridiculously easy answers to such questions as "What's the difference between a spider and a bug?" My immediate reaction was "That wasn't a test." If I ask you your name and you give the correct answer, I don't go, *"Fantastic!!* Congratulations! One hundred percent! Amazing memory!" It's such basic knowledge to you that you answer automatically, and that was how nature study was to me. My next thought was *"Ah!* It *was* a test! So *that* is what it is for Mummery and Apse when they get a perfect mark in history. It doesn't test their ability; it's finding out what they're interested in. That's not a big deal at all."

My next thought was a real quantum shift in my life's thinking up to that date; it was about my best friend, down in the D stream. When we went into the fields together he would run or shout and every living creature would move. He could identify insects by flight pattern. While I was stammering out the names, "Umm . . . uh . . . sparrow! . . . uh . . . cabbage-white! . . ." he was ticking them off like crazy, by flight pattern alone. So sitting up there at the top of the A class I realized the *real* genius was at the bottom—partly because of me because I was now at the top of nature study. And he was defined by the teachers as inadequate, unintelligent, illiterate (which he was, he couldn't read). From that time on I could not accept that system which said "This is right, this is wrong; this is smart, this is not."

That was followed by more observations of similar injustices. For example, an amazingly brilliant child who was good at everything failed the Eleven Plus exam because he didn't know who were the captains of the English cricket and soccer teams.

They didn't bother to find out that in our school he was the captain of both the cricket *and* the soccer teams. He had the highest IQ registered in the school. But just because he did not know who England's top athletes were—and he said in the interview that he "did not care"—he failed. Events like that led me to coach so-called backward kids when I entered the university. I found them all to be amazing geniuses who had all had negative learning experiences at some time in their lives and had begun to assume they were not intelligent. In other words, *insecurity had been placed in their thought system and they began to operate on the basis of it.* "I can't do this." Or they rebelled, but always to their disadvantage. I became increasingly incensed at the damage being done to people by an overall inadequate system. I'm not placing blame; people simply didn't know what they were doing.

I became increasingly insecure about my own lack of knowledge about myself and how I function. I didn't know how my memory, my concentration, motivation, or information-sorting systems worked. I struggled with the exams, produced standardly good results, but I knew it was all ridiculous because in a few weeks I would forget it all; besides, the material didn't seem to have much bearing on who I was or on my life.

I then went out into the big bad world and taught school. I tended to teach delinquent classes. You'd walk into the class and the first thing they'd say was "Fuck off!!" And you knew there was still some life in them and that they were protecting their individuality. Although those were some pretty bad schools, I never found a really intrinsically hurtful person; yet I found thousands of hurt people who were reacting, with violence, to prevent their being hurt. They were filled with insecurity, and it manifested itself in violence. The minute you accepted that this was the case, and you remained quiet and supportive of them in that context, the whole situation became a lot more workable. And they would test and test the teacher to see whether they could trust him, to see if he would make them feel secure—in a sense, *loved.* And if they *did* feel that, then they'd roll with it. In 1970 I decided that I was only spending about fourteen days a year on my hobby, which was teaching people how to learn and mucking around on brain research to understand what was actually going on inside our heads. I decided to formalize what I had found out about learning, thinking, the human brain, the body, and the mind-body relation. So I started writing books and doing television programs on it, and finding other people interested in this with whom to exchange information. I was busy devising courses on it for everybody—and I do mean for *everybody*. I really do feel that everybody needs information on how they function: *the more of that information they have, the more fundamentally secure they become.*

One reason the world is insecure is that it is actually an insecure place and always has been. Wherever you lived you were under threat of some sort: earthquakes, animals, different tribes. The world has always been a basically insecure place, with still pools of security punctuating periods of tremendous violence. Human beings have largely seen other human beings as a threatening element in their environment; you could not trust them. Moreover you could not trust yourself. History is dotted with instances of people saying, "I didn't realize that I could do that!"—that I could kill or harm, and so on. So you have a group of insecure, that is, *unknowledgeable* creatures, not knowing about themselves, about others, or about what was going on around them—bashing in the head of some other fellow who was trying to bash *your* head in, when all they were is what you were, which wasn't much anyway. I mean, you were a ditchdigger or a farmer and most people told you that wasn't much. And life wasn't much and death wasn't much, and maybe there was a God up there who would bash you because you were a no-good, sinning son-of-a-bitch anyway. So what? In that way of thinking there was nothing particularly wrong in killing somebody because that person wasn't worth much anyway.

What we have realized in recent times is that the more people really know about themselves and the world they live in, the more they begin to care about themselves. The more they realize the intricacy of their body and the phenomenal complexity and beauty of their minds, the more precious they become to themselves. Then they realize that this complexity and beauty are patterned in every human being you see. That makes them consider a lot more carefully. If you know you are destroying a most phenomenal instrument when you smash your fists through someone's face, there's a much greater chance you won't do it.

Similarly if you look at animals trapped in a forest fire, their main purpose is to find security. If there is a lake, they swim to the middle or find a log or high piece of land in the water. If you look, you see lions next to deer and foxes next to rabbits. And they are all sitting on this log, looking at the holocaust around them with no thought of combat or eating each other or running from each other, because what is around them is so gigantic that it takes their attention. They become unified in their fear, in their concern about overall survival.

I think the same is beginning to be true for the human race. I don't actually see the main threat as nuclear war. That, to me, is a small threat. People are beginning to realize that the earth is a tiny, tiny ball in the middle of a vast and unknown area of space, out of which could come anything at any time. It could be a meteor (as in the popular film), it could be a gigantic solar flare, it could be most anything that could pop out of there and immediately obliterate everything. Which means that we need to know more about it. There are threats we never knew existed, which really do exist. Major traumas can still take place on our planet: great temperature changes, continents disappearing, and so on. These are similar to my metaphor of the fire. The more human beings realize their own frailty and their own beauty, and the number of events around them that make them insecure, the more they will be inclined to work together for our common good. Most species of animals tend to fight among themselves very little. They go to war against another group, but within their own group they tend to stick together. Human beings haven't yet realized that they are a group; it is still "us versus them." Russians are "different" from Americans; Chinese are "different" from Australians; Africans are "different" from South Americans. They still see themselves as different. But I've begun to notice that people are starting to look at each other, say, a Chinese and an African. And as they talk about what they talk about at home, they find they have the same things at home! What about the war? Pollution? The future? Religion? Wives and marriage and children? Outer space? They are sitting there, looking at each other and increasingly realizing that they are looking at the "same thing." The tribalness of human beings is getting much stronger; we are beginning to realize that we are one and that there is not much point in fighting the tribe. You *protect* the tribe. Sure, you have a fews squabbles over distribution and position, but those are becoming increasingly irrelevant as well.

Things will change as people realize who they are and what

choices they have. They actually do have the choice of to kill or not to kill, to develop or not develop themselves, to make things beautiful or ugly, to be happy or unhappy, to help or not help, to fight or not fight. As they come to realize the capacity of their beauty, the fact that they *do* have choices, to see the various major threats under which their tribe exists and the fact that the more they cooperate the greater chance their tribe has to survive outside threats, then considerations like nuclear weapons will become increasingly minor.

In terms of the weapons problem per se we have to look at how bad the situation actually is. When you look at all the money that has gone into war and war machinery in the past, and into gearing up now for possible war, it is not a large percentage that has actually gone into the weaponry itself, the actual warhead, bullet, or gun. Huge percentages have gone to the education of the soldier in reading, health, responsibility, and basic thinking and mental skills. A lot has gone into invention, which has had, specifically, little to do with the war at all. It is important to be aware that some really positive things come out of military expenditures. In the mind of military people that is a major part of the expense. If you listen to their conversations with their wives and children, you'll find they want pretty much the same things you do. Now you'll probably find they want a military education for their children because in their education they learned about science, art, and morality. And they learned discipline, which is good if it is done well; most great artists and scientists were highly disciplined. You will find these military people have tremendously strong moral relationships with their friends. Most of them are on the side of God, however you interpret God. In *their* minds they are doing something good, and I think it's important that we realize that. It isn't as simple as "bad versus good" and it isn't as simple as "a trillion dollars going down the drain." You also have fantastic scientific offshoots of military spending. Many of the machines that help the handicapped come from military R&D; most of the major brain research comes from the military.

I don't see any really major difference between the Americans and the Russians. If you go to Russia and met the Russians and you go to America and meet the Americans, there's not much difference. You have similar social and family problems. They have as many nudist beaches as the Americans, the same sort of drinking problems, and the people talk about the same things. The actual ideologies are ostensibly different, but the manifestations are not so different. It's still work, reward, and religion of a type. There are certain differences in systems—for example, in the electoral system—but when you examine that it is not so different as it might seem. They have a choice within the same party. When you look at the United States and the choices one gets, it really isn't a choice in the massive sense of the word.

The main thing is that the people who operate in those two systems are the same basic human beings. Their brains and emotions and bodies function in the same way. They are of the same tribe. I see the solution to the problem of national and global security as one of getting people together, which is happening. The more a Russian meets an American, or a Japanese meets a Chinese, or a Japanese meets a Russian, and they talk personally to each other, the less risk there will be. I really think the basic underlying feelings of nations and people tend to hold sway in the end. At the moment there is a definite sense that war is not a good idea.

When people start to think nuclear war is inevitable, that definitely increases the probability of its happening. No doubt about it. I feel that there is also a very rapidly growing, although not very visible yet, belief in the *non*inevitability of war. One of the major differences between one person's believing war is inevitable and another's believing that it is avoidable is the realization on the part of the individual that he or she can influence the course of events. Everything is open and everything can be influenced. People don't realize how incredibly much we affect each other. One person who has one argument with one other person can send that person into an office in a bad mood. And that person in a bad mood can make six others in a bad mood. And those six others in a bad mood can . . . etc., etc. Fortunately the same is true of a good mood. Thus one tiny little individual really can have a tremendous effect. When we realize that, we see that nothing is inevitable. Any one of us can make the choice to influence events. It really is that simple.

Once again it comes back to people's learning how they function. If each one of us realized we are carrying around this phenomenal biocomputer called a "brain," and that we can do all kinds of amazing things with it, war becomes an easy problem to solve if you don't want it to happen.

I recommend massive programs of education on what people are. When they know what they are, things will change automatically. We also need massive programs on how to think. If people knew how to think, a lot of the rubbish spoken and written about war today would not even be considered or written. All the emotionalism and irrational appeals made to people would no longer affect people's thinking. Once they knew how to think, the dialogue would improve. For example, it would no longer be "The Russians have got missiles six times as big as ours!" So what? They would realize that size is not a major factor, particularly in this debate. And yet it is used as if it were.

We then need to teach people what the *real* war is. The real war is about the survival of all of us. When people realize what the *real* war is, I think they will tackle it with the same kind of enthusiasm with which they now to go war. What war really involves is people saying "Hey, friend, let's sail off and fight for what we believe in." Instead of doing that by bashing in everyone's skulls and blowing them all to bits, you do it in terms of improving the environment, enhancing beauty, and so on. You create an environment in which your tribe can live well. That's what war is all about anyway. War is not a negative motivation: to defend my country, to give us more space, and so on. It is only negative when it doesn't create what it wants, when it wipes out your tribe and destroys the tribal environment.

Creating global security comes down to making people aware of themselves, that they are lovable, magnificent beings. If they really feel that, their love of themselves will oblige them to consider the cosmos and all the other creatures on the planet because those things all contribute to their happiness or unhappiness. They will have to consider the environment around them because it affects their well-being and sense of harmony. Happiness, harmony, love, enlightenment, ease, grace—all these are really a function of knowing yourself. And when people come to know themselves, that doesn't mean there won't be any more problems, but it will be far more enjoyable solving them.

Where there is no vision, the people perish.

Proverbs 29:18

I know no safe depository of the ultimate powers of society but the people themselves; and if we think them not enlightened enough to exercise their control with a wholesome discretion, the remedy is not to take it from them, but to inform their discretion by education.

—Thomas Jefferson

Conclusion

We have all seen those pictures in children's magazines where you are asked to "find the horse hidden among the trees." At first glance you only see the trees; the image of the horse is cleverly concealed in the lines of the drawing. It is only when you visually "step back," shifting your focus and concentration, that the horse's image suddenly leaps out at you, making you wonder how you ever missed seeing it. In a very real sense "finding the horse"—a new vision of our nation, our world, and of ourselves—is exactly what this book is about.

For several decades our leaders and we ourselves have defined national security predominantly in terms of weapons and delivery systems. The driving assumption has been that the more we frighten the Russians, the better we can deter them from attacking us and force them to negotiate; thus the more *insecure* we make *them,* the more *secure we* will be. Although the interviewees are, almost to a person, critical of Soviet foreign and domestic policies, they challenge the logic of this fundamental assumption on several grounds. More than one reminds us that fear begets fear: each time we increase our arsenals, they feel compelled to build up theirs—and vice versa. It's the proverbial "Two wrongs don't make a right." Several remind us of the need to offer positive "win–win" options to the Soviet Union. We are reminded that the current high rate of military expenditure is draining resources from other areas of our economy, creating weakness from within. Other interviewees raise important moral considerations about our own nation's role in the world: despite many charitable acts on our part, is it ethical for us, with 5 percent of the world's population, to continue consuming over 30 percent of the world's resources? Is it acceptable in our *own* eyes to continue to support repressive regimes in the Third World in exchange for privileged access to raw materials or military bases? Are we being hypocritical to "play footsie" with some leftist dictatorships when we see it in our economic self-interest to do so? Indeed many of those interviewed are raising the question, is there perhaps a better way of defining our nation's self-interest in a manner more consistent with our highest vision of ourselves and what we aspire to be? What *is* our vision? What are our national goals? Who, indeed, are we? Again, where is the horse among the trees?

To pull together just a few of the threads presented by the interviewees, Dr. Edward Teller reminds us of the pricelessness of freedom, which must be worked for at each moment. While he feels we need great military strength to buy time, he also calls for some sort of world order which springs from practical considerations rather than from any rigid ideological prescription. Eldon Byrd expresses concern that we are on the verge of a whole new breakthrough in weapons technology which makes it even more urgent for us to develop "win-win" solutions to global problems. He joins Buckminster Fuller in noting that we have all we need in the way of scientific breakthroughs to create a higher standard of living and spiritual well-being for all the earth's people than we have ever known—what we need is the political will, born of our individual wills, to commit ourselves to carrying out this great transformation. Dr. B. F. Skinner calls for us to define small steps in which we can succeed and then to positively reinforce our good results. Professor Seymour Melman calls for joint U.S.–Soviet studies in economic peace conversion, noting that our permanent war economy (and that of the Soviets) is destroying our societies from within and that we are doing to ourselves what is traditionally done by the enemy. Both Russell Means and Hazel Henderson feel that the real enemy is indiscriminate industrialization and the loss of reverence for our Mother Earth and life itself. Ina May Gaskin lays much of the responsibility for our present crisis at the way in which women have been systematically disempowered, particularly in the birthing process. Dr. James Prescott presents fascinating evidence that tactile deprivation in early childhood, repressive sexuality, and authoritarian monotheistic and patriarchal structures are at the root of the violence which propels us into wars. Ed Mitchell and others stress the need for a much deeper understanding of the nature of human consciousness and of the creative process. And Howard Kurtz calls for a new "Manhattan style project" which pulls together the positive creative energies of the world's peoples to design an *international* security system which we can test out and refine over the next two or three decades until we trust it to work effectively in promoting the security and well-being of *all* the nation-states. Finally, many of the interviewees call for a more active role to be played by women in developing the new vision and in conducting high level conflict management.

Their views and the others presented in these pages begin to form the outline of a horse among the trees. Although it is not possible in the interviews included herein to lay out the entire blueprint or "critical path roadmap" to a guaranteed future with greater quality of life for everyone, the *outlines* of a logical and intuitive course of action have emerged quite distinctly. It is evident that we are coming to the end of an old set of roads and that we must work together to chart a new course. The more of us who share in this process of defining the new vision, the better our new roadmap will be. This will require the best thinking and intuition of each of us, for as Buckminster Fuller put it, we will have to qualify for survival.

In my own life experience I have discovered too much order in the world and in the cosmos to be able to believe that life and the situation in which we find ourselves is a completely "chance" or "random" process. As Robert Muller and others observe, there are effective ways in which we can "tune in" to a deeper source of wisdom and find the answers. It seems that just as we individuals are individually presented at each moment with choices which lead either to our development or to our deterioration, we are also collectively, as an entire human species, being presented with an enormous choice: either we come together to work for our mutual well-being and fulfillment or we will destroy ourselves. "The saints weren't kidding," says Joanna Macy.

To understand better the nature of the choice we face, I have gone to the people, for it is we, with all our marvelous strengths and insights—as well as our weaknesses and illusions—who make up America and the people of the earth. And in the final analysis it is our voices and actions and collective will that are going to shape our destiny: we will create what we ultimately get.

The night before a major Civil War battle Abraham Lincoln was in a tent reviewing battle plans with one of his generals. The general turned to his commander in chief and said, "Mr. President, let us pray that God be on our side tomorrow." To which Lincoln replied, somewhat sadly, "I think it is more fitting that we pray that *we* be on the side of *God*." Dr. Shigetoshi Iwamatsu is eloquent in his plea that we not succumb to the arrogance of power or blind belief that some divinely endowed invincibility will protect us no matter what actions we engage in.

Looking back at the long road I have come in writing this book and digesting all the insights and ideas people have so generously offered me, I am beginning to see light at the end of the tunnel in front of me. Each person who shared with me thoughtfully and honestly has enriched my life and vision. Rather than my work being tiring and debilitating, I am increasingly refreshed by the growing vision I've been piecing together and by the knowledge that in our essence we do all hunger for the same things. *It is my conviction that we can vastly accelerate the pace of the transformation as more of us begin to ask the "impertinent questions" and as we more consciously contribute our skills and resources wherever we find ourselves.*

Wherever our new path leads us, the act of walking together must be filled with love and celebration, for only that will inspire us to continue and to make the breakthroughs we need in every area of human consciousness and endeavor. Indeed as the following story about my Soviet friend Yuri Antipov illustrates, I believe that integrity, love, and celebration will be the most effective way to reach and "disarm," in a more profound sense, the Soviet Union. After all, as Christ told us, we should love our enemies: it is only when our enemies have truly become our friends and we have discovered we share a common vision that we can vanquish the spectre of fear that separates us from one another. As Tony Buzan put it, "This doesn't mean there won't be any more problems, but it will be far more enjoyable solving them."

When I first met Yuri, a group of five of us (four Americans and Yuri) spent several hours one evening in New York City talking about ourselves and our countries and beliefs. This was my first opportunity to talk in any depth with a Soviet citizen. Toward the end of the evening I leaned forward and said with intensity, "Look, you have your dialectical materialism: thesis, antithesis, and synthesis. Today your country has some good qualities and some things that don't work very well; the same is true for my country. What we need to do is to look together honestly at how we can make both of our countries and *all* the countries of the world work better. We need to select the best from all that the world has to offer."

"You know, Norie," he said, withdrawing slightly, "you believe in your way so much that it makes you more powerful than me. I am a little bit afraid of you."

"Don't be afraid of me, *please*," I said anxiously. "You are my *brother*, Yuri, and those aren't just words. We really do have to work together, otherwise I'm very afraid we won't survive."

"You are right. You are right. We must talk more," he said. Shortly thereafter our first meeting ended.

Several months later, as Alison and I were starting on our long journey around America, some friends organized a farewell party in New York City. Yuri was invited. He arrived somewhat late, arms folded tightly over his chest and a frown on his face. He didn't respond to my enthusiastic greeting.

"What's the matter, Yuri?" I asked. "Did you have a bad day at the office?"

He ignored my question and burst out, "*The problem is that nobody is real.* Everybody is phony. They are all wearing masks to cover up who they really are."

My immediate response was utter grief, and I burst into tears. "That's not true. *I'm* real, and *you're* real when you're not saying dumb things like that. . . . And everyone *here* is real." One of my friends handed me a handkerchief, jerked his head in my direction, and said to Yuri, "She's real, all right."

Yuri was immediately apologetic. "I'm *sorry*, Norie, I'm sorry—I didn't mean to hurt your feelings. But you must understand how difficult it is to be a Soviet citizen living in your country. Everybody hates me just because I am from the Soviet Union."

"*I* don't hate you," I wiped my eyes with the handkerchief and blew my nose, feeling a bit awkward for the tears. "Nobody *here* hates you. You are our *brother*. As I told you, we've got to work *together*."

We patched things up, drank a toast to friendship, and had a wonderful party, telling jokes about our countries and ourselves, and generally breaking through to a new dimension of mutual appreciation. Toward the end of the evening Yuri suddenly leaned back on the couch and started laughing at some inner joke.

"Okay, brother, what's so funny?" I demanded, smiling. His laughter was infectious. "Share it!"

"You know, Norie," he was still laughing and struggling to express his words, "it would be *such* a pity if we destroyed each other: *we're so nice!*"

And that was when I realized that creating this sort of communion, in each moment seeking to be absolutely real with each other and committed to each other's well-being, is truly the Best Game on Earth. This genuine sharing is the only thing that will keep us from destroying each other and ourselves. Yuri is right: in our fundamental being, we *are* nice. And when we are not, it seems to be because the customs and institutions which shape us have suppressed and distorted our natural tendency toward wholeness and aliveness. Although we have been adjusting our institutional structures in accordance with gradual changes in our customs and understanding, we have reached a moment when we need to stop and take fresh stock of who we are, where we are going, and how we will get there. In doing this, each one of us has a unique set of experiences, perceptions and abilities—gifts we can choose to contribute toward making our nation and the world more secure, harmonious, and beautiful.

The people whose voices you have heard through these pages represent only a tiny fraction of what is available to us in the collective wisdom of the people—in the United States and throughout the world. Today, the telecommunications revolution has "conveniently" brought us television, computers, telephones, and a host of other tools to assist us in linking up with one another into a vast network of unified consciousness—a "planetary nervous system." We can begin, on a national and a global scale, to redefine and link up both our images of ourselves and our world, as well as of our goals, our visions, and our ideas for how to achieve these. Everything we need is in place or being created; what most of us have lacked is the broad outline of the vision—again, the outline of the horse among the trees.

It is this great gathering, this coming together in a spirit of global communion and cooperation to create the new rules and new game plan which I have chosen to call the "Best Game on Earth." Only a life-game with the overarching goal of supporting us each to bring forth our wholeness and well-being will be powerful and enjoyable enough to keep us from destroying each other and ourselves: in an oppressive, illusion-filled, violent world, death looks attractive to that part of our being which longs for peace. The only kind of "life-game" which can lift us beyond our "collective death wish" is one whose goal is to create a new world in which we can genuinely realize our desire for peace and for our mutual fulfillment. This process requires the efforts of all of us—idealists and cynics, radicals and conservatives and the apolitical, rich and poor—motivated to "leave the trail better than we found it." As we share our visions, passions, experiences and insights and our love with one another, we can weave the multicolored threads to create a new cloth. This in turn will bring inspiration and renewal to the poor, the hungry, the sick, and the dispirited for, as Richard Falk points out, "The most important statement we can make in creating a new world order is what we each do with our own lives. This has a contagious effect."

In the Best Game on Earth, all of us—all nations, races, religions, ages, and systems of belief—are valuable players. Each of us can make a critical difference in shaping our collective future. And my own experience has taught me that the more wholeheartedly we participate and give, the more we receive and the more joyful the Game becomes. Thus,

> *Whatever you can do or dream you can,*
> *Begin it: Boldness has genius, power and magic in it.*

Questionnaire

A List of "Impertinent" Questions

We perceive the outer world and ourselves through the filter of our personal attitudes, values, habits, and experiences. The following list of questions is not designed to be a "scientific survey"; rather, its purpose is to assist you (either as an individual or as a group) to look more deeply at your attitudes regarding personal, group, national, and global security.

Individual _____

1. Is it your experience that you have an effect on the world around you, or do you usually feel yourself as being affected by the circumstances in which you find yourself? What would make you feel more powerful to effect positive change? What holds you back? How can you overcome that?
2. Are you able to handle [dissent / anger / confusion] with relative ease? Elaborate. What would enable you to handle these more easily?
3. Do you get your physical needs [adequate food / comfortable living conditions / sufficient education / adequate income] met? Why or why not? What would enable you to meet those needs better?
4. Do you get your emotional needs [support from family members / support from friends] met? Are you able to express yourself fully? What would enable you to get your emotional needs met better?
5. Can you say "yes" when you want to say "yes" and "no" when you want to say "no"? Why or why not? What would enable you to do so?
6. Do you get adequate [sleep / exercise / time in nature / time alone / time with your friends / time with your family]? Is this quality time? What would enable you to do so?

Health and Safety _____

1. Are you afraid of [death / growing old]? Why or why not? Do you have friends or relatives who will take care of you if you become unable to care for yourself? Do you take care of

yourself in such a way that you are investing in your future health? Why or why not?

2. Do you eat well-balanced and nutritious meals? Why or why not? Do you routinely indulge in [caffeinated drinks / alcohol / mind-altering drugs / cigarettes / sugary foods / highly processed foods / rich foods]? What would it take for you to choose to clean up your [eating / smoking / drinking] habits? What is stopping you from doing so? Do you experience a relationship between your personal habits and your sense of inner peace and security? Elaborate.

3. If you had a major health problem or accident, could you [afford / borrow money for] medical treatment or an operation? Do you have full health insurance? Why or why not? If not, is this a source of stress for you? How can you reduce that stress?

4. What are the major sources of stress in your life (e.g., noise, pollution, dangerous neighbors, people around you who fight, too much responsibility, poor relations with those around you, etc.)? What [are you doing / can you do] to reduce the level of stress in your life?

Work

1. Is your work [meaningful / stimulating] to you? Why or why not? What would make it more so?

2. How do you define your life's purpose? Does your work further that purpose? Why or why not? If you only had a year left to live, would you continue in the same work?

3. Do you have a good physical working environment (e.g., lighting, air quality, plants, noise level, convenient commute, etc.)? How could it be improved?

4. Do you have good relations with your [boss / co-workers / subordinates / clients]? What would improve them? What can you personally do to improve them?

Political/Social

1. Are you a registered voter? Why or why not? Do you vote regularly? Who or why not? Do you consider yourself well informed about [local / state / national] issues? Why or why not?

2. Did you vote in the most recent [local / state / national] election? Why or why not?

3. Do you do any paid or volunteer work which makes a contribution to the field of [politics / education / social improvement]? Why or why not? If yes, is your work satisfying? What would make it more satisfying?

4. What kinds of changes—if any—do you think need to be made in our [local / state / national / global] systems of [politics / economics / social welfare]? What is the best way to bring about these changes? What are you doing to assist in this transformation?

5. Do you trust your [local / state / national] leaders? Why or why not? How have you come to feel this way? What would make you [trust / distrust] them?

6. Do you follow [local / state / national / global] politics? Why or why not? Do you regularly [read the newspaper / watch the news on television / listen to the news on the radio]? Why or why not? Do you believe what you [read / see / hear]? Why or why not? What would increase the level of credibility for you? What can you do to improve this situation?

Religion / Values / Basic Assumptions ___

1. Do you consider yourself to be a religious person? Why or why not? Do you find a sense of security in your system of beliefs? Elaborate. How have you come to hold this system of beliefs? Are you tolerant of other systems of belief? What are the limits of your tolerance?

2. Do you believe in [a God of love / a God of wrath and vengeance]? What do you experience as the nature of your relationship with God? Do you believe in heaven and hell as actual places or as a creation of the human mind? How have you come to hold these beliefs? Do your beliefs bring you peace of mind? Are you a peacemaker?

3. When do you think it is [safe / unsafe] to trust a person? What enables you to trust someone? What causes you to distrust someone? Have you ever had any experiences where your trust in someone has been abused? If so, were you able to recreate the trust?

4. Do you believe there is order and purpose in the universe? Why or why not? Do you believe in karma? Do you believe in reincarnation? How have you come to hold your system of beliefs? How does your system of beliefs affect your behavior?

5. Do you share similar values on important subjects (e.g., integrity, sexual behavior, child-rearing practices, assuming responsibility, keeping commitments, etc.) with your family (spouse, parents, children, siblings) and friends? Can you communicate with these people on subjects of importance to you? Why or why not? What would make this possible?

6. Do you believe that the [United States / Soviet Union] is acting in a moral and an effective fashion in the world today? Why or why not? What do you think are [our / their] national ethics? What are the areas in which [we / they] most need to improve? What would most enable this to happen? Do you think you can have [are having] any effect on causing this to happen?

7. Have you ever had the experience of being totally at one with the universe? Do you experience this regularly? Has this experience changed your way of looking at the world? What seems to [support / block] your having this experience?

8. Do you believe that there are beings from other [planets / dimensions] who are here to [help / harm] us on earth? How have you come to hold these beliefs? Do you believe you have control over the [positive / negative] influence of such beings? If so, how do you do this? Do you think that these particular questions are "crazy"? Why or why not? How did you come to hold this attitude?

War and National/Global Security _____

1. Do you think there will probably be a [limited / all-out] nuclear war before people wake up to the dangers of nuclear weapons? Would people survive? Elaborate. What do you think we can do to avoid nuclear war? What do you think you can do personally? Do you have any suggestions for how to stop and reverse the arms race?

2. What do you think would be the most likely cause(s) of nuclear war? How can these best be prevented? Which areas of the world do you think are most likely to be the scene of

the outbreak of nuclear war? How can peace be created in those areas? Is there a contribution you can make to help this happen?

3. What do you think are the major sources of national and global [security / insecurity] today? Elaborate. What do you think can be done to make America and the world more secure? How can you personally contribute to doing this?

4. Do you think we need to develop a global security system? Why or why not? If so, what do you think it would look like and how would it best be carried out? How can you personally contribute to doing this?

5. What do you think are the most important questions we must ask ourselves regarding national and global security? Do you have any answers to these questions? Elaborate.

The Soviet Union _____

1. Do you consider yourself to be well informed about the Soviet Union, particularly about its social, political, and economic policies and conditions? What are the major sources of your information? Do you consider these sources to be accurate?

2. How can we accurately assess Soviet military intentions?

3. Describe your current attitudes toward the Soviet [leaders / system of government / economic system / information dissemination / handling of dissidents / people in general]. How strongly do you hold these views? What information and incidents have most affected your attitudes on each of these?

4. What do you [like and respect / dislike and fear] most about the Soviet Union?

5. How can the United States improve relations with the Soviet Union? Elaborate. Are you or your friends/colleagues doing anything to put these ideas into action?

6. [Have you been / Are you interested in going] to the Soviet Union? Why or why not?

The Third World _____

1. Do you consider yourself to be well informed about the Third World and the north-south problem? What are the major sources of your information? Do you consider these sources to be accurate? Have you visited any Third World countries?

2. How do you think the problems of population, poverty, disease, political repression, and development can best be handled in the Third World? What could the [United States / Soviet Union] contribute to solving these problems? What can you contribute?

3. Do you think we need to establish a new global economic order? Why or why not? If so, what would it look like? How would it best be implemented? What do you see as the major blockages and how can those best be surmounted? What can you contribute?

4. Do you see a relationship between economic well-being in the Third World and in the industrialized nations? Elaborate.

5. How do you think that we can improve relations between the United States and the Third World? Elaborate. What can you contribute?

The Future

1. Do you have a positive or negative vision of [your personal / our national / our global] future? What is your negative vision? How can such an outcome best be avoided? What is your positive vision? What concrete suggestions do you have for how to go from the current situation toward that more positive vision? What are you doing to support this happening?

2. Do you know any people or groups who are currently working on national and global security issues in a way that seems particularly effective to you? What is it that makes their work so effective? What are their positive visions of the future? Are you directly or indirectly involved?

3. Are you [now / willing to become] involved in an active fashion? Elaborate on what the form this involvement would take. How would you assess the strength of your personal commitment? What skills or support do you need to be most effective? Is that available?

Miscellaneous

1. If you could communicate directly to the [American president / Soviet premier], what would you say? Have you considered writing him a letter to this effect?

2. With which interviewee(s) do you find yourself in the great-

est [agreement / disagreement]? With which points? Elaborate.

3. What key points have you thought of which were not addressed by any of the interviewees?

4. Did you think any of the interviewees were downright "crazy" in any of their beliefs? Were you able to imagine the world through their eyes? How did that feel?

5. Did any of the questions in this survey make you particularly angry or irritated? If so, which ones, and why?

6. Do you think we really have freedom of speech in America, or do you think that the bus driver quoted in the Introduction is right in saying that the "little men in white coats" will come to "get" the author in the next ten years if she continues to ask such questions?

7. How can you and I best support each other in being all we can?